MW01717137

U'

Instructor's Manual
to Accompany

Allen and Stimpson

BEGINNINGS OF INTERIOR ENVIRONMENT
Seventh Edition

Prepared by
Miriam Stimpson

Macmillan College Publishing Company
New York

Maxwell Macmillan Canada
Toronto

Maxwell Macmillan International
New York Oxford Singapore Sydney

Printed in the United States of America

Macmillan Publishing Company
113 Sylvan Avenue, Englewood Cliffs, NJ 07632

ISBN: 0-02-301822-4

Printing: 2 3 4 5 6 7 8 9 Year: 5 6 7

CHAPTER 1

ELEMENTS AND PRINCIPLES OF DESIGN

Chapter Focus

Chapter l is divided into five major sections to focus the student's attention on the basic elements and principles of design. These sections discuss the development of Good Taste and Style, The Human Factor, the Two Basic Design Directions (structural and applied ornamentation) and the properties of the Elements and Principles of Design.

Text Outline

I. GOOD TASTE AND STYLE:

A. **Capability for making aesthetic judgements:**
   1. Requires a knowledge of elements and principles of design.
   2. Visual appreciation.
   3. Intelligent selection.
   4. New media and technology can be applied in original and creative ways.
   5. Personal style.

B. **Guidelines for Developing Style:**
   1. Acquire knowledge of principles and elements of design.
   2. Observe objects in nature.
   3. Study historical, modern, and contemporary architecture and furnishing styles.
   4. Examine available design periodicals and books.
   5. Question experienced professionals.
   6. Acquire knowledge of accessories.
   7. Realize fashion not always a reliable criterion of good design.

II. THE HUMAN FACTOR:

A. **Introduction.**
   1. Personal needs of end users - physical, emotional, and spiritual
   2. Comfort, security, privacy, and aesthetic satisfaction.

B. **Definition of Design**:
   1. Arrangement of details which make up a work of art.

C. **Goals of Design**:
1. ***Function*** or purpose.
2. ***Economic*** factors - budget.
3. ***Aesthetically pleasing*** or beautiful.
4. ***Character*** and ***individuality.***

III. TWO BASIC DESIGN DIRECITONS:

A. **Structural Design**:
1. Relates to the ***size and shape*** of an object.
2. The design is an ***integral part*** of the structure itself.
3. Attributes essential to successful structural design include:
   a. ***Simplicity***
   b. ***Good Proportion***
   c. ***Appropriateness of Materials***

B. **Applied Ornamentation or Decorative Design:**
1. Relates to ***ornamentation of the basic structure.***
2. Achieved through ***selection*** and ***placement of color, line***, and ***texture.***
3. Four classifications apply to applied ornamentation or decorative design:
   a. ***Naturalistic***
   b. ***Conventionalized*** or stylistic
   c. ***Abstract***
   d. ***Geometric*** design
4. Attributes essential to successful decorative design:
   a. ***Suitability***
   b. ***Appropriateness*** of ornamentation to the object
   c. ***Placement***

IV. ELEMENTS OF DESIGN:

A. **Introduction:**
1. Elements are the basic components that make up a total design.
2. Elements are known as the "***tools*** " of design.
3. Elements relate closely to the principles of design.

B. **Texture:**
1. Refers to the surface quality of objects.
2. Five basic categories: ***soft, smooth, shiny, dull, and rough.***
3. Textures can be combined for interest and variety.

4. Properties and considerations of texture include:
   a. ***Visual interest, beauty, and character***
   b. ***Light reflection***
   c. ***Maintenance***
   d. ***Acoustics***
   e. ***Combining textures for interest***

C. **Pattern:**
1. Pattern is a decorative ***design, figure, or motif***
2. Created through the use of ***line, form, space, light, and color***
3. Too much pattern can create a "busy" and uncomfortable environment
4. Lack of pattern may be stark and uninviting
   (Use and effect of pattern covered in Chapter 5)

D. **Line:**
1. Line is the ***direction*** of an art creation
2. Lines give a room motion or repose
3. Line can alter the proportion of an object or entire room
4. Each line type has a particular psychological effect on a room
5. Basic line types:
   a. ***Vertical lines*** - feeling of height, strength, and dignity
   b. ***Horizontal lines*** - feeling of repose, solidity, and strength
   c. ***Diagonal lines*** - feeling of action and movement
   d. ***Curved lines*** - graceful feeling
   e. Types of curved lines include:
      (1) large convex (upward)
      (2) large concave (downward)
      (3) horizontal curves
      (4) small curves
6. Too much line movement in a room may evoke a feeling of instability
7. Careful balance of the four line types are essential to a feeling of comfort and harmony

E. **Form and Shape:**
1. The ***contour*** of an object is represented by its shape, which is made up of lines
2. When a ***two-dimensional shape*** takes on a third dimension, it becomes ***form or mass***

erceived as objects or furniture that require space
ious locations.
within a room - furniture arrangement-is

into three categories:
res (most dominant shapes used in architecture and
se of unity and stability, are easy to work with, and
nserve space.
(have three sides, for example: diamond and
ides dynamic effect.
re, circle, cone, and cylinder) are constant,
shapes.
often enhanced by combining the three basic forms
duce a feeling of confusion in a space.
ct to another as the eye moves about the room
urable.
nation of forms is currently evident in both modern
and traditional styles.

F. **Space:**
1. Space is "***an interval or area between or within points or objects***"
2. Space is opposite of the element of form.
3. Well-planned and well-organized space makes for a smooth working environment.
4. Generally, there is a lack of sufficient space for comfortable living.
5. Skillful ***application of the elements and principles*** can increase the sense of space. Suggestions for achieving this goal include:
   a. Arrange space so eye can easily travel through a room to outside areas.
   b. Use unobtrusive patterns and textures.
   c. Use a few and lightly scaled furniture pieces.
   d. Select colors that are light in value, muted and cool.
   e. Use artificial lighting around perimeter of room both on ceiling and uplighters on floor.
   f. Provide wall-to-wall floor treatment. Consider simple window treatments.
   g. Create illusion of more space with mirrors.
   h. Explore possibilities of open planning, a projecting window, or skylight.
   i. Select furnishings with "see through" materials and designs.
   j. Keep rooms free of clutter.
   k. Use a few well-chosen accessories.

6. The preceding guidelines may by reversed when the problem of too expansive or undefined space exists.
7. The arrangement of space within the interior framework is discussed in Chapters 4 - Space Planning and 10 - Furniture Arrangement.

G. **Color**

1. Color is considered the most important element of design. (Color is covered in detail in Chapter 2).

H. **Light**

1. Light can be either ***natural*** or ***artificial.*** (The element of light is presented in Chapter 3).

V. PRINCIPLES OF DESIGN:

A. **Introduction:**

1. Through the centuries certain principles of design have evolved.
2. When thoughtfully considered and sensitively applied, they contribute to achieving the "***goals*** " of design.
3. Although there are no absolute rules when creating a design project, most interiors are enhanced by adhering to these basic guidelines.
4. Understanding the principles is central to a designer's creativity.

B. **The Six Principles of Design**:

1. **Proportion:**
   a. Encompasses both the relationship of one part of an object to the other parts or to the whole, and the relationship of one object to another - both aspects involving shape or form.
   b. Over 2,000 years ago the Greeks discovered some secrets of good proportion:
      (1) Greeks felt that the square was the least satisfactory proportion and the rectangle was better - with its sides in a ratio of 2:3. This shape is called the "***golden rectangle*** "
      (2) The ratio of the "golden rectangle" has a progression: 2:5:8:13:21:3: and so on.
      (3) The application of these proportions in architectural planning and furnishing lies in the relationship of sizes or areas.

(4) The ancient Greeks also discovered that the division of a line somewhere between ***one-half and one-third*** its length the most desirable.
(5) This division of a line is called the "***golden mean.***" It can be applied, for example, to tying back drapery or hanging pictures.
(6) The Greeks also discovered that odd numbers are preferable to even ones.

2. **Scale:**
   a. Refers to the ***overall size of an object*** or its parts compared with other objects or their parts, regardless of shape.
   b. Correct use of ***scale and proportion*** is important to the success of a structure and its furnishings.
   c. Because scale is a relative quality, mathematical correctness is not the only solution.
   d. Interior design deals with size relationships geared to ***human scale.***
   e. Good scale and proportion begin with the choice of the structure on the lot and takes into account all furnishings.
   f. The ***material used*** in construction should be in scale with the structure itself.
   g. ***Exterior architectural features*** should be suitably scaled to the structure.
   h. An object is perceived in relation to the ***area*** around it.
   i. ***Accessories*** need to be scaled for the items with which they are to be used.
   j. Not only form but also ***color, texture, and pattern*** are important in the consideration of scale and proportion.
   k. The apparent ***size and proportion*** of rooms and object may be altered. through skillful use of the elements of design.
3. **Balance:**
   a. Is that quality in a room that gives a sense of ***equilibrium*** and ***repose.***
   b. It is a ***sense of weight*** as the eye perceives it.
   c. Generally, human beings have a need for balance in their lives.
   d. The three types of balance are:
      (1) ***Bisymmetrical or Formal, Balance*** : identical objects are arranged equally on each side of an imaginary line.
      This type of balance has the following characteristics:
         (a) Often employed in ***traditionally styled*** environments.
         (b) Predominantly ***formal*** and dignified.
         (c) ***Contrasts*** with nature.
         (d) Conveys a ***restful*** and peaceful sensation.

(2) ***Asymmetrical Balance*** : (also named ***approximate symmetry***) Is often referred to as ***occult or optical*** . Requires more thought and imagination. Objects of different sizes, shapes, and colors may be used in an infinite number of ways. General aspects of this type of balance include:

(a) Tends to ***shift focus*** from the center.
(b) Predominant in ***modern*** interiors.
(c) Tends to be ***informal.***
(d) Generally more ***active*** than symmetrical balance.
(e) More ***compatible with nature.***
(f) Provides a more ***spacious*** appearance

(3) ***Radial Balance*** : The elements of the design ***radiate*** from a central point. Most often seen in a room where chairs surround a round table, in a flower arrangement, and in chandeliers. General aspects include:

(a) Often a visually pleasing alternative to the other two types of balance.
(b) Combines well with bisymmetrical and asymmetrical balance.

4. **Rhythm:**
   a. Assists the eye in moving easily about a room from one area to another.
   b. Effectively creating rhythm, a designer can produce continuity and interest.
   c. The seven types of rhythm are:
      (1) ***Repetition*** : Established by repeating color, pattern, texture, line, light, or form.
      (2) ***Opposition*** : Wherever lines come together at right angles.
      (3) ***Transition*** : Found in a curved line.
      (4) ***Gradation or progression*** : Produced by the succession of the size of an object from large to small or of a color from dark to light.
      (5) ***Radiation*** : Lines extend outward from a central axis.
      (6) ***Contrast*** : Achieved when opposites are placed in close proximity.
      (7) ***Alternation*** : Two forms or lines alternate to create movement.
5. **Emphasis:**
   a. Refers to the ***dominant and subordinate*** components or the focal point and supportive furnishings of this center of interest.
   b. It is effective to have one feature repeatedly draw the eye.
   c. A focal point can bring a feeling of order and unity.
   d. Lack of emphasis can create boredom and uninteresting space.
   e. Too much emphasis can produce chaos and unrest.

f. Four basic levels of emphasis are:
   (1) ***Emphatic*** : include a dramatic view, fireplace, or architectural feature.
   (2) ***Dominant*** : Usually the level where most designers begin. Include a fireplace, art wall, garden view, etc.
   (3) ***Subdominant*** : includes the level of furnishings that support the focal point and might include large pieces of furniture or the window, ceiling, and floor treatment.
   (4) ***Subordinate*** : This level most often includes accessories.

g. Flexibility is important and furnishings can be rearranged within this framework depending on the desired outcome.

h. Emphasis is planned and even manipulated through use of the elements of design.

i. Focal point should be important but not overpowering.

j. Room is enhanced when the elements are linked to other furnishings.
   (1) ***Color*** can help a grouping be brought into immediate focus.
   (2) ***Form*** usually involves arranging furniture within the space so they focus on the point of emphasis.
   (3) ***Texture*** can help draw the eye to a particular item.
   (4) ***Pattern*** can attract the eye to a desired focal point.

6. **Harmony:**

a. A ***unifying theme*** - a common denominator - should run through all the component parts and blend them together.

b. Two goals are combined to create harmony: ***unity and variety.***

c. Exteriors and interiors are attractive when there is a pleasant relationship.

d. Harmony results when all other principles of design come into play.

e. Most common and important considerations when seeking a harmonious living environment include:
   (1) ***Interior architecture*** should be consistent and the furnishings of a room be in harmony with the background.
   (2) ***Furniture*** should seem to belong and scaled accordingly.
   (3) ***Colors*** appropriate to the style and scale of furnishings often considered with a sensitive approach to color harmonies. Often there is great flexibility and creativity when achieving color harmony.
   (4) ***Textures*** of surfaces help determine the success of a room's harmony
   (5) ***Window treatments*** can contribute to the room's total harmony.
   (6) Carefully selected ***floor coverings*** help unify the scheme
   (7) Harmony is often achieved by carrying out a ***basic theme*** or style:
      (a) ***formal modern*** (b) ***informal modern***
      (c) ***formal traditional*** (d) ***informal traditional***

(8) *Accessories* can enhance a room and help tie it together.

Learning Enhancement Options

Good Taste and Style: Ask students what the qualities are of a person who has a sense of style and good taste. Have students express their own opinions regarding personal style and preferences. Have students indicate ways in which they might acquire good taste in regards to making selections for their own environment. Discussion may include observing nature, studying basic styles, visiting design studios, talking with professional interior designers, and going on home tours. Ask students if they have a favorite color, if they prefer certain textures over others, what styles they enjoy, etc. Make students aware of the fact that since they are taking a design class, it indicates that they have an interest in the subject to some degree. Encourage the students to "see" design in everything around them including both residential and nonresidential settings.

The Human Factor: Ask students to express their own ideas involving human needs in an interior space and have them identify various design needs in their own homes. What essential elements are required for a comfortable and aesthetically pleasing environment? Discuss the importance of the human factor in a design project. Ask students how adequate solutions can be found to solve particular problems in regard to human needs and special need users.

Discuss the four goals of design and have students give examples of how these goals relate to their own lives.

Two Basic Design Directions: Ask students to describe structural design and point out these elements in the classroom. Discuss what attributes are essential to successful structural design. Have students discuss the four types of applied ornamentation and identify various examples found in the room, such as clothing. Here is an excellent opportunity to display fabric or wallpaper examples of the four types of applied ornamentation or decorative design. Discuss what attributes are essential to successful applied ornamentation. Another effective way to demonstrate the differences between structural design and applied ornamentation is to display examples of each in similar objects - for example: two salt shakers, two spoons, two vases, two carpets, etc.

Elements of Design: Ask students how the elements of design are used by professional interior designers to achieve particular goals or solve design problems. How do the "tools" of design relate to the principles of design? (See **"Films / Videos"** on pg. 18)

Texture: Have students describe various textures found in their own environments. Discuss the five basic texture categories and how they can be combined for interest and variety. Point out specific textures found in an interior such as rugs, stone, glass, ceramics, plants, fabrics, metals, etc. Discuss the properties to consider when selecting textures for a residential and nonresidential space. (See **"Films/Videos"** on pg. 18)

Pattern: Demonstrate patterned fabrics, carpets, wallpapers, etc. If available, display fabric groupings showing good pattern use.

Line: Ask students to respond to each line type and discuss the importance of line in an interior. Discuss what happens when there are too many lines in a room and how a comfortable balance of line can be achieved. (See **"Films/Videos"**)

Form and Shape: Discuss what form and shape are and their importance in an interior. Ask students to identify the three basic shapes and the properties of each. Examine how to enhance an environment through the use of the three basic forms.

Space: Have students identify the term "space" and how it relates to form or shape. Why is it important to have well-planned and well-organized space? Since space is generally at a premium, discuss ways in which the elements and principles of design can be used to increase the feeling of space. Ask the students to provide personal examples of available space in their own environment and how they have solved any problems.

Color: Mention color as one of the most important elements used by designers and the an entire chapter is devoted to this "tool" of design.

Light: Indicate to the students that like color, light is an essential element of design and covered in a separate chapter.

Principles of Design: Have the students identify the principles of design and how these goals can be accomplished in an interior design project. Ask the students how important it is to become aware of these principles.

Proportion: Have the students identify what proportion means when applied to interior design. Discuss the various contributions to the art world by the ancient Greeks and how they relate to contemporary interiors. (See **Films/Video)**
(See **"Transparencies"** on page 18)

Scale: Ask the students to define the term "scale" and review its importance in an interior. Discuss the relationship of scale to human beings. Have the students give examples of how scale can be used to provide both comfort and beauty in an environment. How does it interrelate with the other elements?

Balance: Discuss the importance of equilibrium and repose in a residential and nonresidential setting. Have students provide examples of the three types of balance and characteristics of each.

Rhythm: Have students define "rhythm" as it relates to interior design. Discuss the seven types of rhythm and how they can be applied to creating continuity and interest in an environment. (The classroom itself could be used as an example for pointing out each rhythm type.)

Emphasis: Ask the students to identify the principle of emphasis and its important role in the interior. Examine the major contributions of the four basic levels of emphasis. Have the students work through the process of designing a particular room and applying each level of emphasis. Discuss how the seven elements of design can be used to accomplish the goal of creating a focal point. Encourage the students to be flexible and allow for creativity.

Harmony: All students have experienced being in a room that is not harmonious and one that is harmonious. Have them discuss these personal experiences. What is harmony as it relates to interior design? What are two goals that create harmony? Ask the students to apply the elements and other principles of design to achieving the goal of harmony. Discuss how harmony results when a basic theme or style is carried out.

Explain the assignment. (**Transparency** available) (This assignment can also be used in class.)

Test Questions

Multiple Choice:

__A__ 1. Good taste is generally:
A. What is appropriate to a particular live-style
B. What is currently popular

__C__ 2. The text outlines all but one of the following guidelines for acquiring good taste:
A. Study the elements and principles of design
B. Observe objects found in nature
C. Apply short-term fundamentals of design
D. Become knowledgeable about historic and contemporary styles

__B__ 3. The four basic goals of design outlined in the text include the following:
A. Space planning, purpose, budget, and beauty
B. Function, economic considerations, beauty, and individuality
C. Function, the elements of design, individuality, and budget

__C__ 4. Structural design involves all but one of the following criteria:
A. Simplicity
B. An integral part of the structure itself
C. Made up of line, texture, ornament and form
D. Relates to the size and shape of the object

__D__ 5. The illustration at the right is an example of what design type?
A. Naturalistic
B. Abstract
C. Geometric (Illustration of Conventionalized design)
D. Conventionalized

__A__ 6. The illustration at the right is an example of what design type?
A. Geometric
B. Conventionalized
C. Naturalistic (Illustration of Geometric design)
D. Abstract

__B__ 7. Criteria for successful applied ornamentation includes all but one of the following:
A. Pleasant to touch
B. Supportive of light effects
C. Relates to the size of an object
D. Is vital in itself
E. All of the above

__C__ 8. The elements of design are often known as the:
A. Goals of design
B. Function of design
C. Tools of design

__E__ 9. The element of texture involves: (Select the best answer)
A. Household maintenance and light reflection
B. Source of beauty
C. Provides a physical and psychological impression
D. Acoustics
E. All of the above

__A__ 10. According to the text, among the most expressive qualities of line is its:
A. Direction
B. Added dimension
C. Informality
D. Dignity

__D__ 11. The following psychological property is generally true of the horizontal line:
A. Stately
B. Active
C. Graceful
D. Repose

__B__ 12. Form falls into three basic categories: (Select the best answer)
A. Circles, diamonds, and rectangles
B. Rectangles and squares, triangles, and curved
C. Squares, cylinders, cones, and triangles

__D__ 13. Reasons for the widespread acceptance of rectangles include all but one of the following:
A. Provide a sense of unity
B. Easy to work with
C. Can conserve space
D. Inexpensive to use

__C__ 14. Curved forms generally:
A. Do not mix well with squares and rectangles
B. Are graceful, but never dramatic
C. Are constant and unifying
D. Usually work best as accent forms

__A__ 15. When space is at a premium, which of the following will help provide a feeling of spaciousness:
A. Use furniture with sections of caning or glass
B. Use a few bold patterns
C. Use artificial lighting toward the center of the room
D. Use tieback draperies

__D__ 16. According to the text, the scale and proportion of an object is perceived in relation to:
A. The surrounding light
B. The color background
C. The textural contrast
D. The area around it

__A__ 17. Over 2000 years ago, the Greeks discovered the direction of a line somewhere between one-half and one-third was the most pleasing. This division is still retained as the:
A. Golden Mean
B. Sacred Quotient
C. Golden Rectangle
D. Point of Entasis

__C__ 18. The Golden Section, discovered by the ancient Greeks, is the division of line or form in the following progression:
A. 3:6:9:12:15
B. 2:4:6:8:10:12
C. 2:3:5:8:13:21
D. 3:7:11:15:19

__B__ 19. Symmetrical balance is known as:
A. Informal
B. Formal

__A__ 20. Asymmetrical balance is known as:
A. Active
B. Passive

__B__ 21. Emphasis planned in a interior primarily deals with four levels:
A. Texture - color - pattern - form
B. Emphatic - dominant - subdominant - subordinate
C. Focal point - furniture arrangement - backgrounds - accessories
D. Dominant - subdominant - subordinate - accessories

16, 19

__D__ 22. Harmony especially results in an environment 16, 19, 29, 30
two aspects are combined:
A. Rhythm and unity
B. Variety and function
C. Function and style
D. Unity and variety

__A__ 23. The following design element is considered by professionalsto be the most unifying tool of a design composition in creating harmony:
A. Color
B. Space
C. Lighting
D. Balance

True / False:

__F__ 24. Current popular fashions are usually a good criterion for determining excellent design.

__T__ 25. The creation of good design in residential and nonresidential environments has no absolute formula.

__T__ 26. The goal of "function" is concerned with the physical and psychological needs of the end users.

__F__ 27. Structural design is not always an integral part of the object itself.

__F__ 28. Conventionalized design is copied exactly from nature.

__T__ 29. Texture can be perceived by memory as well as by touch and sight.

__T__ 30. Perhaps the most important application of the proportions discovered by the ancient Greeks lies in the relationship of sizes or areas.

Matching:

Match the following elements of design to the most appropriate description:

A. Texture
B. Line
C. Form or Shape
D. Space
E. Pattern

__B__ 31. Refers to the direction of an art composition.

__E__ 32. Is created by color, line, and form.

__A__ 33. Takes into consideration maintenance, light reflection, and acoustics.

__C__ 34. The contour of an object.

__D__ 35. An interval between or within points.

Match the following three types of balance with the correct criteria (Answers may be repeated as needed)

A. Bysymmetrical balance
B. Asymmetrical balance
C. Radial balance

__A__ 36. Contrast with nature is the goal.

__B__ 37. Harmony with nature is the goal.

__A__ 38. Primarily used in traditional interiors.

__C__ 39. Seen in chandeliers and flower arrangements for example.

__B__ 40. Provides a more spacious appearance.

Match the following types of rhythm with the appropriate answer:

A. Transition
B. Gradation
C. Opposition
D. Contrast
E. Repetition
F. Alternation
G. Radiation

__A__ 41. Rhythm occuring wherever a curved line is found in the room.

__C__ 42. A type of rhythm established wherever lines come together at right angles.

__G__ 43. Method of rhythm in which lines extend outward from a central axis.

__B__ 44. Rhythm produced by the succession of the size of an object from large to small or a color from dark to light.

__F__ 45. An example of this type of rhythm might be a motif employing a repeating square, circle, square, and so on.

__D__ 46. Rhythm achieved when opposites are placed in close proximity.

__G__ 47. Pattern, color, form and other elements are duplicated to create rhythm in the room.

Essay / Short Answer:

48. Explain the role of the designer in taking into account the human factor in a design project. What goals should be achieved?

The answer to this question is found on page 5

49. Discuss the four basic goals of design and include relevant information on each.

The answer to this question is found on pages 5 and 6.

50. Briefly outline and describe the principle of harmony and how it relates to the other principles and elements of design. What specific ways can the elements be used to create harmony?

The answer to this question is found on pages 21 and 22.

Educational Resources

Publications:

Abercrombie, Stanley. *A Philosophy of Interior Design* . New York: Harper and Row, 1990.
Belvin, Marjorie Elliott. *Design Through Discovery.* New York: Holt, Rinehart and Winston, 1985.
De Sausmarez, Maurice. *Basic Design: The Dynamics of Visual Form.* New York: Van Nostrand Reinhold, 1983.
Desiano. *Principles & Elements of Design* . Trillium Press. 1989.
Faulkner, Ray, LuAnn Nissen, and Sarah Faulkner. *Inside Today's Home.5th ed.* New York: Holt, Rinehart and Winston, 1986.
Maier, Manfred. *Basic Principles of Design* . New York: Van Nostrand Reinhold, 1977.
Papanek, Victor. *Design for Human Scale.* New York: Van Nostrand Reinhold, 1983.
Zelanski, Paul, and Mary Pat Fisher. *Design: Principles and Problems* . NewYork: Holt, Rinehart and Winston, 1984.

Movies / Videos:

Why Man Creates : 25 min / Pyramid Films
Eye for Design:: 22 min / 1991 / #HK38 Insight Media
Discovering Line : 17 min / Phoenix Films/BFA
Discovering Texture : 17 min / Phoenix Films/BFA
The Golden Section:: 18 min / Fleetwood Films, Inc.
Greece and Rome - Classical Ideal : 1989 / Public Broadcasting Co.

Transparencies:

Proportions Discovered by the Ancient Greeks and Applications
Design Assignment

CHAPTER 2

COLOR

Chapter Focus

Chapter 2 is divided into fourteen major sections covering basic information relevant to understanding the element of color and its properties. These sections discuss Color in History, the Psychology and Physiology of Color, Color Groups, the Effects of Individual Colors, Color and Pigment, Color Systems, Color's Three Dimensions, Creating Livable Color Harmonies, Other Considerations in Color Applications, Color Considerations for Nonresidential Settings and Color Forecasts for the 1990s.

Text Outline

Introduction:

A. Designers agree that color provides a visual sensation that is considered the most vital and expressive of the seven elements of design.
B. A thorough knowledge of color associations, color theory, the properties and character of various colors, historic colors, color systems, and other considerations of color is essential for the professional interior designer.
C. Color is an international language
D. Color has always had symbolic importance
E. Many colors signify certain character traits, and expressions using color names have specific meanings commonly used and understood.

I. COLOR IN HISTORY:

A. Color can reveal much about the civilizations of people
B. Greatest value of color is its power to create beauty
C. Since the dawn of history, humans have toiled to bring beauty into their environments through the use of color.
D. Cultures that have had a significant influence on color use through the centuries include:
    1. ***Ancient Egypt*** (ca. 4000-660 B.C.): blue, tangerine, green, carmine, dull reds, various browns, rust, yellow, white and black

2. ***Ancient Greece and Rome*** (ca. 6th Cent. B.C.-450 A.D.): cream, brown, white, black, purple, mauve, pink, deep green, red, gold, blue, blue-green, black, gold, and dull red called Pompeian red.
3. ***Medieval Europe*** (ca. 500-1500): brilliant blues, reds, purples, yellows, golds, and greens
4. ***Renaissance*** (ca. 1400-1600):Vibrant reds, greens, golds, and blues. Deep browns, greens, blues, golds, and reds,, cream and some pale blue
5. ***Louis XV and Rococo*** (1730-1774): Light pale colors
6. ***Neoclassic France*** (1760-1789): Color more delicate and softly pastel
7. ***Early Colonial America*** (1607-1700): Dark reddish brown, various greens, dark grayish blue, natural colors (cream, brown, and white)
8. ***Eighteenth-Century Georgian*** (1714-1790): Rich reds and golds. Dull medium colors: Williamsburg green and Williamsburg blue
9. ***Neoclassic England and America*** (1790-1820): Delicate colors. Adam green, peach, pink, soft yellow and Wedgewood blue
10. ***Empire and Greek Revival*** (ca. 1804-1860): Black, white, Empire green, gold, and vibrant colors like purple, red, yellow, and blue
11. ***China:***: Peacock blue, white, gold, chrysanthemum yellow, cherry blossom pink, celadon green, jade-green, red-orange, red, and black
12. ***Japan:***: "Shibui" colors derived from nature
13. ***Spain and Mexico*** (1600 to present): Vivid colors: blue, red, gold, pink, and orange - coupled with white and black
14. ***Southwest Indian*** (ca. 1500 to present): Deep red, turquoise, grey, purple, black, and cream
15. ***Victorian period*** (1837-turn of the century): Dull or vivid reds, bottle greens, tobacco browns, and deep purple, and mauve
16. ***Arts and Crafts Movement*** (ca. 1860-turn of century): Natural dyes. Blue greens, deep orange, rich greens, reds, blues, and golds.
17. ***Art Nouveau*** (Soft apricot, greens, and golds. White, rose, pink, purple and black. Tiffany blues, greens, and purples.
18. ***Santa Fe Style*** (1920s to present): Desert colors of sand, soft purples, blues, blue-greens, greens, corals, cream, and white
19. ***Bauhaus, International Style*** (1919 to present): White. Sometimes accented with black, gray, red, blue, and yellow
20. ***Art Deco*** (ca. 1909 to outbreak of WWII): White, black, gray, silver, red, purple, chocolate brown, turquoise, gray-blue, gray-green, peach, and pink
21. ***Post-World War II*** (1940s-1960s): Light colors, beige or off-white. Turquoise, orange, brown, rose and blue. Vivid Spanish colors. New color combinations.
22. ***The 1970s:*** Wide range of color fashions. Red, white and blue.

23. ***The 1980s:*** New architectural and design styles. Muted purples, blues, pinks, greens, and peach. Gray, pastel hues, and muted colors popular.

II. THE PSYCHOLOGY AND PHYSIOLOGY OF COLOR:

A. Research has shown that the human **body responds to color** both psychologically and physiologically.
1. Color affects individual's ***moods or feelings*** in regard to space.
2. Color affects the eye's perception of ***weight and size*** .
3. Color affects a person's perception of ***temperature*** .
4. Color can ***cause feelings*** of boredom and calmness, or stimulation and liveliness.

B. This **information** is immensely **valuable to the designer** when planning both residential and nonresidential spaces

C. Many **color studies** have indicated that:
1. People prefer to eat from a white dinner plate.
2. Most flags of the world use red, white, blue, green, yellow, orange, and black,
3. Bulls react to the movement of the matador's cape rather than the color red - the crowd reacts to the excitement of red.
4. Soft colors are calming in a doctor's office.
5. Fast-food restaurants use bright warm colors in order to stimulate the appetite and hurry patrons through their meals.
6. After factory works complained how heavy their black boxes were, the boxes were painted light blue. The workers believed the boxes were lighter.

III. COLOR GROUPS:

A. The simplest psychological division of color results in two major groups: ***warm*** and ***cool*** , with ***neutral*** in between:

1. **Warm Colors:** red, red-orange, orange, yellow-orange, yellow, and yellow-green. When at full chroma, warm colors tend to be:
   - engaging
   - active
   - positive
   - cheery
   - cozy
   - advancing
   - stimulating
   - somewhat informal
   - tend to blend objects

2. **Cool Colors:** blue, blue-green, green, violet, and blue-violet. When a tint, cool colors tend to be:
   - relaxing
   - restful
   - soothing
   - receding
   - somewhat formal
   - tend to make individual objects stand out
   - expand space

3. If used in strong intensity in large areas, warm colors may cause psychological irritation
4. Rooms done in all cool colors may be perceived as too cool and unfriendly and may lack unity

B. *Neutral and Neutralized Colors*

1. **Neutral Color**: Technically, neutral colors are gray, white, and black. These neutrals are often called "achromatic" - or without color
2. **Neutralized Colors:** Fall midway between the warm and cool color groups A warm neutralized color may be a tint, tone, or shade of a warm hue, a cool neutralized color is a tint, tone, or shade of a cool hue.
   a. Warm neutralized colors are generally easier to work with than cool neutralized colors
   b. Neutralized colors are generally important to every color scheme.
   c. Tend to be restful, tranquil, livable, unobtrusive, and supportive
   d. Can be boring and wearisome when not used effectively

IV. PSYCHOLOGICAL AND PHYSIOLOGICAL EFFECTS OF INDIVIDUAL COLORS:

A. In addition to the division of colors into warm and cool, each color contains peculiar properties that produce certain psychological and physiological effects:

1. ***Red*** **:** Courage, passion, love, excitement, danger, martyrdom, anger, etc. Conspicuous. Mixes well. When darkened and muted it becomes maroon, and when lightened becomes pink. Pink is delicate and flattering
2. ***Yellow*** **:** Cowardice, deceit, sunlight, optimism, warmth, enlightenment, communication. High-noon yellow most revealing and demanding. Gray-yellows more fragile. Yellow family also includes gold. All yellows are reflective, take on tones of other colors, add flattering highlights.
3. ***Orange*** **:** Cheerfulness, stimulation, sunset, excitement. Similar properties as red, but not as demanding. When lightened and muted, becomes a peach tone. Orange mixes well with cool colors.
4. ***Blue*** **:** Honesty, truth, loyalty, masculinity, formality, repose, tranquility, sobriety, sky, depth of sea. Difficult to mix and varies greatly under different lighting. Affected by the different materials it colors.
5. ***Green*****::** Nature, serenity, hope, envy, safety, peace, passive, security. Fresh and friendly. Is a good mixer. White brings out green's best qualities. When grayed, warmed, or cooled, green makes an excellent background. Deep dark green a favorite for floor coverings.
6. ***Violet*** **:** Royalty, nobility, snobbery, power, drama, opulence, mystery, worship, dignity. Combines well with pink and blue. A light value of violet is lavender. Often used in small amounts.

7. ***White:*** (neutral) Purity, cleanliness, sterility, sophistication, and freshness. White and off-white (neutralized) make all colors in a room look cleaner and livelier. Off-white is considered unequaled as a mellow background color. Used in traditional and modern interiors
8. ***Black:*** (neutral) and off-black (neutralized color): Mourning, sorrow, depression, sophistication, mystery, magic, night. Usually used in smaller amounts. Can add an important accent that makes other colors crisp and clear. Too much black can be claustrophobic and oppressive.
9. ***Gray:*** (neutral) Penance, gloom, storm, fog, depression, wisdom, intelligence, business, high-tech, sophistication. May be tiring without colorful accents. A good mixer with other colors, especially pinks, purples, and blues. Good background color when lightened.
10. ***Brown:*** (neutralized color): Earth, wood, warmth, comfort, security, support, stability. Homeyness of brown makes it a favorite - especially in wood furnishings. Ranges from pale cream beige to deeper chocolate brown. Can be used together for variety. Light browns make excellent backgrounds.

V. COLOR AND PIGMENT:

A. Scientists have been developing new color theories and systems for many years
B. Many different scientific approaches to color exist.
   1. The ***physicist*** works with ***colors in light.***
   2. The ***chemist*** is mainly concerned with the ***production of pigments***
   3. The ***psychologist*** has theories based on ***visual perception***
   4. The ***interior designer*** benefits from an understanding of ***all three approaches.***
C. The most practical approach to understanding color derives from personal experience.
D. Colors in objects are referred to as ***pigment colors*** and the colors from the sun and from lamps are called ***light colors.***
E. The process of combining the primary colors of light (red, green, and blue) is said to be an ***additive*** one. (i.e., the sensations produced by different wavelengths of light, or spectral colors, are added together).
F. When pigments are mixed, the resulting sensations differ from those of the spectral colors. In this case, the method is a ***subtractive*** one, since subtraction or absorption of the wavelengths of light occurs.
G. In reality, a ***ray of light is the source of all color***, for without light, color does not exist.
H. For the designer, pigment colors are of greater concern than spectral colors.
I. Before people learned out to produce color by chemical means, they were derived from ***animal, mineral***, and ***vegetable*** sources.

VI. COLOR SYSTEMS:

A. A number of color theories, or systems have been developed and are in use today.

B. Some incorporate psychological as well as physical factors.

C. A variety of color wheels have been produced, each based on a different group of basic colors:

1. ***The Brewster System:*** Is the simplest and best known of the color systems. (Also known as the ***Prang*** color wheel or ***Standard Color Wheel***)
   a. Based on three primary colors:***yellow, red, and blue*** . **Primary** means the colors cannot be mixed from other pigments.
   b. Theoretically, with five tubes of paint - the three primaries plus black and white, one could produce the entire range of colors.
   c. Equal amounts of any two primary color result in **secondary colors**: green, violet, and orange.
   d. **Tertiary, or intermediary** hues are composed by mixing equal amounts of a primary color and a secondary color.
2. ***The Ostwald System*:** Named after is creator, Friedrich W. Ostwald.
   a. The Ostwald color wheel uses *yellow, orange, red, purple, blue, turquoise, sea green, and leaf green,* is based on hue plus the *white* content and the black content of the hue.
   b. Theoretically, 24 hues can be derived from mixing these hues plus pure white and black.
   c. There are 28 variations of these 24 hues with a resulting total of 672 hues and 8 neutrals.
   d. The cool group of hues is arranged on one half of the circle and the warm group of hues arranged on the other half of the circle.
   e. Ostwald arranged the hues in a conical configuration
3. ***The Munsell System:*** Is essentially a scientific concept of describing and analyzing color in terms of three attributes:
   a. **Hue (H)**, or the color name, is indicated by the capital letter H.
   b. **Value (v),** or the lightness and darkness of a color, is indicated by the central axis, which shows nine visible steps.
   c. **Chroma (c),** is shown by the horizontal band extending outward from the value axis.
   This complex color system can be simplified to the following basics:
   (1) The chromatic colors are based on five principal hues: *red, yellow,* green, blue, and purple. The five intermediate colors are yellow-red, green-yellow, blue-green, purple-blue, and red-purple.
   (2) Each of these 10 hues is subdivided into four parts, indicated by the numerals 2.5, 5, 7.5, and 10. These hue names are symbolized by capitalized initials, such as R for red or YR for yellow-red

(3) When finer subdivisions are required, these 10 hues may again be combined, such as R-YR, etc.
(4) The segment lying between each of the 10 color hues is divided into 10 color steps. In each case, the basic and intermediate color is in the center and is marked by the number 5, which indicates it is the strongest degree of pure color of that particular hue.
(5) By using the correct letters and numbers, a designer can describe any given hue and locate it on the color tree.

4. Other Color Systems include:
   a. **Paint Manufacturer Color Systems** - coded for their own products
   b. **Johannes Itten's Color Theories** - known for his *"Four Seasons - Personal* Color Analysis. "
   c. **Josef Albers Color Theories** - known for his theories on color perception.
   d. **Color Consultant Manufacturers** color matching based on the latest computerized technology.

VII. COLOR'S THREE DIMENSIONS:

A. Already referred to in the Munsell notation. The qualities of hue, value, and chroma include:

1. ***Hue*** **:** or the color name, is the singular characteristic that sets each color apart from all the others.
   a. A color may be lightened or darkened, made more intense or less intense but it is still a hue - such as light blue, dark blue, bright blue or dull blue.
   b. In all, about 150 variations of full chroma of hue exist, of which only 24 basic hues of full chroma have enough variation to be of practical use.
   c. When neighboring hues on the color wheel are mixed, they produce new hues.
   d. When hues opposite from each other on the color wheel are mixed, the result is a neutral hue
   e. In beginning a color scheme, generally one dominant hue is the starting point
2. ***Value:*** is the degree of luminosity, or lightness or darkness of a hue in relation to black and white.
   a. Nine gradations are easily visible to the eye
   b. The value of any hue can be raised by adding white and lowered by adding black.
   c. When black is added to a hue, the value is lowered and the result is a ***shade.***
   d. When white is added to a hue, the value is raised, and the result is a ***tint.***
   e. Tints are most frequently used for large background areas

f. When mixing tints, certain pigments are not perfect.
g. In addition to shades and tints, a third classification is ***tone.***
h. As an object is raised in value, its *apparent size* increases.
i. The use of sharp value contrast *emphasizes* an object.
j. Black tends to make *adjacent colors* look richer.
k. White *reflects* light into adjacent colors.
l. The manner in which *tonal value* is distributed throughout a room is important. Each room usually contains three tonal values: *light* , *medium* , and *dark* with varying amounts of each.

3. ***Intensity or Chroma:*** is the degree of saturation or pure color.
   a. It describes the *brightness and dullness* and strength or weakness of the pure color that a hue contains.
   b. Intensity may be *strengthened* by the *addition of pure chroma* or *lessened* by the *addition of that color's complement*
   c. A color may be made to *appear more intense* by placing it *against* its *complementary color.*
   d. When two complementary colors are mixed in equal amounts, they tend to *neutralize* each other.
   e. Strong chroma is *conspicuous* and size-increasing.
   f. "***The law of Chromatic Distribution*** " is often used by designers
   g. Color is a great *mood setter.* Strong chroma tends to create a feeling of informality, soft neutralized tones are generally reserved for a more formal atmosphere. However, these rules are often broken for an opposite effect.

VIII. CREATING LIVABLE COLOR HARMONIES:

A. Endless color possibilities are available to the designer and consumer, derived from traditional organized methods or sparked by original ideas.
B. Harmonizing colors from the standard color wheel is a popular approach.
C. In general, color schemes derived from the color wheel fall into two categories: related and contrasting.
D. The basic color scheme are:

1. ***Monochromatic:*** are developed from a single hue, but with a range of values and different degrees of intensity.
   a. Unity is probably the most notable element in this type of scheme
   b. A danger in this scheme may be monotony
   c. Are often further enhanced by the use of textures and pattern
   d. Black and white can be used without changing the character
2. ***Neutral (Achromatic)*** is utilizing black, white, or variations of gray.
   Neutralized or Monotone: created from colors with low chroma
   a. Can be employed as tints, tones, or shades.

   b. Can also be categorized as a type of monochromatic scheme.
   c. Neutrals and neutralized colors are easy to live with
3. **Analogous:** or related color schemes, are produced from any segment of colors that are in juxtaposition but contain no more than half the colors on the color wheel.
   a. Widely used and easy to achieve,
   b. The colors may be warm, cool, or a combination.
   c Harmony is established because they often have one color in common.
   d. Generally, one dominant color should be present
4. ***Complementary, or contrasting*** color schemes are probably the most widely used because they have more variety.
   a. These may be developed in a number of ways, but each scheme uses colors of contrasting hues
   b. Always have some warm and cool colors
   c. One dominant hue usually sets the mood
   d. Six types of complementary schemes are:
      (1) *Direct Complement* (two-color plan)
      (2) *Split complement* (three-color plan)
      (3) *Triad complement* (three-color plan)
      (4) *Double complement* (four-color plan)
      (5) *Alternate complement* (four-color plan)
      (6) *Tetrad* (four-color plan)

IX. ADDITIONAL WAYS OF CREATING COLOR HARMONY:

A. A ***fabric*** might be a starting point for a color scheme
B. A color scheme can be established drawing colors from a ***wallpaper***
C. An ***area rug, art rug, custom rug, or wall-to-wall carpeting*** can be the inspiration for a color scheme
D. A ***painting, print, or art object*** can determine a color scheme
E. ***Nature*** can provide an unlimited number of color schemes

X. THE SHIBUI COLOR HARMONY:

A. Shibui expresses on one word the ***Japanese*** approach to beauty
B. Shibui suggests an appreciation of serenity and a protest against ostentation.
C. The effect is one in which colors are brought together to enhance each other in a harmonious whole
D. The following ideas are incorporated in the shibui scheme:
   1. Looking to nature, on which the color scheme is based
   2. Colors do not match

3. The darker colors occur underfoot and become lighter upward
4. A matte finish with little high shininess or glitter
5. Pattern and texture in nature are subtle
6. Pattern in nature is not uniform

XI. NATURAL EARTH COLORS:

A. Natural earth colors are ***inorganic pigments*** found in minerals, principally from oxides, from the soil.
B. Earth colors have been used for millennia.
C. Earth colors are still used today - especially to help protect from corrosion.
D. Earth colors are the most permanent colors available, are usually non-toxic, and are not affected by atmospheric conditions.

XII. OTHER CONSIDERATIONS IN COLOR APPLICATION:

A. The effect of ***adjacent colors*** on each other
B. The effect of ***natural and artificial light*** on color
C. ***Metameric Colors:*** how various types of natural and artificial light can change the visual perception of a surface
D ***The light source:***
   1. ***Incandescent light*** casts a warm glow
   2. ***Fluorescent tubes*** come in white, warm, and cool tints. *White* light is the most natural
   3. *Warm light* is most flattering
   4. Warm light *accentuates* warm colors and *neutralizes* cool colors. Cool light *intensifies* cool colors and *deadens* warm colors.
   5. Both single and mixed colors take on a different look when subjected to artificial light

E. The ***surface*** that reflects light
F. The ***level*** of illumination
G. The ***methods*** of lighting
H. The effect of ***texture*** on color
I. The effect of ***distance and area*** on color
J. The effect of color and ***temperature***
K. Some ***uses*** of color for the interior
   1. ***Off-White***
   2. On the ***ceiling***
   3. When selecting a ***window treatment***
   4. For ***wood trim***
   5. When walls are ***paneled***
   6. In altering apparent ***size and proportion***

7. In bringing ***balance*** to a room
8. In achieving a pleasing color ***transition*** from one room to another:
   a. Keep the floor covering consistent from room to room
   b. Similar or matching wall and ceiling colors from room to room
   c. Consistent use of moldings and architectural trim
   d. Related colors employed on various pieces of furniture and window treatments
   e. Accessories that carry colors from one interior space to another
9. In ***period rooms***
10. In ***hue distribution***
11. Reflecting the ***mood*** of the room: General color moods can be evoked for specific areas of the house, including: the entrance hall, formal and informal living areas, eating areas, kitchens, bedrooms, and bathrooms.
12. Reflecting ***personality***
13. Color in ***wood***

XIII. COLOR CONSIDERATIONS FOR NONRESIDENTIAL SETTINGS:

A. Keep in mind that human beings respond to color psychologically and physiologically.
B. With this in mind, the designer can more successfully evaluate the functional needs for nonresidential projects.

XIV. COLOR FORECASTS FOR THE 1990s:

A. No absolute color rules can be applied at any particular time.
B. It is good to be award of color trends, but ultimately, personal preferences for comfortable and pleasing colors are the most valuable consideration
C. A number of organizations help determine color preferences for American residential and nonresidential design
D. Research collected by color consultants and experts indicate the palette for the 1990s will be electric compared to the pastels of the 1980s.
C. Colors will be rich and darker in value.
E. Lively colors will be popular.

Learning Enhancement Options

Color in History: Discuss how color can reveal much about the civilizations of people in both primitive tribes and highly developed cultures. Ask students to respond to the colors used by various cultures and its relevance or application in today's interior design.

The Psychology and Physiology of Color. Discuss these aspects of color with the students and have them respond to how color makes them feel and relate to their environment.

Color Groups. Display the standard color wheel or draw on the board the color groups. Show slides or other visual materials of rooms showing cool and warm color schemes and have the students respond to how these groups make them feel and how they might be used in a particular setting to evoke a certain mood..

Psychological and Physiological Effects of Individual Colors. Have students respond to each individual color as they view these colors in both residential and nonresidential settings. Discuss the importance of the designer's role in regard to the psychological and physiological effects of individual colors.

Color and Pigment and Color Systems. Review with the students how pigments are used in interior design field and the best known color systems. If available, demonstrate these color systems with color wheels and other teaching aids.

Color's Three Dimensions. Further explore the three properties of color derived from the Munsell Color System. Support with visual materials, especially examples from the Munsell Color System organization. If this is not available, refer to the text.

Creating Livable Color Harmonies. Using the illustrations in the text or actual visual materials, explore the various ways of creating color harmonies and the advantages and disadvantages of each harmony. Support with slides of these color harmonies applied to interiors. Fabric layouts showing color harmonies, including Shibui and earth color harmonies can help the student visualize the application of these color harmonies.

Other Considerations in Color Applications. Discuss with the students the numerous points brought out in the book concerning various design criteria and how it relates to color use. Provide examples and ask the students to share their own experiences regarding color applications in specific situations.

Color Considerations for Nonresidential Settings. Have the students discuss how they feel about colors used in nonresidential settings, such as in a fast foot restaurant, a hospital, a hotel, a mall, a recreation center, etc. Discuss how they feel about the colors in the classroom they are using this semester. Further discuss how the designer can apply knowledge of color to create a successful nonresidential environment. Examples of good and poor use of color in nonresidential projects can help the student be sensitive to the importance of using color to best advantage in a public place.

Test Questions

Multiple Choice

__A__ 1. One of the following sets of colors would be most characteristic of ancient Egypt:
- A. Brilliant blues, tangerine, green, and carmine
- B. Soft pastel colors such as light blue, green, and orange
- C. Deep red, gray-blue, gray-green, and mauve
- D. Pink, orange, cobalt blue, and purple

__B__ 2. Pastel colors were particular popular with the following style or period:
- A. 17th Century Colonial America
- B. 18th Century French Court
- C. The Renaissance
- D. Art Nouveau

__D__ 3. The following colors are historically popular for the Victorian interior:
- A. Intense pinks, greens, golds and blues
- B. Soft pale colors
- C. White, black, gray and brown
- D. Rich brown, green, purple, and mauve

__C__ 4. Typical colors used during the Art Deco period are:
- A. Pale pink, apricot, lime green and blue
- B. Rich tobacco brown, bottle greens and golds
- C. White, black, silver, red, peach and pink
- D. Strong pink, cobalt blue, orange and white

__B__ 5. Which of the following <u>is not</u> correct concerning the effects of color:
- A. Affects an individual's moods in regard to space
- B. The red color of the matador's cape excites the bull
- C. Color can cause feelings of boredom
- D. Color affects a person's perception of temperature

__C__ 6. Which following sets of color best describe COOL COLORS?
- A. Blue, orange, green, red, violet
- B. Green, yellow-green, blue, red-violet
- C. Blue, green, violet, blue-green
- D. Blue-green, blue, blue-violet, violet, red-violet

__C__ 7. When working with color, the physicist is mostly concerned with:
A. Pigments C. Light
B. Visual perception D. All three criteria

__A__ 8. Which of the following best describes what is meant by "The Spectrum Colors?
A. Colors included in white light from the sun
B. Colors with white added
C. Colors straight from the tube
D. Primary and secondary colors

__B__ 9. "Pure Chroma" as it relates to color describes which of the following?
A. Colors of low intensity
B. Undiluted color
C. A shade
D. A tone

__D__ 10. Which system of color notation is most employed by designers around the world?
A. The Brewster System
B. The Ostwald System
C. The Standard Prang Color Wheel
D. The Munsell System

__D__ 11. When describing a blue tone of high value, the following is accurate:
A. A dark blue of high intensity
B. A dark blue of low intensity
C. A light blue of high intensity
D. A light blue of low intensity

__A__ 12. How would a neutralized hue be described?
A. A color that has been lowered in intensity
B. A primary color
C. Color in pure chroma
D. The spectrum colors

__B__ 13. Intensity is a term interchangeable with:
A. Value C. Hue
B. Chroma D. Luminosity

10, 15, 16

8, 9, 10, 15
16, 17, 18

__D__ 14. If a designer describes a color as Hue: red, Value: h
muted, what kind of color is described?
A. A strong pure red
B. A bright hot pink
C. A dull brick red
D. A pastel pink

__B__ 15. An object will increase in apparent size in the following situations:
A. When a cool color is used
B. When a warm color is used
C. When an off-white is used
D. When a neutral color is used

__A__ 16. To emphasize an art object designers may employ the following:
A. Contrasting hues and values
B. White or off-white
C. Dark values
D. Bright warm colors

__C__ 17. Intensity of a hue will increase by:
A. Adding white
B. Adding more of the complementary hue
C. Adding more of the dominant hue
D. All of the above

__D__ 18. In a small room facing north (with a few small windows), which of the following could be employed to help make the room feel spacious, a comfortable temperature, and properly lit?
A. Light values, cool hues, rough textures
B. Low values, cool hues, rough textures
C. Low values, warm hues, smooth textures
D. Light values, warm hues, smooth textures

__B__ 19. Name the following law: "The large areas should be covered in the most neutralized colors of the scheme. As areas decrease in size, the chromatic intensity many be proportionally increased."
A. "The Law of Hue Distribution"
B. "Law of Chromatic Distribution"
C. "Shibui law"
D. "Natural law of Harmony"

__B__ 20. Incandescent light on a red fabric will have the following effect:
A. Neutralize the color
B. Enhance the color
C. Give the true color
D. Make the color darker

__D__ 21. Incandescent light on a blue fabric will have the following effect:
A. Enhance the color
B. Give the true color
C. Make the color lighter
D. Neutralize the color

__A__ 22. Generally, color will be seen at its truest character in which kind of light?
A. White light
B. Fluorescent
C. Incandescent
D. Daylight

__C__ 23. An off-white is best described as:
A. White with a warm hue added
B. White with any neutral added
C. White with any hue added
D. White with a cool hue added

__D__ 24. The main consideration in using off-whites in a room is:
A. Compatibility of light and dark hues
B. Compatibility of warm and cool hues
C. The amount of hue added to the white
D. Have a basic hue in common

__C__ 25. Color transition may be best described as:
A. Color harmony from furniture to accessories
B. Color harmony for all backgrounds
C. Color harmony from room to room
D. Color harmony within a room

True / False

__F__ 26. Color use by a particular civilization does not especially reveal information about their culture

__T__ 27. Despite popular studies, the knowledge on which popular assumptions about color are based is often superficial.

__F__ 28. It is known that color affects humans psychologically, however, there is very little evidence to support the fact that color affects humans physically.

__T__ 29. The way we see color is affected by the way the object absorbs and reflects the light and the light source.

__F__ 30. The same color in a deep pile carpet will appear lighter than on a smooth shiny fabric.

__F__ 31. Color chosen from a paint chip will appear lighter when applied to an entire wall surface.

__T__ 32. The color of wood should always be taken into account when planning a color scheme.

Matching

Match the following color clans to the most appropriate description:

A. Warm colors
B. Cool colors
C. Neutral colors
D. Neutralized colors

22, 29, 32, 38

22, 23, 25

__B__ 33. Tend to be receding and make indiv
Tranquil and soothing.

__D__ 34. Tints, tones, or shades of hues. For example: off-black, brown, off-white, cream, beige and taupe

__C__ 35. White, black, and gray

__A__ 36. Tend to soften the edges of objects and close in space. Positive and engaging.

Match the following hues with the most appropriate psychological and physiological description:

A. Red
B. Yellow
C. Blue
D. Green
F. Violet

__D__ 37. Hope, envy, peace, security, safety and passivity

__A__ 38. Danger, courage, passion, strength and anger

__F__ 39. Drama, royalty, nobility, opulence, mystery, and worship

__C__ 40. Honesty, truth, loyalty, formality, sobriety. Soothing.

__B__ 41. Cowardice, deceit, optimism, enlightenment and communication.

Match the following color systems with the correct answer:

A. Brewster Color System
B. Ostwald Color System
C. Munsell System

__B__ 42. Color wheel uses yellow, orange, red, purple, blue, turquoise, sea green, and leaf green

__C__ 43. Color system uses red, yellow, blue, green and purple

__A__ 44. Color wheel uses red, yellow, blue, orange, green, and purple

Match the following color harmonies with the appropriate description:

A. Monochromatic
B. Analogous
C. Complementary

__B__ 45. A segment of colors that are in juxtaposition

__A__ 46. Depends heavily upon hue, value, and chromatic distribution for interest

__C__ 47. Always contains both warm and cool colors. The most widely used harmony.

Essay / Short Answer

48. Why is color considered the most vital and expressive of the seven elements of design. What does a study of color involve?

Answers to these questions are found on page 26.

49. Outline the various methods of creating color harmonies and what is involved in the selection each approach. Include information on the Shibui philosophy.

Answers to these questions are found on pages 41 through 48.

50. Briefly discuss the important of planning colors for nonresidential projects. What are some of the considerations and applications for the professional interior designer?

Answer to this question is found on page 55.

Educational Resources

Publications:

Albers, Josef. *Interaction of Color.* New Haven, Conn: Yale University Press, 1975.
Birren, Faber. *Color and Human Response.* New York: Van Nostrand Reinhold, 1978.
Gerritsen, Frans. *Theory and Practice of Color.* New York: Van Nostrand Reinhold, 1975.

Halse, Albert O. *The Use of Color in Interiors, 2d ed.* New York: McGraw-Hill, 1978.
Hope, Augustine, and Margaret Walch. *The Color Compendium.* New York: Van Nostrand Reinhold, 1990.
Itten, Johannes. *The Art of Color.* New York: Van Nostrand Reinhold, 1973.
Kuppers, Harold. *Color: Origins, Systems, Uses.* New York: Van Nostrand Reinhold, 1973.
House Beautiful Magazine Editors. *House Beautiful Color.* Hearst Books. 1993.
Ladau, Robert F., Brent K. Smith, and Jennifer Place. *Color in Interior Design and Architecture* . New York: Van Nostrand Reinhold, 1989.
Libby, William Charles. *Color and the Structural Sense.* Englewood Cliffs, N.Y.: Prentice-Hall, 1974.
Marbery, Sara. *Color in the Office: Design Trends from 1950 to 1990 & Beyond.* Van Nostrand Reinhold, 1993.
Ostwald, Wilhelm. *The Color Primer.* New York: Van Nostrand Reinhold, 1969.
Poore, Jonathan. Interior Color by Design. Rockport Publishers. 1993.
Sharpe, Deborah T. *The Psychology of Color and Design.* Chicago: Nelson-Hall, 1975.
Verity, Enid. *Color Observed.* New York: Van Nostrand Reinhold, 1982.

Movies / Videos:

Basics of Color: 20 min / Insight Media
Color Communicates: 20 min / Insight Media
Color in Everyday Life: 25 min / 1992 / Insight Media
Discovering Color: 15 min / Phoenix Films/BFA
Discovering light and dark: 18 min / Phoenix Films/BFA
Living with Color: 2 parts, 29 min each / Insight Media
Nature of Color: 11 min / Coronet Films

Transparencies

The Standard Brewster Color Wheel
The Ostwald Color Wheel and Cone
The Munsell Color System

CHAPTER 3

LIGHTING

Chapter Focus

Chapter 3 presents eight sections representing the most important aspects, considerations, and applications regarding the element of light. These sections include: Natural lighting, Artificial Lighting, Types of Lighting, Psychological Effects of Lighting, Lighting Fixtures, Switches and Outlets, Lighting for Areas and Activities, and Economy and Energy Conservation.

Text Outline

Introduction

A. Through our sense of vision we perceive the world around us and function in our environments.

B. Vision depends on both natural and artificial light

C. A well-planned lighting system:

1. Creates an environment that is comfortable and functional.
2. Provides a sense of safety and security.
3. Creates a mood or atmosphere.
4. Focuses attention on a specific object or draws attention to the room's focal point.
5. Helps change the apparent size and proportion of a space.
6. Supports the style selected.
7. Effectively shows the texture and form of an object or entire room.
8. Aids in creating an environment that is both emotionally uplifting and aesthetically pleasing.
9. Allows color to be perceived in various ways.

I. NATURAL LIGHTING:

A. The principal source of natural light is the *sun.*

1. Its properties, including ultraviolet light, warmth, and radiant energy, are of significant importance to people's health and well-being.

2. Sunlight emits all visible ***wavelengths of radiant energy*** , as well as ***invisible infrared wavelengths*** and ***ultraviolet wavelengths*** .
3. ***White light*** is ***electromagnetic energy*** emitted in the visible portion of the ***spectrum*** .

B. The ***human eye*** sees the color of an object when light of mixed wavelengths is reflected into the eye from the object's surface
1. A particular surface absorbs or reflects a color of the spectrum depending on its composition.
2. The process of vision depends on:
   a. ***light***
   b. ***an object*** to be seen
   c. ***a receptor*** (our eyes)
   d. ***a decoder*** (our brain)

C. Light is measured in four different ways:
1. ***Footcandle*** : unit of measure for amount of light falling on a surface.
2. ***Lumen*** : measure of light produced by one lamp.
3. ***Footlambert*** : unit of measure for amount of light reflected from a surface
4. ***Candela*** : unit of measure for the intensity of light in a given direction.

D. Often, the challenge for the designer is to control natural light within a living space to contribute to the occupant's comfort and aesthetic enjoyment.

E. Design can also determine the most suitable window treatment for a particular structure.

F. ***Combustion Lighting:*** Until the development of electric lighting, the only method of producing supplementary light.
1. It still deserves consideration as a decorative element in residential and some nonresidential projects.
2. Fire, oil lamps, candles, and gaslights are all methods of combustion.

II. ARTIFICIAL LIGHTING:

A. A ***man-made source*** of illumination derived from electricity.
1. Electrical energy is transformed into visible light and identified as wattage.
2. Using today's versatile artificial lighting sources created for function, comfort, and visual pleasure, designers can fully employ all aspects of their ingenuity in illumination.

B. Through the art of man-made lighting, space can be modified, structural elements can be emphasized or subordinated, color, texture, and form can be enhanced art objects can be brought into focus, and an atmosphere of cool formality or warm intimacy can be imparted to a room.

C. The designer needs to understand both the aesthetics and techniques of lighting.
D. In most rooms a variety of lighting is desirable, because comfort, beauty, and mood are influenced by the source, color, amount, placement, and quality of illumination.
E. Before selecting lighting fixtures for particular needs, the type of light source should be considered.
F. The most familiar light sources are ***incandescent, tungsten-halogen, fluorescent, HID lighting*** and ***neon.***
G. These sources use a bulb, called a **lamp** in the industry
   1. ***The Incandescent Filament Lamp:*** comes from the familiar light bulb invented by Thomas Edison. Electricity flows through a tungsten filament sealed in a bulb. heating it and creating light. It is the most common type employed for residential designs. Attributes include the following:
      a. Available in wide variety of sizes, shapes, colors, and types.
      b. Small and adaptable. Easy to control quantity of light.
      c. Do not flicker, hum, or cause significant interference.
      d. Produce white light that casts a slight red and yellow hue.
      e. Generally flattering to human skin coloring.
      f. Effectively highlight textures and forms.
      g. Relatively inexpensive, although not as productive in terms of energy conserved.
      h. Permit precise optical control for effective accent and task lighting.
      i. Disadvantages: Exposing lamp can cause unpleasant glare. Warm incandescent light tends to neutralize cool colors.
   2. ***The Tungsten-Halogen Lamp:*** A relatively new high-performance lighting source for both residential and commercial design (also known as a quartz-halogen lamp). It is a type of incandescent lamp and operates on the same principle, although the shape of the lamp is different. Instead of a filament, the halogen lamp has a piece of hard quartz in a small enclosure that when heated attains higher temperatures and therefore produces a more intense light. When halogen gas is introduced into the enclosure the result is better performance output. Major advantages include:
      a. Although initially more expensive to buy and operate, they last much longer than incandescent lamps - from 2,000 - 4,000 hours.
      b. Produce more intense light than incandescent lamps.
      c. Light source is smaller, so can be used with smaller fixtures and still provide intense light.
      d. Can be used with a dimmer to provide a variety of lighting levels.
      e. Can be used in elegantly designed torcheres or uplighters.

f. Available in wall-mounted units that provide excellent background or spot lighting.
g. Low-voltage halogen lamps are small and flexible enough to focus as a narrow beam suitable for task lighting.
h. Disadvantage: Halogen lamps are expensive. May require special sockets.
Require careful installation and if exposed should not be touched without gloves. Emit high levels of heat and tend to blacken when used with a dimmer. Must be carefully shielded, so cannot be used as direct lighting.

3. ***Fluorescent Lighting:*** is produced in a glass tube lined with a fluorescent coating, filled with mercury vapor and argon, and sealed at the ends with cathodes. When gases are activated by an electric current, ultraviolet rays stimulate the phosphorous bulb coating, which emits visible light. Lamps are made in straight, U shaped, circline, and circlete shapes. Most familiar type is the T12 tubular lamp. Attributes include the following:
a. Emit less heat than incandescent lamps.
b. Although expensive, use less energy to produce a greater amount of light.
c. New family of small fluorescent straight lamps being used in many applications where incandescent lamps were formally used.
d. Sources are larger and create broader areas of light than incandescent.
e. Provide diffused, shadowless light.
f. Particularly efficient for commercial lighting.
g. Disadvantages: Fixtures and lamps can be more expensive. Light quality somewhat flat and monotonous. Can distort colors and details. Cold light can be unflattering. Have a tendency to hum and flicker. Not as flexible and easy to control.
h. Designers often mix both fluorescent and incandescent light in a space to combine the most desirable qualities of each lighting source.

4. ***The HID Lamp:*** (High intensity discharge) incorporates some of the desired qualities of both incandescent and fluorescent lighting. The lamp is similar to the incandescent bulb but is slightly larger. It is most commonly used for commercial and public spaces, however, with technology advances, will eventually be used in the home. There are three types of HID lamps: (1) ***mercury*** (2) ***high-pressure sodium*** and (3) ***metal halide*** . Advantages and disadvantages include:
a. Lasts from 16,000 to 24,000 hours
b. Highly suitable for commercial and institutional demands for energy-saving lighting. Poor color and noise limit their use in small spaces.
c. Require up to nine minutes to reach full light capacity. Strong glare can occur if not shielded properly.

5. *Cold Cathode (Neon) :* contains an inert gas at low pressure that emits a reddish glow when voltage is applied. Can be fashioned in many decorative forms, especially curved, and available in almost any color. Lasts for many years, however, does require a transformer and is quite fragile. Most often employed for commercial projects. Interesting effects can also be created for home use.

III. TYPES OF LIGHTING:

A. Three main types of lighting are:

1. ***General or Ambient Lighting***
   a. Background or fill light that spreads an even, overall luminosity and reduces harsh contrasts between pools of concentrated light.
   b. Can be produced by large area light sources, by a number of small sources by direct or indirect light; or by pendants, chandeliers, downlights, spotlights and reflected light from portable fixtures.
      (1) *Direct Lighting:* Often used for general lighting, it is light thrown directly downward onto a particular area, resulting in shadows and sharp contrast between dark and light.
      (2) *Indirect Lighting:* Is light that shines onto the ceiling or wall and is reflected back into the room. Tends to expand space visually and when reflected from the ceiling provides general illumination. Tends to be flat and usually needs to be supplemented by portable fixtures. Can be used to dramatize a particular area.
2. ***Task or Local***
   a. Is functional and localized for a particular activity such as sewing, office work, reading, writing, preparing food, or grooming.
   b. Lighting is placed near the activity but aimed to avoid glare.
   c. Most tasks require a high level of illumination.
   d. Placement, shade design, socket location, and shielding all contribute to controlling glare and supplying good light.
   e. Recessed or ceiling-mounted fixtures should have dimmers..
   f. The choice of lamps or tubes will determine the quantity of light.
3. ***Accent***
   a. Employs a concentrated beam of light focusing on a particular object or area.
   b. Can be placed at any desired angle and be precisely controlled to provide the required amount of intensity and color.
   c. Can separate one area from another, highlight a treasured item, establish a focal point, or create a touch of drama.

IV. PSYCHOLOGICAL EFFECTS OF LIGHTING:

A. Successful lighting can provide a sense of emotional well-being in addition to satisfying physical requirements. With respect to human psychology, light has the following attributes:

1. Associated with the exuberance of life itself and with human well-being.
2. Can convey a sense of security, warmth, and comfort.
3. Can evoke a mood
4. If not enough light in the environment, may provoke feelings depression or fear. (Light therapy is often used to treat depression.)
5. Too much light or glaring light can be agitating, uncomfortable, even resulting in physical ailments and an inability to function adequately.

B. Designers take into account the psychological impact of light to satisfy both physical and emotional human needs.

V. LIGHTING FIXTURES:

A. Fixtures, or luminaires, for artificial lighting sources can be divided into two groups: ((l) architectural, or built-in, and (2) portable, or nonarchitectural.

1. ***Architectural Lighting:*** Includes wall-mounted and ceiling-mounted fixtures and is closely correlated with the structure of the room. It should be included in the wiring plans of the original structure. The flexibility of these fixtures can be fairly limited.

   a. ***Wall-Mounted Fixtures:*** Types of wall-mounted fixtures include:
      (1) Valance lighting - a horizontal fluorescent tube is placed behind a valance board above a window
      (2) Bracket lighting - similar to valance lighting, but fixture is placed either high on the wall for general wall lighting or low for specific tasks.
      (3) Cove lighting - is placed near the ceiling directing light upward
      (4) Wall sconces - or lighting fixtures permanently attached on the wall.

   b. ***Ceiling-Mounted Fixtures:*** several kinds include:
      (l) Recessed downlighters - may focus on a definite object or produce general lighting.
      (2) Wall-washer - an adjustable unit that can be directed at any angle to "wash" the wall with light.
      (3) Eyeball - is similar to a wall-washer but can swivel, allowing light to be angled where desired.
      (4) Cornice - usually built on ceiling to direct light downward only.
      (5) Soffit - enclosed light attached to the ceiling
      (6) Track lighting - is flush-mounted to the ceiling (can be wall-mounted). Fixtures clip anywhere along a track.

(7) Suspended fixtures or pendants - are hung from the ceiling.
(8) Flush-mounted lighting - as opposed to recessed. May project a few inches into the room and reflect direct or indirect lighting.
(9) Luminous panels - consist of recessed light diffused through ceiling panels.
(10) Custom-design architectural lighting - created for a particular purpose or design effect.

c. Floor lighting may be used in dark hallways and the base of steps as a safety device.

2. ***Portable or nonarchitectural Lighting:*** indicates the ability to transport fixtures from location to location as desired, considering the purposes they serve and the area in which they are used. Portable fixtures (both table and floor models) are the oldest forms of electrical interior lighting. They provide flexible lighting in the residential or public environment and may be purely functional, decorative, or both. Considerations include:
   a. ***Placement*** - generally are positioned as part of a furniture grouping near an electrical outlet, and out of the line of traffic.
   b. ***Function*** - fixtures should be chosen with purpose in mind. Usually a combination of both portable and ceiling and wall-mounted fixtures satisfies lighting needs for function and visual interest.
   c. ***Shades*** - Most portable fixtures come with shades to help diffuse and direct the light. A table lamp used for reading is most effective when the bottom of the shade is at the eye level. The shade works well when it is at least 16 in. across the bottom. When the shade is lined with white, maximum light is provided. Glare is eliminated when the shade covers the bulb and fixture.
   d. ***Light diffusion*** - A soft white bulb provides the best light diffusion. An opal glass diffuser bowl also improves the quality of light over standard lass because it helps reduce glare. A flat dishlike diffuser helps soften and mask direct light from horizontal bulbs.
   e. ***Scale and Proportion*** - should be considered in relation to other furnishings and to the size of the room and the lamp itself. Decorative fixtures generally work best when the design is simple, unobtrusive, and suitable to the room's style and design. Structural fixtures devoid of ornamentation usually work best when simple, well proportioned and suitably scaled, and constructed of materials and textures that complement the room's style.

VI. SWITCHES AND OUTLETS:

A. The convenient location of switches and outlets is essential and must be indicated on the blueprint and electrical plan of the structure.
   1. Each room requires a light switch.
   2. Switches may be conveniently placed on the latch side of each access door.
   3. Switches are necessary at both ends of hallways and at the top and bottom of stairways.
   4. Where task lighting is necessary, switches should be place within easy reach.
   5. Dimmers on switches allow great flexibility

B. Outlets: Throughout interior spaces, outlets should be plentiful and located for specific tasks.
   1. When a room's function is determined, outlets can be conveniently located in accordance with local building codes.
   2. Outlets placed in regular intervals approximately 3 to 6 ft. apart between doorways and floor-length windows decrease the need for hazardous extension cords.
   3. Outlets mounted 12 in. from the floor and wall switches located 50 in from the floor are workable.
   4. Where heavy mechanical devices are power driven, special heavy-duty outlets should be provided.
   5. Outdoor outlets must be weather-proof, made ground-fault interruptible, and situated safely.

VII. LIGHTING FOR AREAS AND ACTIVITIES:

A. Since humans are psychologically and physically affected by light, it is an important factor when planning each interior space.

B. Glaring light is disturbing and hampers activities.

C. Bland or inefficient light can actually result in physical fatigue.

D. Designers can alleviate lighting problems by controlling the light source and causing the light to be reflected, absorbed, or redirected.

E. Lighting considerations for specific areas and activities in residential settings:
   1. ***Entrance area:*** is the keynote to the decor of a home and can provide a cordial air of hospitality where lighting plays an important role.
   2. ***Living rooms:*** need soft general background lighting supplemented by special area lighting to support the function of this space which includes conversation, playing and listening to music, reading, studying, etc.) Both direct and indirect lighting sources are desirable. Well-chosen lamps at necessary locations add a feeling of comfort and hospitality conducive to conversation. Lighting can help establish the room's focal point.

3. ***Dining rooms:*** deserve versatile lighting around the table area that can be adjusted for a variety of functions.. A low-level background can be provided by general lighting. A chandelier or pendant using incandescent globes and hung about 30 in. above the table provides a pleasant setting. Dimmer controls allow for a change of mood. Creative use of accent light helps in avoiding flat downlights and adds interest.
4. ***Family and recreation rooms:*** accommodate a variety of activities and require particularly flexible lighting. General lighting is essential, with area and task lighting supplied for specific activities.
5. ***Kitchens and utility rooms:*** function best when generous overall lighting for safety and efficiency is planned. Task lighting is necessary for mixing, cooking, and sink centers.
6. ***Bedrooms:*** need comfortable general lighting with appropriate task lights for reading, desk work, grooming, and other activities, depending on the use of the space. Direct lighting is also efficient when placed over chest of drawers, in closets, close to seating, and other beds. Dim circulation lighting for safety at night is required. Accent lighting can be effectively used.
7 ***Bathrooms:*** require shadowless lighting for shaving and grooming, which can be supplied by lights from overhead and from both sides of a mirror. Mirror lighting is usually sufficient to illuminate an average-sized bath or powder room, however, general lighting overhead and over tub areas is needed.
8. ***Halls and Stairways*** - require overall illumination for safe passage.
9. ***Outdoor lighting*** - at night enhances the exterior architecture, gardens, etc., in both residential and nonresidential structures and aids in safe passage. Also helps alleviate the black glass look inside. Weatherproof luminaires for outside use are available.

VIII. ECONOMY AND ENERGY CONSERVATION:

A. Knowledgeable planning and purchasing can give a space sufficient lighting and still save watts and dollars. Following are guidelines to help conserve energy in lighting:
   1. Lighting should fit specific needs.Sufficient light is important, but using more light than necessary wastes electrical energy.
   2. Dimmers are useful in adjusting light levels, increasing lamp life, and saving energy.
   3. Installing multiple switches makes it possible to use only the amount of light required.
   4. Fixtures should be energy effective, allowing maximum light to be emitted.
   5. Fixtures that can be adjusted and placed where light is needed is a wise choice.

6. A reflectorized lamp is good for accent or task lighting. Low-voltage spotlights are especially effective.
7. Light sources should be efficient. Light output varies in efficiency according to wattage and color.
8. Three-way incandescent lamps allow selectivity in the amount of light used.
9. Where appearance is not a consideration, as in garages and some basements, industrial reflectors are an economical option.
10. When ceilings, walls, floors, and furniture have light colored finishes they reflect more light and require less lighting.
11. Keeping reflectors, diffusers, and lamps clean helps to maintain lighting equipment.
12. Lights should be turned off when not needed.

Learning Enhancement Options

Natural Lighting: Ask students to respond to feelings of well-being generated from sunlight. Discuss the important of natural lighting in planning both residential and nonresidential environments and what problems are involved. Show transparencies of how the human eye sees color of an object when the light of mixed wavelengths is reflected. Discuss the process of vision and the four different ways in which light is measured. Talk about the functional and decorative qualities concerning combustion lighting.

Artificial Lighting: Ask students to provides examples of how they respond to various types of artificial lighting in their personal environments as well as in public places, for example, doctor's offices, restaurants, schools, malls, etc. Discuss how through the art of man-made lighting, environments can be both functional and aesthetically satisfying. Show the transparencies of the various lamps and discuss the advantages and disadvantages of the five lamp types. If a light box is available, demonstrate the effects of cool and warm light.

Types of Lighting: Ask students to respond to the three main types of lighting: general, task, and accent. Discuss the difference between direct and direct lighting. Back up the discussion with visual materials.

Psychological Effects of Lighting: This section presents an excellent opportunity to have students relate personal experiences on how various lamps, types and sources of has lighting affected them. Further reinforce these experiences with those of your own, especially examples from design projects.

Lighting Fixtures: Outline the various types of lighting fixtures and the difference between architectural and nonarchitectural lighting. Discuss with the students the various fixture types and how they are mounted. Cover each fixture, both wall-mounted and ceiling-mounted. Brief sketches of these fixture types illustrated on the board are helpful to students. Show visual material to support each fixture and its use and effect in both residential and nonresidential settings.

Switches and Outlets: Discuss with the students how switches and outlets function and can be conveniently located for the end user.

Lighting for Areas and Activities: Review with the students the psychological and physical properties of lighting in regard to its use in each room of the house. This is an excellent section for having students relate personal experiences and to provide additional examples of your own. Visual materials depicting the use of light in the basic rooms in the home will enhance the student's appreciation and knowledge of this element.

Economy and Energy Conservation: Discuss the various ways in which people can help in energy conservation. Stress the importance of everyone contributing to helping the economy and saving energy. Even though the little things you can do may not seem like much, when millions of people adhere to these ideas, it can make a difference.

Test Questions

Multiple Choice

__A__ 1. The process of vision depends on all but one of the following:
- A. A lumen
- B. A decoder
- C. A receptor
- D. An Object

__D__ 2. Electrical energy is transformed into visible light and identified as:
- A. A lamp
- B. As electromagnetic energy
- C. A receptor
- D. Wattage

__B__ 3. In the industry, a bulb is called a:
A. Fixture
B. Lamp
C. Filament
D. Lumen

__C__ 4. An incandescent filament lamp:
A. Produces a white light that cast a slight blue hue
B. Tends to flicker
C. Is relatively inexpensive
D. Is generally expensive

__B__ 5. The tungsten-halogen lamp:
A. Contains a tungsten filament
B. Contains a piece of hard quartz
C. Contains mercury and argon
D. Produces less intense light than an incandescent lamp

__A__ 6. The fluorescent lamp:
A. Uses less energy to produce a greater amount of light
B. Uses more energy to produce a greater amount of light
C. Is only available in straight tubes
D. Generally should not be mixed with incandescent lamps within a space

__D__ 7. The HID lamp:
A. Has a good quality of color, so suitable for residential use
B. Requires only a few seconds to reach full light capacity
C. Is similar to the incandescent bulb but is slightly smaller
D. Is similar to the incandescent bulb but is slightly larger

__C__ 8. The cold Cathode (Neon) lamp:
A. Has a relatively short usage period
B. Is strong and durable
C. Requires a transformer
D. Contains an inert gas at high pressure that emits a bluish glow when voltage is applied

__B__ 9. Lighting can be divided into three distinct types: (which does not belong?)
A. Local
B. Perimeter
C. General
D. Accent

__A__ 10. Which of the following best describes "ambient lighting"?
A. General
B. Accent
C. Mood
D. Luminescent

__D__ 11. The two basic methods of artificial lighting are: (Select the best answer)
A. Structural and architectural
B. Functional and structural
C. Portable and nonarchitectural
D. Nonarchitectural and architectural

__C__ 12. Cove lighting placed near the ceiling directs all the light:
A. Outward from each side of the fixture
B. Downward
C. Upward
D. Downward and Upward

__B__ 13. Cornice lighting, usually built on the ceiling, directs the light:
A. Upward
B. Downward
C. Downward and Upward
D. Outward from both sides of the fixture

__A__ 14. Electrical outlets are usually placed in regular intervals approximately:
A. 3 to 6 feet apart
B. 2 to 5 feet apart
C. 4 to 8 feet apart
D. 8 to 10 feet apart

__D__ 15. When the goal is to conserve energy, which guideline does not apply?
A. Use dimmers
B. Fixtures that can be adjusted
C. Use a reflectorized lamp
D. Install only a few switches in the room

True / False

__T__ 16. The apparent size of a space can be affected by light.

__T__ 17. The principle source of light is the sun.

__F__ 18. Electromagnetic energy is a major force in producing electric current.

__F__ 19. Incandescent lamps last from about 2,000 to 4,000 hours.

__T__ 20. A soffit is an enclosed light attached to the ceiling.

Matching

Match the following units of measure with the correct answer:

A. Footcandle
B. Lumen
C. Footlambert
D. Candela

__D__ 21. Intensity of light in a given direction.

__A__ 22. Amount of light falling on an object.

__B__ 23. Measure of light produced by one lamp.

__C__ 24. Amount of light reflected by a surface.

Match the following basic light sources with the appropriate criteria:

A. Natural light
B. Combustion light
C. Artificial light

__C__ 25. Visible light identified as wattage.

__B__ 26. Oldest method of producing supplementary lighting.

__A__ 27. Visible wavelengths of radiant energy.

Match the following lamps with the correct description:

A. Incandescent lamp
B. Tungsten-halogen lamp
C. Fluorescent lamp
D. HID lamp
E. Cold Cathode lamp

__E__ 28. Inert gas at low pressure emits a red glow.

__D__ 29. Mercury, high-pressure sodium or metal halide.

__A__ 30. Tungsten filament sealed in a lamp.

__B__ 31. Lamp has a piece of hard quartz in a small enclosure.

__C__ 32. Lamp filled with mercury vapor and argon.

Match the three types of lighting to the correct criteria:

A. General B. Task C. Accent

__B__ 33. Placed near the intended activity.

__A__ 34. Reduces harsh contrast between pools of concentrated light.

__C__ 35. Separates one area from another and highlights.

Match the following wall-mounted fixtures with the best description:

A. Valance B. Bracket C. Sconce

__C__ 36. Decorative or structure fixture placed on wall for visual interest.

__A__ 37. Horizontal fixture directs light upward and downward.

__B__ 38. Placed high or low on the wall for general or task lighting.

Match the following ceiling-mounted fixtures with the most appropriate description:

A. Eyeball
B. Cornice
C. Soffit
D. Track
E. Flush-mounted
F. Luminous panels

__E__ 39. Opposite of recessed. Projects into the room a few inches.

__F__ 40. Recessed light diffused through translucent material.

__B__ 41. Directs the light only downward from the ceiling.

__A__ 42. Similar to a wall-washer, but can swivel.

__C__ 43. Light fixture is enclosed in a box-like structure and attached to the ceiling.

__D__ 44. Fixtures can be clipped along a course.

Essay / Short Answer

45. Briefly discuss the benefits of a well-planned lighting system in a residential or nonresidential environment.

Answer to this question is found on page 60.

46. Outline five basic types of lamps and the advantages and disadvantages of each.

Answer to this question is found on pages 63 through 66.

47. List the three main types of lighting and indicate the effects and use of each type..

Answer to this question is found on pages 67 through 70.

48. Successful lighting can provide a sense of emotion well-being in addition to analyzing physical requirements. With respect to human psychology, list light's attributes:

Answer to this question is found on page 70.

49. Portable lighting indicates the ability to transport fixtures from location to location as

desired. They provide flexible lighting in the residential or public environment and may be purely functional, decorative, or both. Considerations include:

Answer to this question is found on pages 74 through 77.

50. In outline form, list the general lighting considerations for specific areas and activities in residential settings.

Answer to this question is found on pages 78 through 80 .

Educational Resources:

Publications:

Design Criteria for Lighting Interior Living Spaces. New York: Illuminating Engineering Society of North America, 1980.

Gardner, Carl and Barry Hannaford. *Lighting Design: An Introductory Guide for Professionals* . New York: Wiley. 1993.

General Electric. *The Light Book.* Cleveland, Ohio: Nela Park, 1981.

Gilliatt, Mary, and Douglas Baker. *Lighting Your Home: A Practical Guide.* New York: Pantheon, 1979.

Grosslight, Jane. *Light: Effective Use of Daylight and Electric Lighting in Residential and Commercial Projects.* Englewood Cliffs, N.J.: Prentice-Hall, 1984.

Kaufmann, John E. *IES Lighting Handbook Reference Volume.* New York: Illuminating Engineering Society of North America, 1981.

Lightolier. *The Light Book.* Jersey City, N.J.: Lightolier, 1981.

Mahnke, Frank H. and Rudolf H. Mahnke. *Color and Light in Man-made Environments.* New York: Van Nostrand Reinhold, 1987.

Nuckolls, James L. *Interior Lighting for Environmental Designers.* New York: Wiley, 1976.

Phillips, Derek. *Lighting in Architectural Design.* New York: Holt, Rinehart & Winston, 1968.

Rooney, William F. *Practical Guide to Home Lighting.* New York: Van Nostrand Reinhold, 1980.

Movies / Videos

Interior Lighting: Bringing Rooms to Life : 22 min / 1990 / Insight Media

Transparencies

How the Human Eye Sees Color and an Object
The Basic Lamp Types

Ch 3 - 11 more
28 total

CHAPTER 4

SPACE PLANNING

Chapter Focus

Chapter 4 presents seven sections covering the impact of the physical interior environment on the occupant's life and how space can be well-planned to meet the basic goals of space planning. These sections include: The Basic Goals of Design and Space Planning, Programming and the Design Process, Site Selection and Orientation, The Floor Plan, Analyzing Basic Types of Floor Plans, Floor Plan Shapes, and Attached and Multifamily Plans.

Text Outline

I. **THE BASIC GOALS OF DESIGN AND SPACE PLANNING:**

A. The designer's ultimate goal when planning a residence or commercial structure should be the integration of the basic requirements for:

1. An efficient and aesthetically pleasing space
2. Functional needs
3. Physical and psychological comfort
4. Economic considerations
5. Aesthetics
6. Individuality

B. Other criteria worth considering when planning space include:

1. Conserving energy
2. Incorporating ideas for "greening the environment"
3. Ensuring a healthy and safe environment
4. Addressing the needs of all users, including the physically challenged, children, or the elderly

C. ***Functional Needs:*** To be livable, an interior should fulfill its intended function of satisfying the needs of the people for whom it is designed.

1. Careful consideration of functional space should commence in the initial planning stage.

2. For a residential project, designers should ask numerous questions concerning lifestyles, design preferences and requirements of the end users.
3. Part of the early planning phase, or program, involves completing a personal profile for each occupant
4. In the case of a nonresidential project, spelling out the needs of the client in detail is required.
5. Spatial requirements should be planned after carefully evaluating this information.
6. Specific design requirements may be necessary for the special needs of users such as children, the elderly, or physically challenged.

D *Physical and Psychological Comfort:* of the occur is anoints important aspect of the space planning process.

1. This includes being comfortable in relation to the scale and proportion of the architecture.
2. Selection and arrangement of line, color, form, lighting, and texture to create a sense of balance and harmony.
3. Furniture should be suitable scaled for comfort and arranged for purpose and efficiency.

E. *Planning for the Physically Challenged* is of utmost importance when planning a nonresidential space and the design must meet certain code and legal requirements. Even in residential design, physically challenged and elderly individuals are often members of a household or may be the only occupants. The environment needs to function well for convenience, safety, and security. Some criteria include:

1. Home should be free of architectural barriers
2. Bathrooms and fixtures must be conveniently and safely located with ample room for manipulating a wheelchair.
3. Clearances between furnishings in all rooms of the house should be adequate.
4. Lighting throughout the home should be located with access to switches, controls, and outlets.
5. Floor coverings in hard, smooth surfaces that are slip resistant work most efficiently
6. The kitchen should be arranged with heights, clearances and other measurements planned for convenience and safety.
7. Climate-control boxes should be approximately 2 to 4 feet above the floor

F. *Economic Considerations:* A home is probably the largest single investment a consumer will every make. Receiving the best value possible is essential.

1. The designer should study costs on paper and look carefully at such criteria

as available resources or allocated budget, client needs, materials and components required, time limits, building requirements and codes.

2. The cost of a structure is related to the amount of square footage within the space and varies depending on many factors, such as site, geographic location, materials specified, cubic square footage, special construction features, and the cost of local labor.
3. Average building costs per square foot depend on the region where the structure will be built.
4. In residential projects the initial cost is only the beginning: payments and upkeep must continue.
5. Most home-financing agencies recommend that the monthly payment should not exceed 28 percent of the gross income.
6. A general formula is that monthly payment of approximately $500.00 is due for every $50,000 borrowed.
7. Suggestions concerning methods and materials that can help minimize project costs include:
   a. A well-designed floor plan.
   b. A basic and simple plan.
   c. A unified theme.
   d. Adequate insulation.
   e. Solar orientation.
   f. Centralized plumbing and fireplaces
   g. Use of indigenous materials
   h. Use of standard milled items
   i. Consideration of long-term upkeep

G. ***Aesthetics*** Interior spaces should be pleasing to the users and ought to have a certain intrinsic appeal.

1. Sensitivity to the aesthetics of all interior environments, such as private dwellings, financial or educational institutions, offices, retail and hospitality spaces, health care centers, and other nonresidential interiors is essential for interior designers.
2. A knowledgeable designer has a trained eye for discriminating between good and poor design.
3. Beauty has been described as that quality which pleases the senses and lifts the spirit and is most often a personal reaction.
4. Authorities in the design field generally agree that beauty in any object is achieved through the thoughtful application of the principles of design and a skillful use of design elements, unified by a basic theme.

H. ***Individuality:*** is an elusive quality, particularly when considering its properties in a private dwelling.

1. Individuality often develops slowly and naturally, revealing the personality of the occupants.
2. Often, individuality or projecting a particular character is expressed in nonresidential projects.

II. PROGRAMMING AND THE DESIGN PROCESS:

A. As the designer begins a residential or nonresidential project, it is essential to understand how the end users will function in the space and to collect all relevant background information.

B. After this information has been gathered, a plan or design process can be determined. This initial planning stage is called the Program.

C. The program is also a written or typed design statement summarizing all the requirements, goals, and objects for one specific project and its users.

D. In the case of a residential project, this is often referred to as a client profile. A nonresidential project may require a more extensive program.

E. The basic steps involved in the design process include:

1. ***Commitment to the problem:*** The written program outlines the client's expectations and the designer's commitment and responsibility.
2. ***Define the problem:*** This step in the design process requires confronting the problems involved with the design project and then defining what these problems are:
3. ***Gather information:*** This step requires collecting information essential to the design's success. (This step is involved in the programming as mentioned previously).
4. ***Analyze the facts***: Once the information is gathered, the designer can examine and analyze the data that will have an important bearing on the final solution.
5. ***Generate ideas***: This is the most creative step for the designer. Once the problems have been identified, and the facts have been gathered and analyzed many design concepts for possible solutions can be explored.
6. ***Select the most effective solution***: The designer can evaluate which ideas will best meet the needs, preferences, and budget of the client or clients. Often, input from the client will aid in determining the most suitable solution.
7. ***Implement the ideas.***: At this point in the design process, action is taken to implement the ideas generated. This may include communicating the ideas through drawings and renderings, specifying materials to be incorporated, working with contractors, and writing and signing contracts. The ideas and solutions are then carried out and completed.
8. ***Design Evaluation*** : Following completion of the project, the designer should critically evaluate its outcome.

F. ***Residential Projects:*** involve designing spaces for single individuals or families in an environment that is often called a "home" and generally involves an entirely different design focus from planning nonresidential spaces. These private dwellings include:
   1. Detached houses, townhouses, condominiums, apartments, prefabricated houses, mobile homes, and dormitories.

G. ***Nonresidential Projects:*** The numerous types of commercial spaces on which a designer may work will have a variety of functions, therefore space planning involves a more complex procedure than the residential projects.
   1. To meet the needs of the client and end users, extensive study and research on the part of the designer are required.
   2. The general categories of nonresidential design include:
      a. ***Business office design***
      b. ***Health care*** (hospitals, medical offices, physical therapy ctrs., etc.)
      c. ***Industrial design*** (factories, workshops, warehouses,etc.)
      d. ***Retail design*** (stores, shops, galleries, showrooms, etc.)
      e. ***Financial institutions*** (banks, credit unions, stock exchanges, etc.)
      f. ***Educational institutions*** (universities, colleges, schools, etc.)
      g. ***Government and public*** (courthouses, municipal bldgs, libraries, etc.)
      h. ***Hospitality*** (restaurants, hotels, resorts, inns, motels, etc.)
      i. ***Recreational*** (sports clubs, health clubs, golf and tennis resorts, etc.
      j. ***Transportation*** (stations for airplanes, ships, buses, trains, etc.)

H. Following the programming and design process specified for residential projects, the designer is particularly concerned with the following space planning criteria for specific nonresidential projects:
   1. ***Functional requirements*** of the end users met.
   2. ***Spatial organization.*** Lay out the space by zoning and diagramming the various functions.
   3. ***Shape and size of the space.*** The available cubic and square footage helps determine the total design of the space.
   4. ***Traffic lanes or patterns.*** Users should be able to travel effectively within all interior spaces.
   5. ***Building laws, codes, and restrictions.*** Codes set by state and local government must be followed.
   6. ***Interior systems.*** Electrical, heating, and cooling systems, ventilation, plumbing, sanitary drainage, fire protection systems, elevators, escalators, ramps, acoustical control, and other systems must be carefully planned for efficiency and safety.
   7. ***Specifications of materials and components.*** Lighting, style, colors,

textures, accessories that will contribute to the physical and psychological well-being of all users must be chosen.

8. ***Planning for the physically challenged.*** The space must be made accessible for wheelchairs.

III. SITE SELECTION AND ORIENTATION:

A. On certain projects, the designer may have imput into selecting the site for a residential or nonresidential structure.

B. Before making a selection, the designer should have the general plan of the structure in mind.

C. Not until the site has been analyzed should the plan be finalized.

D. Depending on the building's intended function, criteria when selecting a site for a nonresidential structure might include public convenience, efficiency, accessibility, and aesthetic appeal.

E. For a residence, a desirable topography is often a gently sloping lot that provides good natural drainage and allows sewer lines to be connected easily.

F. Effective positioning of the structure on the site and orienting the structure to take advantage of solar proerties are also important criteria.

IV. THE FLOOR PLAN:

The Floor Plan: The graphic details of a floor plan indicate the spatial boundaries of the structure and strongly influence the efficiency and comfort of interior spaces.

A. Intelligent appliction of basic design requirements to the general floor plan is conducive to the smooth working of an interior space.

B. Generally, users appreciate well-planned circulation patterns whether in public or private spaces.

C. In recent years, skyrocketing building costs and interest rates , along with dramatic changes in the family structure, have forced people to live in small spaces, making multipurpose areas a necessity.

D. It is essential to be able to read and understand an architect's working drawing of a floor plan.

1. This graphic design is referred to as the ***blueprint.***
2. The floor plan is a ***two-dimensional drawing*** indicating the walls, floors, partitions, windows, stairs, cabinets, and other structural components.
3. Floor plans are drawn precisely to ***scale.***
   a. A commonly used scale in a residential floor plan is ***1/4 in. to 1 ft.***
   b. In a nonresidential project ***1/8 in. to l ft.*** is often used.
4. To understand the blueprint, it is necessary to become familiar with basic architectural drafting symbols.

5. With this knowledge the designer can intelligently examine the blueprint while "walking through" the spaces.

Interior Zoning: Defining basic areas in residential and nonresidential projects is helpful to the design in the space planning process. The functions in a residential structure fall into three zones that combine related activities (l) ***service or work zones,*** (2) ***social zones,*** and (3) ***private zones.***

A. ***Service or Work Zones*** (Kitchen, utility, sewing room, workshop, office, and other work related zones.)

1. ***The Kitchen Area:*** Is usually the "hub" of the home - where food preparation, serving, eating and other activities take place. An area for socializing and relaxing with friends and should be planned for flexibility. Kitchens should be efficient. Planning kitchen space includes the following considerations.

a. ***Shape or Arrangement*** should determine the location of work centers, accommodate physical limitations, and facilitate various everyday household activities. The basic kitchen arrangements are: (U-shape, (2) L-shape, (3) island, (4) parallel, and (5) one-wall.

b. ***The Work Centers:*** (1) sink area (preparation and cleanup), (2) cooking area (range and oven), and (3) refrigerator area.

c. ***Placement of Work Centers:*** walking distance between the three work centers should not be less than seven ft. or more than twenty ft.

d. ***Physical Limitations of the User:*** Cabinet and countertop heights should be comfortable scaled to the person working in the space.

e. ***Sufficient Cabinet and Counterspace:*** Efficient and adequate cabinet and counter space is necessary. There must be storage for: (l) food, (2) tableware, (3) appliances, (4) cleaning supplies, and (6) cooking utensils.

f. ***Pantry Space*** is a convenient addition.

g. ***Food Preparation:*** Surfaces for mixing, washing, cutting, blending, etc. should be adequate and conveniently placed

h. ***Eating:*** Countertop space or bars are popular for quick meals can be logically incorporated.

i. ***Appliances:*** Cabinets should accommodate ***permanently placed appliances*** : refrigerators, ovens, cooking tops, ranges, sinks, etc, and ***portable appliances:*** microwaves, blenders, mixers, etc.

j. ***Lighting:*** Adequate artificial and natural lighting is essential.

k. ***Style:*** whether modern or traditional depends on the taste of the users. Colors, textures, materials, flooring, countertops, window treatment and accessories are the major elements to consider.

2. ***Utility Area***
   a. **Function**, convenience, and transition are major considerations.
   b. ***Laundry*** room often placed near dressing or hygiene area but may be relegated to space near the kitchen or garage. Convenient placement of washer and dryer. Sufficient work space, storage and lighting necessary.
   c. ***Sewing, workshop, office, garden and other work areas*** should be conveniently located with well-arranged space.

B. ***Social Zones*** (entry, living, dining, recreation, and entertainment areas) are where people meet for various activities.
   1. ***The Entrance Area:*** Introduces the home and directs traffic. A place to enhance the home's theme. Select floor covering with traffic in mind. Scale and amount of furnishings are determined by the size of room. Lighting should be adequate and welcoming.
   2. ***Formal Living Area:*** Provides for all household members and guests as well. Works well when placed away from major traffic lanes for privacy. Activities usually include conversation, listening to music, reading, and relaxing. Considerations for space planning include:
      a. ***Floors, Walls, Ceilings, and Other Backgrounds.***
      b. ***Fireplace Treatment***
      c. ***Window Type and Treatment***
      d. ***Furniture Selection and Arrangement***
      e. ***Lighting***
      f. ***Accessories***
      g. ***Incorporation of Principles and Elements of Design***
   3. ***Informal Living Areas:*** The family room has become one of the most important rooms in the house. The designer takes into account the tastes, interests, and activities of all household members. This room may take many forms, but the main objective is to provide a flexible area to serve many purposes. Sometimes the room is combined with the kitchen and informal eating area and called "***the great room.***" Considerations include:
      a. ***Mood or Atmosphere Desired***
      b. ***Floors, Walls, and Fabrics***
      c. ***Furniture***
      d. ***Storage***
      e. ***Entertainment***
      f. ***Lighting***
   4. ***Formal Dining Area:*** An area for gracious dining. Requires privacy and should be close to the food preparation area, but shut off from the clutter of the kitchen. Planning considerations include:

a. ***Floor Coverings***
b. ***Furniture***
c. Defining the Space
d. ***Lighting***

5. ***Informal Dining Areas***: for quick snacks and everyday family meals are most conveniently located in or near the kitchen. Eating area close to kitchen can vary depending on the space and shape allocated. Adequate space is necessary to accommodate furnishings, lighting and supportive furnishings and accessories.
6. ***Entertainment, Recreation, and Educational Centers:*** Usually found in larger homes and may include indoor swimming pools, Ping-Pong, billiard and pool tables, a bar, space for dancing or television viewing, music centers, and computer and study centers. These various activities requires careful consideration when planning for convenience, safety, comfort, and aesthetics. With the vast array of new electronic products for the home, new design problems have arisen and new solutions are being explored. These products include the home computer with its many hardware and software components, video cassette recorders, etc. Some considerations for securing adequate space and equipment include:
   a. ***Choosing the Space***
   b. ***Floor and Wall Treatments***
   c. ***Furnishings***
   d. ***Fireplace treatment***
   e. ***Additional Furnishings***
   f. ***Lighting***

C. ***Private Zones*** (Sleeping, dressing, and hygiene) For maximum quiet and privacy, these areas function best when away from the social and work zones. A bathrooms, however, may be placed near both.

1. ***Bedrooms for Adults:*** Has become a refuge from pressures and stress - a place where relaxation and activities other than sleeping may take place. Often it is a luxurious part of the home. Because it is so personal and private, the designing may be different from any other room in the house. The main consideration should be twenty-four hour comfort. Each occupant should have input. Some considerations include:
   a. ***The bed***
   b. ***Other Functions the Room Will Serve***
   c. ***Lighting***
   d. ***Window Treatments***
   e. ***Fabrics***
   f. ***Style and Mood of the room***

2. ***Bedrooms for Children and Young Adults:*** A child's room requires good storage, adequate lighting, a desk for study, a comfortable bed, and space for play.
   a. The room can be planned with the child's input so it reflects his or her personality.
   b. Safety, with simple, sturdy, small-scaled furniture is a paramount concern.
   c. As a child grows and changes, flexible furnishings are practical.
   d. The room should be planned to accommodate the child's personal accessories.
   e. Durable and cleanable backgrounds are wise choices.
3. ***Dressing and Clothes Storage***: The dressing area may be in a separate space, in a closet, in the bedroom itself, or adjacent to or in the bathroom. Storage for clothing items should be close to the dressing area and bathroom and planned for convenience. A space for soiled clothed should be well located. Adequate storage for clothing, jewelry, and other dressing items is be planned to best advantage.
4. ***Personal Hygiene:*** Bathrooms are usually placed between social and private areas for the convenience of the users. Today, function and luxury are combined. Most homes have more than one bathroom. Major considerations for the designer are to:
   a. Determine the ***space available***
   b. The ***needs*** of the end users
   c. The most efficient arrangement of ***plumbing fixtures*** and supportive furnishings
   d. The ***accessories*** for function and aesthetic pleasure
   e. ***Upkeep*** requirements
   f. ***Lighting*** requirements
   g. ***Storage***

D. ***Additional Considerations:***
   1. ***Efficient Traffic Lanes***
   2. ***Well-Placed Openings***
   3. ***Adequate Space***
   4. ***Legal and Environmental Concerns***
   5. ***Projected Changes and Remodeling***

V. **ANALYZING BASIC TYPES OF FLOOR PLANS:** Spatial planning of interiors falls into two basic design approaches:

A. ***The Closed Plan:*** Provides separate and distinct rooms for specific activities and allow more individual privacy. Each room is enclosed by four walls with access through a door.

B. ***The Open Plan:*** Space for various activities flows from one area to another, broken by few or no wall barriers or partial divisions.
1. An Advantage of this plan is that it seems to expand space visually.
2. More efficient heating and cooling and more flexibility within the living spaces.
3. Most homes today incorporate both closed and open planning.

VI. FLOOR PLAN SHAPES: Most floor plans for residential design fall into nine basic shapes or styles. These floor plan shapes often have a few jogs, angles, or window extensions that do not change the basic shape of the structures.

A. The advantages and disadvantages associated with each shape can be evaluated by the following criteria:
1. How ***positioned on the site*** and the ***landscaping potential***
2. ***Expense***
3. ***Zoning and interior arrangement***
4. ***Traffic patterns***
5. ***Heating and cooling***
6. ***Light and ventilation***
7. **Interest and individuality**
8. ***Private outdoor living space***

B. The most typical floor plan shapes the following can be evaluated in terms of the criteria outlined above:
1. ***Rectangle Plan***
2. ***Square Plan***
3. ***Multistoried Plan***
4. ***L-Shaped Plan***
5. ***T, U, and H Plans***
6. ***Atrium***
7. ***Circular***

VII. ATTACHED AND MULTIFAMILY PLANS: Architects are currently designing high-density units accommodating a variety of lifestyles and tastes.

A. In all cases, main concerns include: (1) efficient use of space, (2) privacy, (3) easy upkeep, (4) security, and (5) energy conservation.

B. ***Apartment houses, duplexes, garden apartments, clustered condominiums, and townhouses*** are planned much like single detached houses.

Learning Enhancement Options

The Basic Goals of Design and Space Planning: Ask students to relate personal experiences involving functional needs, physical and psychological comfort, economic considerations, aesthetics, and individuality. Visual material drawn from completed projects can provide added insight into how these goals can be achieved. Review basic human needs and how space can be planned to accommodate these requirements.

Programming and the Design Process: Briefly outline the basic steps involved in the design process. A transparency of the steps involved in the design process is available, or these steps may be sketched on the board. Visual material, including student projects or professional drawings, etc. would make the process more understandable for the student.

Site Selection and Orientation: Discuss the importance of selecting the best site for a project and what criteria is involved. Have students relate information, including personal experiences, concerning proper orientation of the structure to the sun.

The Floor Plan: This is an excellent section to show actual working blueprints. (Most professional architects will provide an instructor with a set of plans.) Also, transparencies of floor plans are available to present in class. Work through interior zoning with the students relating personal experiences and asking them for input. Visual material depicting each room in the home helps the student to understand this concept.

Analyzing Basic Types of Floor Plans: Discuss the criteria used to analyze a floor plan. This information can be supported with visual material.

Floor Plan Shapes: Draw the basic floor plan shapes on the board or have them already illustrated for class presentation. Apply the criteria for analyzing types of floor plans to each floor plan shape.

Ask the students to compare a good floor plan with a poor floor plan. Discuss with the students the difference between ***open planning*** and ***closed planning***. Briefly examine the advantages and disadvantages of each.

Attached and Multifamily Dwellings. Review various types of attached and multifamily dwellings available to homeowners today and the challenges for the designer and architect. Outline the major concerns the designer must address in providing a functional, comfortable and economical environment.

Test Questions

Multiple Choice

__B__ 1. The basic goals of design involve all but one of the following:
A. Aesthetics C. Psychological Comfort
B. Client presentation D. Individuality

__C__ 2. What factor is not particularly related to economic space considerations:
A. Region where the structure will be built
B. The amount of square footage
C. Character
D. Upkeep

__A__ 3. Home-financing agencies recommend a monthly payment should not exceed:
A. 28 percent of the gross income
B. 20 percent of the gross income
C 15 percent of the gross income
D. 35 percent of the gross income

__D__ 4. Which of the following criteria is not a general step in the design process:
A. Commitment to the problem C. Design evaluation
B. Gather information D. Analyze the space

__A__ 5. Which of the following is not a major category of nonresidential design:
A. Hospital design C. Retail design
B. Industrial design D. Hospitality design

__C__ 6. Planning interior systems includes: (Select the best answer)
A. Cabinets and storage C. Elevators, plumbing, and ventilation
B Entertainment centers D. Educational centers

__B__ 7. Graphic details of a floor plan involve all but one of the following:
A. Spatial boundaries C. A two-dimensional drawing
B. The principle of harmony D. The blueprint

__D__ 8. A commonly used scale in a nonresidential floor plan is:
A. 1 in. to 1 ft. C. 1/4 in. to 1 ft.
B. 1/2 in. to 1 ft. D. 1/8 in. to 1 ft.

__A__ 9. Interior zoning refers to: (Select the best answer)
A. A separation of basic functional areas
B. Government and state codes
C. Local building codes
D. Location of plumbing and electrical systems, etc.

__C__ 10. The three basic kitchen work centers include all but one of the following:
A. Sink
B. Cooking
C. Storage
D. Refrigerator

__A__ 11. Generally, walking distance between the three work centers should not be:
A. Less than 7 ft. or more than 20 ft.
B. Less than 6 ft. or more than 15 ft.
C. Less than 8 ft. or more than 15 ft.
D. Less than 10 ft. or more than 25 ft.

__C__ 12. Select the most correct definition of a "closed plan":
A. A floor plan with traditional small window walls
B. A floor plan with free flowing interior space and perimeter walls with fewer windows.
C. Interior spaces enclosed by four walls with an entry door
D. A traditional or modern house with some interior partitions and solid exterior walls.

True / False

__T__ 13. Space planning includes incorporating ideas for "greening the environment"

__T__ 14. Programming includes completing a client profile.

__F__ 15. For the physically challenged, climate-control boxes should be approximately 3 to five feet from the floor.

__F__ 16. A general formula for house payments is $1000 for every $50,000 borrowed.

__T__ 17. Use of indigenous materials can help lower building costs.

__T__ 18. Experts generally agree that beauty in any object is achieved through application of the principles and elements of design.

__F__ 19. The most creative step in the design process is implementing the ideas.

__F__ 20. Zoning interiors is related to strict government building codes.

__T__ 21. Specifications for a design project refers to materials and components.

__F__ 22. The floor plan can be finalized before the site is analyzed.

__T__ 23. In recent years, high building costs have forced people to live in smaller spaces.

__F__ 24. The U-shape plan is generally an economic choice.

__F__ 25. The open plan is not heating and cooling efficient.

Matching

Match the general categories of nonresidential design with the correct answer:

__B__	26. Resort	A.	Industrial design
__D__	27. Credit Union	B.	Hospitality design
__C__	28. Showroom	C.	Retail design
__A__	29. Factory	D.	Financial design

Match the following steps involved in the design process with relevant criteria:

A. Commitment to the problem
B. Define the problem
C. Generate ideas
D. Select the most effective solution
E. Implement the ideas

__D__ 30. Evaluate which ideas will best meet the needs, preferences, and budget of the client.

__A__ 31. Involves a written program outlining the client's expectations

__E__ 32. Includes communicating ideas through drawings and specifying materials to be incorporated.

__B__ T 33. Involves confronting the problems related to the project.

__C__ + 34. Design concepts for possible solutions can be explored.

Essay / Short Answer

35. Briefly outline and discuss the basic goals of design and space planning:

Answer to this question is found on pages 86 through 91.

36. Outline specific ways in which the environment should function for the well-being of the physically challenged.

Answer to this question is found on pages 87 and 88.

37. List and provide information on nine ways to cut building costs:

Answer to this question is found on pages 88 through 90.

38. Outline the basic steps involved in programming and the design process. Provide relevant information for each stage.

Answer to this question is found on page 91.

39. Following the programming and design process specified for residential projects, what eight additional planning criteria should be considered for specific projects?

Answer to this question is found on pages 92 through 94.

40. On certain projects, the designer may have input into selecting the site for a residential or nonresidential structure. Before making a selection, what criteria should be taken into consideration?

Answers to this question is found on page 94.

41. The graphic details of a floor plan strong influence the efficiency and comfort of interior spaces. Briefly outline four major points brought out in the text to evaluate when working in this planning stage.

Answer to this question is found on pages 94 through 96.

42. List and define the three basic areas or zones in a residence.

Answer to this question is found on page 96.

43. Provide information helpful in the space planning process regarding kitchens.

Answer to this question is found on pages 96 and 97.

44. Provide information helpful in the space planning process regarding formal and informal living areas.

Answer to this question is found on pages 99 through 101.

45. Provide information helpful in the space planning process regarding formal and informal eating areas.

Answer to this question is found on pages 101 through 103.

46. Provide information helpful in the space planning process regarding recreation, entertainment, and education centers.

Answer to this question is found on pages 103 through 105.

47. Provide information helpful in the space planning process regarding bedrooms.

Answer to this question is found pages 105 and 106.

48. Provide information helpful in the space planning process regarding bathrooms areas.

Answer to this question is found on pages 106 through 108.

49. Most floor plans for residential design fall into nine basic shapes or styles. List these nine shapes and briefly outline the advantages and disadvantages of each.

Answer to this question is found on pages 109 through 114.

50. Study the copy of a floor plan attached to this text. Evaluate the advantages and disadvantages based on information presented in the test regarding space planning.

Educational Resources

Publications:

Brandt, Peter B. *Office Design: The Complete Process from Concept to Move-in.* Whitney Library of Design, 1992.
Brett, James. *The Kitchen: 100 Solutions to Design Problems* . New York: Whitney Library of Design, 1977.
Deasy, C.M., and Thomas E. Lasswell. *Designing Places for People* . New York: Whitney Library of Design, 1985.
DeChiara, Joseph, Julius Panero, and Martin Zelnik. *Time-Saver Standards for Interior Design and Space Planning* . New York: McGraw-Hill, 1991.
Harness, S., and J.Groom. *Building without Barriers for the Disabled* . New York: Whitney Library of Design. 1976.
Harris, David A., et al. *Planning and Designing the Office Environment* . New York: Van Nostrand Reinhold, 1981.
Jankowski, Wanda. *Kitchens & Baths.* Glen Cove, NY: PBC International, Inc., 1993.
Loasby, Wren. *Creative Interiors.* David & Charles, London. 1992
Malkin, Jain. *Hospital Interior Architecture: Creating Healing Environments* . New York: Van Nostrand Reinhold, 1992.
Malnar, Joy Monice and Frank Vodvarka. *The Interior Dimension: A Theoretical Approach to Enclosed Space.* New York: Van Nostrand Reinhold, 1992.
McAlister, Marcia. *With House in Hand: Organize Your Decorating. A Step-by-Step Planner for Home or Office* . McAlister Enterprises, 1984.
Mazzurco, Philip. *Bath Design..* New York: Whitney Library of Design, 1986.
Panero, Julius, and Martin Zelnick. *Human Dimensions and Interior Space* . New York: Whitney Library of Design, 1979.
______*Programming the Built Environment* . New York: Van Nostrand Reinhold, 1985.
Shoshkes, Ellen. *The Design Process* . New York: Whitney Library of Design, 1989.
Stanley Project Planners: *Kitchen Design*
______. *The Interiors Book of Shops and Restaurants.* New York: Watson-Guptill, 1981.
Wise, Herbert. *Kitchen Detail.* New York: Quick Fox, 1980.

Movies / Videos:

Why Man Creates : 25 min / PBS Production
Decorating: The Interior Design Zone : 15 min / 1990 / Insight Media
Finishing Touch : 46 min / 1991 / Insight Media

Transparencies:

Steps Involved in the Design Process
Floor Plan A
Floor Plan B

CHAPTER 5

TEXTILES

Chapter Focus

Chapter 5 is divided into thirteen sections to present an overall view of the various aspects involved with textiles and the profession of interior design. These sections include: Textiles for Interiors, Fibers, Construction of Fabrics, Textile Coloring, Finishing, Decorative Textiles for Interiors, Combining Fabrics, Solving Design Problems with Textiles, Textiles for Period and Contemporary Rooms, Textiles for Nonresidential Projects, Textile Presentation Layouts, Textile Terms and Textile Care and Maintenance.

Text Outline

I. TEXTILES FOR INTERIORS:

A. Skilled use of fabric, with the right color, texture, and design is a sure means of creating a successful room. For centuries fabric has been used to cover walls, drape windows and beds, and upholster chairs and sofas. Fabrics can enhance both residential and commercial interiors in many ways. Fabrics:

1. Are ***flexible, functional,*** and ***versatile.***
2. Are ***easy to work with.*** They can be sewn, draped, bent, folded, wrapped, pleated, gathered and stretched.
3. Can be used for any room in the house or in a commercial setting.
4. ***Humanize*** living spaces. They provide a ***transition*** between architecture, furniture, and people and can lift our spirits and soothe our emotions by bringing ***comfort, warmth,*** and ***softness*** to our homes and public places.
5. Are **visually appealing.**
6. ***Express our lifestyles and personality.***
7. Set a mood of ***formality*** or ***informality.***
8. ***Establish an authentic period*** or capture the feeling of a particular style.
9. Are ***acoustically absorbent..***
10. Can be used to give ***privacy*** and ***seclusion..***

11. Are ***readily available*** to the designer and consumer.
12. Are relatively ***inexpensive.***
13. Are relatively ***durable, easy to clean, and maintain.***

B. The term ***fabric*** is applied to textiles or cloth manufactured by machine or by hand, which includes ***weaving, knitting, twisting, felting, lacing,*** and ***fabrication of plastics.***

C. The appearance and durability are dependent on the type and qualities of materials used and method of construction, as well as the color, pattern, finish, and other surface embellishment.

II. FIBERS:

A. ***Fibers*** are the raw material of textiles, derived from nature or man-made.
1. A perfect fiber that will adequately serve every general purpose does not exist.
2. Each fiber has its own desirable properties and limitations.
3. ***Yarns*** are made by spinning various lengths of fibers (the raw material) into strands in preparation for fabric construction.
4. Performance and appearance of the fabric are affected by the method and the amount of twisting of the fibers.
5. ***Ply*** is the result of twisting two or more single yarns together before weaving to give added strength or create novel surface effects.

B. Natural Fibers: come from nature and fall into four classifications:
1. ***Protein,*** or ***animal fibers:***
   a. ***Wool:*** Taken from the fleece of sheep or from Angora goat, camel, and other animal hairs. The advantages of wool: It is resilient, resists abrasion, is a good insulator, is flame retardant, and can be used woven fine or coarse, loose or tight, dyed from palest to deepest colors, cleans well, resists dirt, and can absorb moisture. Disadvantages include: A tendency to yellow with age, shrink, and be damaged by moths and other insects. Can be expensive. Requires professional cleaning. May cause allergies.
   b. ***Silk:*** is an ancient fiber. The process of producing it from the larvae of silkworms, is known as ***sericulture.*** Advantages: beautiful long fiber, soft and luxurious, surpassed in strength only by nylon. It takes and holds dye well. Disadvantages: Sun's rays break down the fiber, is susceptible to deterioration by soil, beetles, and moisture. It is expensive. ***Raw silk:*** or uncultured silk, is a shorter and coarser fiber with less luster.
   c. ***Leather:*** An animal product (particularly the hides of cattle and swine). Advantages: Is pliable and durable, may be dyed or used natura, and can be embossed or sueded. Disadvantages: Can be expensive. It is susceptible to marks, holes, and tears.

2. ***Cellulosic Fibers:*** or vegetable, include stems, leaves, and seed hairs.
   a. ***Cotton:*** is a product of the cotton plant. Advantages: plentiful, takes and holds color well, washes easily and can be woven any way. Flexible use. Inexpensive. Disadvantages: Not as durable, wrinkles, mildews and fades.
   b. ***Linen:*** is made from flax fibers. Advantages: it is strong, pliable, lustrous, washable, takes and holds color, and is absorbent. Disadvantages: Wrinkles unless chemically treated, fades and is stiff in nature. Difficult to clean.
   c. Other vegetable fibers: ***ramie, yucca, milkweed, hemp, jute, kapok, palm leaves,*** and ***sisal.***
3. ***Metallic Fibers:*** include strips of gold, silver, or copper used chiefly as accents. Fibers glitter without tarnishing and are washable. Metallic fibers are a type of mineral fiber.
4. ***Mineral Fiber:*** found in asbestos, is difficult to spin without the addition of another fiber. Is best known for its fire-retardant quality, but has been found to be unhealthy.

C. ***Man-Made Fibers:*** are derived either form chemicals or natural solutions chemically treated. Have been improved in quality; durability; resistance to soil, mildew, and moths; ease of care, and other desirable properties. Man-made fibers fall into two categories: regenerated cellulosic and synthetic.
1. ***Regenerated Cellulosic Fibers:*** are produced by changing the physical and chemical formation of natural ingredients. Some examples are rayon, acetate, and triacetate.
2. ***Synthetic Fibers:*** are produced from chemicals and carbon compounds. Some examples are nylon, acrylic, modacrylic, polyester, olefin, and glass.
   a. To alleviate confusion among the huge array of manufactured fibers, the Federal Trade Commission established rules and regulations under the Textile Products Identification Act.
      (1) Under these regulations, each manufactured fiber is defined in specific terms and give a ***generic*** name, which must appear on the label.
      (2) The trade name identifies the manufacturer. (See Table 5.1)
   b. During the past five decades, the production and consumption of man-made fibers has steadily increased. (See Figure 5.5)

III. CONSTRUCTION OF FABRICS:

A. The history of textile arts is almost as old as the history of humanity.

B. Although modern mechanization has brought about great changes in textile production, weave structures are much the same as they were at the beginning of the Renaissance.

C. More intricate weaves are produced on ***Jacquard*** looms.

D. ***Woven Textiles:*** The most common weaves, as well as some more intricate ones, used in today's decorative fabrics include:

1. ***Plain weave:*** Simple interweaving of warp (vertical or lengthwise) and weft or woof (horizontal or crosswise) threads.
2. ***Twill weave:*** Two or more threads pass over or under another set of threads, skipping at regular intervals to produce a diagonal effect.
3. ***Satin Weaves:*** Have few interlacings or filling yarns with long floats.
4. ***Jacquard:*** Is a loom machine system capable of created multicolored fabrics of intricate patterns. Invented in France in 1801 by Joseph-Marie Jacquard.
5. ***Tapestry:*** An art known since ancient times. originally handwoven and made with bobbins. Now, the Jacquard loom is most commonly used.
6. ***Pile weaves*** : Produced by loops or tufts of yarn that stand out from the surface of the fabric. May be cut, uncut, or a combination.
7. ***Extra warp and weft pattern weaves:*** Extra warp and weft yarns are added to the fabric during weaving.
8. ***Double-cloth weaves:*** Are woven in two attached layers, often resulting in a quilted appearance.
9. ***Open, lacelike weaves:*** Can be obtained in a number of ways. One is the *leno* - a loose weave in which the warp threads are wound in half twists around each other, alternating in position on each row. The *gauze* weave is similar to leno.
10. ***Tension and texture-treated weaves:*** are those in which uneven tension in either weft or warp yarns produces an uneven surface. *Brocatelle* is an example.
11. ***Combination weaves:*** are produced by combining two or more weaves.

E. ***Nonwoven Textiles:***

1. ***Knitting:*** is a process of interlocking a series of yarn loops by means of blunt needles.
2. ***Twisting,*** interlocking, and knotting of yarns account for various types of mesh construction such as nets and laces.
3. ***Felting:*** is a nonwoven process of subjecting a mass of fibers to moisture, heat, and pressure to produce a compact sheet that does not fray.
4. ***Bonding:*** results when two fabrics are adhered (bonded or laminated) together chemically or by heating methods.

IV. TEXTILE COLORING (Dyeing):

A. Fibers and textiles are dyed through various processes, providing an attractive visual element to the fabrics. These include:

1. Direct physical action, in which the structural elements of the fiber absorb the color.

2. Chemical action, in which particular dyes have the ability to unite chemically with certain fibers.
3. Intermediate action, in which a mordant is used to unite the dye and fiber.

A. The various methods of dyeing yarns, fibers, and fabrics include:
1. ***Solution dyeing:*** the coloring agent is added to the viscous liquid of the synthetic before it is forced through the spinnerette to be formed into a fiber
2. ***Stock dyeing:*** the dye is applied to the fibers before they are processed into yarns.
3. ***Yarn dyeing:*** the skeins or hanks of yarns are dyed before they are woven into fabrics
4. ***Piece dyeing:*** fabrics after they are woven. Usually produces a solid color. Piece dyeing can be done in several ways:
   a. ***Jig:*** passes the open fabric back and forth through a stationary dye bath.
   b. ***Pad dyeing*** runs the fabric through the dye bath and then between rollers that squeeze the dye deeper into the yarns of the fabric.
   c. ***Winch, reel, or beck dying:*** immerses the fabric continuously without strain to the fabric.
   d. ***Continuous machine dyeing*** : has compartments for wetting out, dyeing, after treatments, washing, and rinsing.

B. <u>*Dye Lots:*</u> Each time a new dye solution or bath is mixed, the new solution may slightly change, or vary form the pervious bath. Each solution is called a dye lot.

V. **FINISHING:** The finish is a treatment that may be applied to the fiber or yarn before or after construction to change the appearance and performance. When the unfinished fabric comes from the loom it is referred to as ***greige*** or gray goods.

A. <u>*Prefinishes:*</u> of the gray goods consist of a variety of treatments including:
1. ***Bleaching:*** (to whiten)
2. ***Shrinking:*** (to prevent fiber contraction when exposed to moisture)
3. ***Beat setting:*** (to add stability especially for permanent pleating)
4. ***Beetling:*** ((to give luster)
5. ***Gigging or napping:*** (to produce a flannel-like texture)
6. ***Calendering:*** (to provide a smooth finish and tighten the weave)
7. ***Durable finishing:*** (to strengthen the textile)
8. ***Preshrinking:*** (intense heat shrinks the textile to make it ready for finishing)
9. ***Boiling:*** (to rid the fabric of grease or other unwanted substances)
10. ***Singeing:*** (to remove surface fuzz or lint)

B. <u>*Functional Finishes:*</u> are applied to improve performance. These standard textile finishings include:
1. ***Anti-bacterial:*** (to help prevent mold and mildew)

2. ***Water-repellent:*** (to resist stains)
3. ***Soil-repellent:*** (to help resist soiling)
4. ***Flame-retardant:*** (to help retard a textile from burning)
5. ***Moth-proofing:*** (to help prevent damage from insects.
6. ***Anti-static:*** (to help guard against static)
7. ***Insulating:*** (a coating bonded to the fabric to insulate against heat, cold, and noise)
8. ***Carefree:*** (to help resist creasing or wrinkles)

C. ***Decorative Finishes:*** include printing and embroidery.
1. Printing may be done by hand or by machine.
2. ***Hand Processes.*** With the exception of warp printing, fabrics are printed in the piece (after weaving). Hand processes require labor by the human hand. Some popular hand processes include:
   a. ***Batik.*** Section not to be colored are blocked out in a design with wax, the cloth is immersed in a dye solution. The wax is then removed to create a pattern.
   b. ***Hand block printing.*** Carved block is inked and stamped onto a piece of fabric.
   c. ***Tie dye.*** A hand resist process that employs strings or knots tied on the fabric then immersing it in dye, creating abstract patterns.
   d. ***Silk-screen.*** A specially prepared fabric screen resists the color penetration except in desired areas.

D. ***Mechanical Processes***.
1. Many prints are produced mechanically by the transfer of color from an engraved copper roller onto the fabric. This process os called ***roller printing.*** Other types of roller printing include:
   a. ***Embossing.*** Engraved rollers produce a pressed high-low design)
   b. ***Moire.*** (presses a watermark design onto fabrics)
   c. ***Warp.*** (printing done on the warp yarns before woven)
2. Other decorative finishes include ***etching chemically treated textured finishes, flocking, softening, and brightening.***

E. Printed fabrics come in designs of unlimited styles, including ***documentaries*** - designs copied from patterns of a particular historical period.

VI. **DECORATIVE TEXTILES FOR INTERIORS.** Today's interior designer has a wider choice of fabrics than ever before. The market abounds with fabrics available for every taste, style, and decorative and functional use.

A. Following are the principal decorative uses of fabrics:
1. ***Sheers or Glass Curtains*** . Lightweight. May hang permanently over a glass window. (All commercial textiles must comply with strict fire codes.)

D. Sheers filter the light and provide daytime privacy. Fabric should be sheer enough to permit light, be sun proof and wash or clean well. Any sheer fabric that qualifies can be used.

2. ***Casements or Semisheers.*** Informal. Lightweight to mediumweight fabrics. Serve as side drapery during the day and drawn at night for privacy. Fabric should be heavy enough for nighttime privacy but permit some light. Should be drapable, sun resistant and nonsplitting and should wash or clean well. Leno weaves especially help control sagging.
3. ***Drapery.*** Should have a light to medium weight. Can serve as stationary side drapery or be designed to draw for privacy. Drapery can add beauty, height, and dignity to a room. Fabric should drape gracefully, clean without shrinkage, and meed needs of a particular room.
4. ***Upholstery.*** Medium or lightweight fabric that covers furniture permanently, adds beauty and comfort, conceals or emphasizes furniture and adds to or sets the theme of the room. Should have a tight weave, be durable and comfortable, and clean well.
5. ***Slipcovers.*** May cover worn upholstered furniture, protect more expensive fabrics, and brighten or change a room's atmosphere. Are light to mediumweight and should be durable, tightly woven, nonsnag and nonstretch (unless of a stretch variety).
6. ***Walls.*** Fabrics can be used on walls to add beauty or to solve a decorative problem. Fabric should have a tight weave with firm body.

VII. COMBINING FABRICS:

A. Combining fabrics is a matter of training and skill.

B. Although an unexpected combination of materials may create a feeling of great interest and charm, some general principles are helpful when combining colors, textures, and patterns.

1. ***<u>Patterns.</u>*** Pattern indicates the fabric has a motif or design. Many people are afraid of patterned fabrics and avoid them entirely, others use them ineffectively. Often, well chosen patterned fabrics can enhance a room. As with color, no absolute do's and don'ts govern the successful use of pattern. A few general guidelines, however, may be helpful:
   a. Patterns used within the same room should be ***related.***
   b. The ***principal*** pattern need not be repeated as long as one or more of the colors in that pattern are carried over into another area.
   c. The use of no more than one ***bold patterns*** of the same type of design is usually more effective.
   d. Once the dominant motif is established it can be interestingly supplemented by ***small patterns, stripes, checks,*** or ***plaids*** with complementary

textures added.

e. ***Scale or size*** of the pattern should be considered.
f. ***Unusual juxtaposition*** of fabric may create a dramatic effect. This usually develops from knowledge and practice that produce confidence to do the unexpected.
g. Consider the ***style and color*** of the pattern.
h. The pattern's ***proportions and motifs*** should be well designed.
i. Success in combining patterns can be achieved with ***practice, experience,*** and consideration of basic guidelines.

2. ***Texture.*** The surface quality of a textile is also an important element to consider when combining fabrics. Knowledge of what makes a fabric formal or informal is essential:
   a. ***Formal fabrics*** are primarily those with smooth and often shiny textures such as silks, brocades, taffeta and satin.
   b. ***Informal fabrics*** are generally those with a rougher texture and matte finish, such as burlap, canvas, tweed, and boucle.
   c. The unique ***surface quality*** (rough, smooth, shiny, or dull) of each fabric should be considered and evaluated when coordinating them.
   d. The ***character*** of the texture should be appropriate for its intended use or purpose.
3. ***Color.*** When coordinating fabrics, another goal is to select colors that are compatible and harmonious. A few guidelines may be helpful:
   a. ***Hue, Value, and Chroma.*** Remember that color has three dimensions. Hues fall into warm or cool color clans with neutral in between. One of these categories can be selected to dominate the scheme. Fabrics are either light, medium, or dark in value. Fabrics are either muted or bright in chroma.
   b. ***Natural and Artificial Light.*** to be certain the colors of the fabrics are harmonious, compare them under all types of lighting in the space, both natural and artificial.
   c. ***Style.*** Select a color scheme appropriate for the chosen style.
   d. ***Mood.*** A feeling of formality or informality may be achieved through the selection of various colors.
   e. ***Colors in a Pattern.*** Many designers draw on the colors in a patterned fabric or rug to skillfully coordinate other fabrics for room.
   f. ***New and Creative Color Combinations.*** Often, predictable color combinations and those that exactly match are not as interesting as those that are creative. Experience in training the eye while trying out fabric combination along with general guidelines, will help develop a sense of what fabric selections are complementary.

VIII. SOLVING DESIGN PROBLEMS WITH TEXTILES:

A. Problems can often be solved through the skillful use of fabric, with unlimited possibilities. A well-chosen fabric can:
1. *Lighten or darken a room.*
2. *Emphasize walls, windows, or furnishings.*
3. *Conceal walls, windows, or furnishings.*
4. *Bring harmony and unity to a room.*
5. *Provide balance to a room.*
6. *Change the apparent size and proportion of a piece of furniture or an entire room.*
7. *Establish the room's color scheme.*
8. *Establish the historic or modern style of a room.*
9. *Change the look of a room for different seasons.*
10. *Add softness and comfort.*

IX. TEXTILES FOR PERIOD AND CONTEMPORARY ROOMS:

A. With the increased sophistication in today's interiors, it is popular to draw on historic designs to establish an authentic feeling of a specific period or style.

B. Documentary fabrics bearing designs from a wide range of historic periods are being produced by manufacturers.

C. The following is a list of historic styles: (See text for brief outline of typical fabric types, colors, and patterns.)
1. ***English Tudor*** (in Colonial America: ca. 1608-1700)
2. ***Early American Colonial*** (ca. 1608-1700)
3. ***Early Georgian*** (ca. 1700-1750)
4. ***Late Georgian*** (ca. 1750-1790)
5. ***French Rococo (Louis XV)*** (ca. 1750-1774)
6. ***French Neoclassic (Louis XVI)*** (1760-1790)
7. **Country French** (ca. 1730-1760)
8. ***Neoclassic American Federal*** (ca. 1790-1820)
9. ***Neoclassic English*** (ca. 1790-1820)
10. ***French Empire*** (ca. 1800-1820)
11. ***American Empire*** (ca. 1820-1850)
12. ***Spanish Southwest*** (ca. 1600s-present) ***Santa Fe Style*** (ca. 1920s to present)
13. ***Spanish Colonial***
14. ***Victorian*** (1837-ca. 1910)
15. ***China and Japan***
16. ***Early Modern: Arts and Crafts Movement*** (ca. 1860 to present)
17. ***Early Modern: Art Nouveau*** (ca. 1885-present)
18. ***Modern*** (ca. 1920s to present)

X. TEXTILES FOR NONRESIDENTIAL PROJECTS:

A. ***Textile Specifications Safety Codes, and Government Labeling***

1. Selecting textiles for commercial projects requires steps similar to those outlined for residential projects.
2. The interior designer plays a significant role in specifying fabrics that meet testing standards for high quality, required safety codes, and other criteria.
3. As the design process steps are followed, the functional needs of the client are determined, contracts are signed, and the specifications for installation of textiles are written.
4. The textiles selected must meet standard tests for: (1) ***durability,*** (2) ***colorfastness,*** and (3) ***flammability.***
5. The textiles selected must be labelled to indicate their flammability and fiber content (with percentages of natural and man-made fibers when applicable), and whether they have been treated with durable finishes.
6. The designer should select colors, textures, and patterns that are attractive and suit the requirements of the client or end users.

B. ***Environmental Concerns.*** Currently, many designers, manufacturers, and others involved in the design field are conscientiously dealing with environmental issues such as pollution control, "greening" the earth, and recycling.

1. Seminars, conferences, classes, and other means of communication are being held regularly and environmental organizations are helping to inform designers, consumers, and manufacturers on how to deal with these issues and become involved.

XI. TEXTILE PRESENTATION LAYOUTS:

A. Presenting the specified textiles arranged in a professional layout is immensely helpful for the designer in communicating to the client how the colors, textures, and patterns are coordinated and allocated for a particular space.

1. Fabric samples are collected from various sources and cut to appropriate sizes indicating how each fabric will be used in a single room or in spaces in the project.
2. The samples are then attached to a mat or presentation board.
3. The textile presentation layout is then shown to the client.

Learning Enhancement Options

Textiles for Interiors: Discuss with the students how fabrics can enhance both residential and commercial interiors. Review the specific ways in which this may be achieved and provide examples. Visual material demonstrating these ways is helpful.

Fibers. Outline both natural and synthetic fibers. Show fabric examples and discuss the advantages and disadvantages of each fiber.

Construction of Fabrics. Demonstrate the construction of fabrics. Show the transparency of the various types of woven textiles

Textile Coloring and Finishing. Review the various ways textiles are dyed and finished. Show fabric examples if available.

Decorative Textiles for Interiors. This is an excellent section to demonstrate actual samples of sheers, casements, drapery, upholstery, slipcovers, and wall fabrics. Slides or other visual materials showing the use of these particular fabric types in residential and nonresidential settings aids in supporting the criteria.

Combining Fabrics. Group fabrics together for the students while they watch or have coordinated fabrics displayed. Show fabric layouts put together by advanced students or professionals. Stress the important of pattern, texture, and color when combining fabrics.

Solving Design Problems with Textiles. Review with the students how design problems can be solved through the skillful use of fabric. Support the points brought out in the text with actual fabric samples and pictures of these solutions in an interior space.

Textiles for Period and Contemporary Rooms. Demonstrate samples of typical fabrics used in particular period and contemporary rooms. Show pictures of authentic fabrics used in the historic interiors or where documentaries have been used.

Textiles for Nonresidential Projects. Discuss the points outlined in the text involving meeting textile specifications, safety codes, and government labeling and environmental concerns. Have students respond to why designers, manufacturers, and others involved in the design field are dealing with environmental issues.

Textile Presentation Layouts. Show students how designers present textile layouts to a client and what is involved in this stage of the design process.

Textile Terms. Review various textile types and show examples. With so many terms presented, the instructor may want to select only the most commonly used types.

Textile Care and Maintenance. Review with the students how to care for various textile types and necessary maintenance requirements.

Test Questions

Multiple Choice

__B__ 1. Yarns are made by:
A. Twisting two or more single strands
B. Spinning various lengths of fibers into strands
C. Weaving long lengths of fibers into strands
D. Felting various lengths of fibers into strands

__C__ 2. The raw materials is:
A. Yarn
B. Ply
C. Fiber
D. Fabric

__A__ 3. Natural fibers fall into 4 classifications. Which one does not belong?
A. Regenerated cellulose
B. Animal
C. Metallic
D. Vegetable

__ D__4. Wool has all but one of the following properties:
A. Resilient and resists abrasion
B. Is flame retardant
C. May cause allergies
D. Does not yellow with age

__C__ 5. Linen has all but one of the following properties:
A. Strong
B. Lustrous
C. Soft in nature
D. Difficult to clean

__A__ 6. Mineral fibers are found in:
A. Asbestos
B. Gold and silver
C. Ramie
D. Flax

__B__ 7. The warp threads are:
A. Horizontal or crosswise threads
B. Vertical or lengthwise threads

__C__ 8. Dyeing textiles is achieved in all but one of the following ways:
A. Structural element of the fibers change color
B. Particular dyes unite chemically with fibers
C. A bonding agent is used to unite dye and fibers
D. A mordant is used to unite dye with fibers

__D__ 9. All but one of the following are functional textile finishes:
A. Carefree finish
B. Anti-static finish
C. Insulating finish
D. Singeing finish

__B__10. All but one of the following are decorative mechanical textile finishes:
A. Etching
B. Tie-dye
C. Flocking
D. Chemically treated textured finish

__A__11.Which of the following fabrics are typical of the English Tudor style:
A. Linen, chintz, crewel embroidery. The flamestitch.
B. Homespun, broadcloth. Small plaids and quaint prints.
C. Silk, damask, satins. Ribbon and hearts motifs.
D. Lace, fringe, matelasse. Laurel wreath and honey bee motifs.

__C__12.Which of the following fabrics are typical of the Late Georgian style?
A. Cottons and linens. Plaids and quaint prints.
B. Lace and fringe and plush velvets. Animal and figure motifs.
C. Imported damask, brocades. Pineapple motif.
D. Taffeta, moire, and pastel formal fabrics. Toile de Jouy patterns.

True / False

__T__13. A perfect fiber that will adequately serve every household purpose does not exist.

__F__14 In a successful room, the principal patterned fabric should be repeated

__T__ 15. Synthetic fibers are produced form chemicals and carbon compounds

__F__ 16. With modern mechanization, weave structures have seen significant changes since early historic times.

__T__ 17. The most intricate weaves are produced on Jacquard looms.

__F__ 18. Felt is constructed by a woven process of subjecting fibers to heat.

__F__ 19. Dye lots refer to the process of solution dyeing

__T__ 20. A fabric that has a pressed watermark design is called a moire.

Matching

Match the following fibers with the appropriate description:

A. Wool B. Cotton C. Silk D. Linen

__D__ 21. Used in Egypt as early as 4000 B.C. Made from flax fibers.

__B__ 22. Known in India since the 4th century B.C. Most plentiful of natural fibers.

__A__ 23. Absorbs moisture up to 20 percent of its weight.

__C__ 24. Uses a process called sericulture. Sun rays break down the fiber.

(attached xeroxed illustrations of each weave above its label)

A. (Plain weave) B. (Twill weave) C. (Satin weave) D. (Jacquard)

(Attached a xeroxed illustration of each type of weave)

__B__ 25. Twill weave __C__ 26. Satin weave __D__ 27. Jacquard __A__ 28. Plain weave

Match the following dyeing processes with the correct answer:

A. Solution dyeing
B. Stock dyeing
C. Yarn dyeing
D. Piece dyeing

__A__ 29. Coloring agent is added to the viscous liquid of the synthetic.

__B__ 30. Dye is applied to the fibers before they are processed into yarns.

__C__ 31 The skeins of yarns are dyed before woven into fabrics.

__D__ 32. Fabrics are dyed after they are woven.

Match the following printing processes with the correct description

A. Batik
B. Hand-block printing
C. Tie-Dye
D. Silk Screen

__C__ 33. A process that employs knots or strings to print an abstract design.

__D__ 34 A special prepared cloth resists the color penetration except in designed areas.

__A__ 35. Sections not to be colored are blocked out in a design with wax.

__B__ 36. Carved designs are inked and stamped onto the fabric.

Match the following decorative textiles with the best description:

A. Glass curtains
B. Casements
C. Drapery
D. Upholstery

__A__ 37. Filter the light and provide daytime privacy

__D__ 38. Medium or lightweight fabric. Should have a tight weave.

__C__ 39. Usually draw or hang permanently. Can add beauty, height, dignity, and style to a room.

__B__ 40. Also known as semisheers. Usually a loose weave.

Match the following historic or contemporary styles with typical fabrics used:

A. Early American Colonial
B. Country French
C. Art Nouveau
D. Spanish Colonial

__C__ 41. Flowing vines and flower motifs. Themes from nature.

__B__ 42 Ticking, stripes, plaids and country scenes.

__D__ 43 Plain and cut velvets, leather. Bold geometric designs.

__A__ 44. Simple homespun fabrics. Quaint prints and floral needlework.

Essay / Short Answer

45. Authorities in the design field recognize that skillful use of fabric is a sure means of creating a successful room. List and briefly discuss how textiles can enhance both residential and nonresidential spaces.

Answer to this question is found on page 122.

46. Outline the principal decorative uses of fabrics in private and public spaces. Provide relevant information for each fabric use.

Answer to this question is found on pages 131 through 134.

47. Outline some general principles often used by designers when combining fabric colors, textures, and patterns.

Answer to this question is found on pages 134 through 138.

48. Design problems can often be solved through the skillful use of fabric. A well-chosen fabric can may serve many purposes. Provide suggestions outlined in the text concerning solving design problems with textiles.

Answer to this question is found on pages 138 through 140.

49. Discuss the use of textiles for period and contemporary rooms. Why is a knowledge of historic fabric types, colors, and patterns valuable to the designer?

Answer to this question is found on pages 140 through 142.

50. Selecting textiles for commercial projects involves a number of tasks for the designer. Briefly discuss the material presented in the text outlining textiles for nonresidential projects. Include information regarding the interior designer's role in environmental concerns.

Answer to this question is found on pages 142 and 143.

Educational Resources

Publications:

Alexander, Patsy. *Textile Fabrics and Their Selection.* Boston: Houghton Mifflin, 1976.
Corbman, Bernard P. *Fiber to Fabric.* New York: McGraw-Hill, 1983.
Gains, Patricia Ellisior. *Fabric Decoration Book.* New York: Morrow, 1975.
Hardingham, Martin. *The Fabric Catalog.* New York: Simon & Schuster, Pocket Books, 1978.
Jackman, Dianne R., and Mary K. Dixon. *The Guide to Textiles for Interior Designers.* Winnipeg: Peguis, 1983.
Joseph, Marjory L. *Essentials of Textiles. 3d ed.* New York: Holt, Rinehart & Winston, 1984.
Joyce, Carol. *Textile Design.* Watson-Gupthill, New York. 1993.
Larsen, Jack Lenor, and Jeanne Weeks. *Fabrics for Interiors.* New York: Van Nostrand Reinhold, 1975.
Lyle, Dorothy Siegert. *Modern Textiles* . New York: John Wiley, 1983.
Peverill, Sue. *Fabric Decorator, Vol. l* . Little, Brown & Company, 1990.
Tortora, Phyllis G. *Understanding Textiles.* New York: Macmillan, 1982.
Yeager, Jan. *Textiles for Residential and Commercial Interiors* . New York: Harper & Row, 1988.

Movies / Videos:

Textiles : 17 min / 1990 / Insight Media

Transparencies:

Illustration of Basic Types of Weaves

CHAPTER 6

FLOORS, WALLS, AND CEILINGS

Chapter Focus

Chapter 6 is divided into nine sections covering floors, walls, and ceilings as backgrounds in the interior The sections presented are Floors and Floor Coverings, Hard Flooring, Soft Floor Coverings, Walls and Wall Treatments, Nonresilient (or Rigid) Wall Coverings, Paints and Finishes, Resilient (or Flexible) Wall Coverings, Ceilings, and Insulating Against Noise and Heat Loss.

Text Outline

Introduction.

A. The general scheme of any room is established by the architectural backgrounds: walls, floors, and ceilings, plus such items as fireplaces, doors, windows, paneling, and moldings.
B. The decorative treatments added to these backgrounds, as well as to the movable objects in the room, should be in keeping with the overall feeling to give the room harmony and unity.

I. FLOORS AND FLOOR COVERINGS:

A. Because of their function-primarily to be walked on and provide the foundation for other furnishings - floors, more than any other surface, take a great amount of abuse.
B. After the floor's construction is complete, the task of covering this area is a major concern for the designer and client.
C. The market a bounds in a variety of selections for every purpose and decor.
D. Perhaps the most notable characteristic of today's materials is the merging of beauty and practicality.
E. When deciding what type of floor covering is most suitable, the designer and client need to determine whether the specific room requires a hard or soft floor

covering. Considerations include:

1. The intended ***function.***
2. The ***number, age,*** and ***special needs of the occupants.***
3. The lifestyle of the occupants - ***formal*** or ***informal.***
4. The ***location*** and ***climate.***
5. Surface quality as a ***safety factor.***
6. ***Code requirements.***
7. ***Acoustic properties*** required for a specific area.
8. ***Economic considerations*** - initial expense plus long-term maintenance.
9. ***Durability*** required for a particular area.
10. ***Style qualities*** for a certain design direction.
11. ***Personal preferences*** of the occupants.

II. HARD FLOORING.

A. ***Nonresilient Flooring--Masonry:***

1. The term ***resilient*** flooring refers to the material's ability to spring back when pressed. ***Nonresilient*** flooring is not flexible.
2. The initial cost of hard-surface nonresilient flooring is generally high. In long-range planning, however, this is more than compensated for by its extreme durability, versatility, ease of maintenance, and timeless usage.
3. Hard-surface masonry flooring such as brick, stone, and tile remains popular.

B. ***Wood Flooring:***

1. Wood is considered the most versatile and is the most widely used of all flooring materials.
2. It combines beauty, warmth, some resilience, resistance to indentation, durability, availability, and ease of installation.
3. Provide a background for any style of furnishings.
4. ***Methods of Laying Wood Floors.*** The three basic methods of laying wood floors are in ***strips, planks,*** and ***parquetry.***
5. ***Wood Veneer.*** Sometimes a thin layer of hardwood is veneered to a less expensive wood. These veneers are less expensive, but will not hold up as well under heavy wear. Sometimes thin layers of flood are laminated to a backing making it more durable.
6. ***Plastic- (Acrylic-) Impregnated Wood Floors*** are surfaces in which real wood is impregnated with liquid plastic hardened throughout the pore structure by irradiation. The result is a floor with the warmth of wood and remarkable durability
7. ***Particle Board*** is made of pressed sawdust and small wood chips. Most often used for subflooring.

8. ***Stained Wood Floors.*** Wood flooring may be stained in a variety of colors. Colored stain may be applied in basically the same way as a natural finish without obliterating the natural grain of the wood.
9. ***Stenciled and Painted Wood Floors.*** Stenciling is a process of applying paint through a stencil. Hand painted floors have endless design possibilities.

C. ***Resilient Flooring--Vinyl.*** The development of vinyl for floor use is in a large measure responsible for the new interest in hard floor coverings. The effects that are being produced in vinyl are limitless. Vinyl can be clear or vividly colored, translucent or opaque, textured or satin smooth. It comes in 6 and 12 ft sheets and tiles, or in a can. Vinyl is most often used in an informal scheme. Vinyl can be used in almost any residential or commercial room. One drawback might include the negative appearance vinyl can have when simulating a natural material.

III. SOFT FLOOR COVERINGS:

A. ***History of Rugs and Carpets***

1. Carpets were used in ancient times in Egypt, Greece and Rome.
2. Oriental rugs have been produced in Persia, Turkey, China and other countries for centuries.
3. In the 11th century, the Crusaders carried back to Europe many of these fine rugs from the Near East.
4. Since the 13th century, when the first rug looms were established in Aubusson France, weaving of fine floor coverings has been a continuously growing industry.

B. ***Machine-Made Carpets***

1. A number of factors have been responsible for the demand for machine-made carpets: (l) New and improved fibers, (2) American view carpeting as a necessity, (3), Carpeting is one of the few products offering more value per dollar than it did thirty years ago.

C. ***Functional Values***

(1) Insulates against drafts, (2) muffles noise, (3) gives a feeling of comfort, (4) provides safety, and (5) is easy to maintain.

D. ***Decorative Values***

Carpet can (1) be the basis for the room's entire decor, (2) bring furnishings into harmony, (3) create harmony, (4) create personality, (5) create a feeling of luxury, (6) alter the apparent size and proportion of a room, (7) serve as a transition from room to room, and (8) be a room's focal point.

E. ***Quality of Soft Flooring***

1. Quality in carpeting depends on four ingredients:
   (1) **The type and grade of fiber.** The generic name is the key to determining fiber content: Fibers include: nylon, acrylic, polyester, olefin, wool, cotton, sisal, jute, and hemp.
   (2) ***Depth and density of the pile.***
   (3) ***Construction methods.*** Most carpets on the market today are tufted. The performance of a carpet also depends on the degree of twist and the heat setting of the fiber.
   a. ***Tufting*** accounts for approximately 90 percent of all carpet construction today.
   b. ***Weaving*** once accounted for 90 percent of all broadloom. The tree types of woven carpets are: ***Wilton, Axminster*** and ***Velvet.***
   c. Other types of construction methods include: ***needle-punching, flocking, braiding*** , and ***hooking.***
   d. ***Carpet backings*** are important because a good foundation prevents stretching, buckling, shrinking and other problems.

F. *Style Characteristics of Carpets.* Definite style characteristics may be chosen within the categories of ***cut pile uncut*** and ***loop pile,*** with a variety of lengths determining the texture and design. These styles include: (1) ***Level-loop pile*** (2) ***Plush*** (3) ***Velour*** (4) ***Tip or random shear*** (5) ***Multilevel loop*** (6) ***Embossed,*** (7) ***Custom-designed hand-sculptured,*** (8) ***Frieze,*** (9) ***Splush,*** (10) ***Shag,*** (11) ***Saxony,*** (12) ***Flat-woven,*** and (13) ***Patterned.***

G. *Carpets for Specific Needs*
   1. ***Room size*** is important in determining what carpet to select.
   2. For ***heavy-traffic areas*** it is wise to select a good-quality carpet.
   3. ***Furniture style*** is a consideration.
   4. A room's particular ***lighting situation*** must be evaluated.
   5. ***Color*** is one of the most important decisions.
   6. Each carpet has a unique ***texture*** which should be compatible with other furnishings.
   7. If the carpet is ***patterned*** other background are usually complementary when kept fairly plain.
   8. ***Upkeep and maintenance*** are determining factors when selecting a carpet.

H. *Codes and Regulations*. Federal, state, and local laws or codes and regulations set particular standards regarding the performance and quality of a floor covering.

I. *Rug and Carpet Sizes.* Size is another consideration in selecting a carpet or rug.

1. A ***rug*** is a floor covering made in one piece.
2. ***Wall-to-wall carpeting*** has many advantages.
3. A ***room-size*** is one that comes within a few inches or even a foot or so of the walls.
4. An ***area rug*** does not cover the entire floor but is used to define an area of the room.
5. An ***art rug*** , which is usually smaller than an area rug, is generally handcrafted and used as an accent.

J. ***Carpet Underlay*** Before a carpet is laid, a pad or cushion is installed directly on the hard floor surface. Cushioning improves and helps to maintain the appearance of the carpet; enhances the resiliency, which helps prevent pile matting, and prolongs the life of the carpet. The six basic types of carpet underlay are: (1) ***Solid foam,*** (2) ***Bonded foam,*** (3)***Waffle sponge,*** (4) ***Flat sponge rubber,*** (5) ***Fiber,*** and (6) ***Carpet with attached cushioning.***

K. ***Measuring and Installation*** Before installing the selected floor covering it is necessary to figure the amount of material needed and plan for installation. This is almost always done by a profession.

L. ***Handmade Rugs***
1. ***Oriental Rugs.*** The making of Oriental rugs is a great art, and the rugs have been coveted possessions for hundreds of years.
2. ***Oriental Rugs from Persia and Turkey'.*** The great majority of Oriental rugs imported into America have come from these countries.
   a. The beauty of an Oriental rug depends on (1) the ***quality of the wool fiber***, (2) the ***fineness of the weave***, (3) the ***intricacy of the design*** and (4) the ***mellowness of color.***
   b. The three Oriental rugs particularly pleasing to American tastes are: (1) ***Kirman,*** (2) ***Sarouk,*** and the (3) ***Bokhara (Tekke)***
3. ***Oriental Rugs from China.*** The art of rug making has been practiced in China for over twelve centuries and can be recognized by particular colors, geometric designs, religious symbols and flowers.
4. ***Oriental Rugs from India.*** Today many rugs of excellent quality are handmade in India. Rugs employing old and authentic designs from China, Iran, Turkey, and France are made of top-quality wool. ***Dhurries*** are flat-weave rugs particularly popular in America.
5. ***French Rugs.*** Two French-style carpets have been produced with little interruption since the seventeenth century: the ***Savonnerie*** and the ***Aubusson.***
6. ***Moroccan Rug.*** Is a type of Oriental rug made primarily in northwest Africa and are of two types: ***Berber*** and ***Rabat.***

7. ***The Spanish Matrimonia*** is the traditional bridal gift in Spain. It is a fringed bold-figured rug.
8. ***The Navajo Rug*** is a handwoven rug or blanket made in the Southwest.
9. ***Similarity in Folk Rugs*** (l) Simple geometric designs adapted from nature, (2) quaint representations of human and animal forms, (3) color that are from nature, and (4) construction done by hand on a simple loom.
10. ***The Rya Rug*** . Rya is a name derived from an old Norse word meaning "rough." This hand-hooked rug is from Scandinavia.
11. ***Rag Rugs*** were one of the first floor coverings made by American colonists. It is made from scraps of fabrics.
12. ***Braided Rugs*** were originally made in homes from scraps of clothing and blankets and braided then stitched together.
13. ***Hooked Rugs*** are made by hooking colored rags or yarns through a tightly stretched piece of burlap, canvas, or wool.
14. ***Needlepoint Rugs*** were originally made by embroidering with wool yarn on a heavy net canvas. Intricate to plain designs.

IV. WALLS AND WALL TREATMENT:

A. Walls, floors, ceilings, windows, doors, and fireplaces are all part of the room's enclosure and are rarely hidden.

B. Although these background elements provide a setting for furniture and fabrics, their most important function is to provide a background for people.

C. Walls occupy the largest area of a room, define its size and shape, and serve purposes of both function and beauty.

D. The design of today's walls not only includes traditional approaches but also other innovations.

E. Walls can function as wall systems.

F. There are many materials available for treatments. Each type has advantages and disadvantages.

G. When selecting wall materials, consider beauty, function, economy and character. Some basic questions might include:

1. Should walls be ***emphasized*** or **unobtrusive**?
2. Will a ***formal*** or ***informal*** mood dominate?
3. What is the ***scale*** of the room and furnishings?
4. Do walls need to have ***acoustical properties*** ?
5. Is ***light reflection*** or ***absorption*** required?
6. Is the material supportive of the home's ***style*** and ***character*** ?
7. What are the ***maintenance properties*** of the wall material?
8. Does the wall material need to be ***durable*** for its function?

V. NONRESILIENT (OR RIGID) WALL COVERINGS.

A. The most frequently used nonresilient wall coverings with information on the general characteristics, fire ratings, insulation properties, uses and care are found in Table 6.3 in the text. These wall coverings include:

1. ***Plaster*** is the simplest and most versatile of all wall treatments.
2. ***Wallboard*** is used for ***drywall*** construction.
3. ***Wood*** has been a favorite background treatment for centuries.
4. ***Masonry*** includes brick, tile, concrete block, and stone.
5. ***Mirrors*** can expand an area visually.
6. ***Metal*** includes stainless steel, copper, and aluminum.
7. ***Plastics*** are available in sheets or tile in a wide range of colors and styles.

VI. PAINTS AND FINISHES

A. To change the character of a room quickly and with a minimum of expense, nothing works like paint.

B. Paints are made from a vast array of synthetic and natural materials

C. Common types of paint include:

1. ***Alkyd paints***
2. ***Acrylic paint***
3. ***Latex paint***
4. ***Enamel paint***
5. ***Epoxy paint***
6. ***Varnish***
7. ***Shellac***
8. ***Lacquer***
9. ***Polyurethane***
10. ***Stain***
11. ***Sealers and Fillers***

VII RESILIENT (OR FLEXIBLE) WALL COVERINGS.

A. <u>Wallpaper</u>: Using decorative paper as a wall covering has been important in enhancing interiors since the late sixteenth century. Wallpapers are a valuable tool in transforming the visual aspect of interiors.

1. ***History of Wallpaper:***
   a. Hand-painted wallpapers are known to have been made as early as 200 B.C. in China.
   b. The first manufacture of wallpaper was in France (16th century).
   c. Marbleized papers (***domino papers***) were produced in France.
   d. Henry IV granted a charter in 1599 to the Guild of Paperhangers.

e. ***Flocked papers*** were introduced early in the 17th century
f. A new printing method was developed in France by ***Jean Papillon*** that produced matching patterns. He is known as "***the Father of wallpaper.***"
g. Other developments were made by ***Baptiste Reveillon*** in France and ***John Baptiste Jackson*** in England. (Pictorial murals)
h. ***Carrington House*** in Providence, RI, was one of the first wallpaper firms in America.
i. In 1739, ***Plunket Fleeson*** established his Philadelphia factory for printing wallpapers.
j. During the mid-19th century, copper rollers turned by a rotary machine were invented.
k. Wallpapers went out of fashion for a period in the 1920s. Since the 1930s, the wallpaper industry has flourished.

2. ***Methods of Producing Wallpaper:***
   a. The three most common methods of producing wall coverings are ***roller printing*** (the most common method), ***hand blocking***, and ***silk-screen printing. Embossed*** and ***flocked*** wallcovers are additional processes.
3. ***Common Wallpaper Terms:***
   a. ***Washable.*** Paper can be washed with lukewarm mild suds.
   b. ***Scrubbable.*** Paper is more resistant to rubbing than washable.
   c. ***Pretrimmed.*** The selvage on the paper has been trimmed.
   d. ***Semitrimmed.*** Selvage has been trimmed from only one edge.
   e. ***Prepasted.*** Paper has had paste applied during the manufacturing process.
   f. ***Single roll.*** Contains 36 square feet.
   g. ***Double and triple roll.*** Double roll contains 72 sq. ft. Triple: 108 sq. ft.
   h. ***Dye lot.*** Original or first production of a color or colors. Each dye lot has a number. Each dye lot may vary in color.
   i. ***Pattern repeat.*** If paper is patterned, the patterns need to line up.

B. ***Vinyl-Coated Coverings:*** The most common include:
   1. ***Vinyl-protected.*** Wallpaper with a coating of vinyl plastic.
   2. ***Vinyl-latex.*** Paper impregnated with vinyl, laminated to lightweight fabric or paper, then vinyl coated.
   3. ***Coated fabric.*** Wall covering with a woven cotton backing treated with an oil or plastic coating before the design is applied.
   4. ***Plastic foam*** is a soft, flexible material available in rolls, squares, or rectangles. Absorbs sound and insulates.

C. ***Fabric Wall Coverings.***
   1. For centuries, fabric on walls has given warmth and beauty.
   2. Today, fabrics of many varieties are used on walls.

3. The best choice, except when using the shirred method of application, is a medium weight, closely woven fabric.
4. Some popular methods of applying fabric wall coverings include:
   a. ***Shirring method***
   b. ***Double-face masking tape***
   c. ***Velcro method***
   d. ***Staple method***
   e. ***Paste method*** (the most professional and permanent method)
   f. ***Fabric applied to panels***

D. Other Resilient Wall Coverings
1. ***Japanese grass cloth***
2. ***Wood veneer with fabric backing***
3. ***Real leather tile***
4. ***Cork***

E. Decorative and Functional Values of Wall Coverings.
1. Bring ***beauty, charm,*** and ***interest*** into an uninteresting room.
2. Add ***architectural detail.***
3. Establish the ***period or theme.***
4. Set the mood of the room: ***formal*** or ***informal.***
5. Supply an ***effective background*** for display.
6. Provide a ***dramatic focus.***
7. Change the***visual aspect*** of a room.
8. Conceal ***architectural defects or damaged walls.***
9. Change the apparent ***size and proportion*** of a room.
10. Bring ***harmony*** into a room.
11. ***Low in cost, easy to apply*** and ***relatively easy to clean.***
12. Flexible. Can be used in any room of the house.

As with carpets, federal, state, and local building codes and safety regulations pertain to wall coverings specified for nonresidential projects.

VIII. CEILINGS:

A. The ceiling--the largest unused area of a room--has been given special attention for hundreds of years.

B. ***Functions*** of the ceiling include providing (1) protection from the elements, (2) insulation for heating and cooling, (3) a source for artificial lighting (and in some cases, natural lighting when skylights are used), (4) an important element of the character and atmosphere of a room, (5) an acoustic barrier for absorbing or reflecting sound, and (6) a flame-resistant barrier that meets standard fire codes.

C. ***Ceiling Illusions.*** If a ceiling is much above or below the average main-floor height of 8 ft, it tends to alter the general feeling of the room.

1. A high ceiling emphasizes space and tends to create a feeling of dignity and formality.
2. A low ceiling, which decreases space, can produce a warm, informal atmoshpere. Ceilings may be made to appear higher or lower.
3. ***For height:***
   a. Run the wall color or covering a short distance onto the ceiling.
   b. Use a light color on a ceiling
   c. Use a predominance of vertical lines
   d. Add a skylight
   e. Use diagonal beams
4. ***For a lower ceiling:***
   a. Paint it a darker color or use a patterned wall covering.
   b. Extend the color or covering down onto the wall (dropped ceiling)
   c. Use a predominance of horizontal lines.
   d. Use wood ceilings and horizontal beams.
5. ***Types of Ceilings:***
   a. ***Flat***
   b. ***Shed or lean-to***
   c. ***Gabled, double-pitched or cathedral***
   d. ***Sculptured***
   e. ***Coved***
   f. ***Vaulted and domed***
   g. ***Coffered***
   h. ***The dropped ceiling***
   i. ***Custom-design ceilings.***
6. ***Types of Ceiling Materials:***
   a. ***Plaster and Wallboard***
   b. ***Tiles***
   c. ***Glass and Plastic***
   d. ***Stamped Metal***
   e. ***Fabric***
   f. ***Wood***

IX. INSULATING AGAINST NOISE AND HEAT LOSS:

A. A major challenge facing architects and builders today is combating noise. Sound is being muffled by an increase in the mass and density of sound-deadening materials.

B. With energy conservation a major concern, the use of solar energy is increasing. In addition, architects and builders are using a variety of means to control heat loss.

Learning Enhancement Options

Floors and Floor Coverings. Review with students the function of floors and the task of covering this area. Discuss the considerations when determining what floor covering will be the best selection for a particular space.

Hard Flooring. Show examples of the various types of rigid floor coverings. Support this review with pictures of residential and nonresidential interiors where these floor coverings have been used. Discuss the advantages and disadvantages of each type.

Soft Floor Coverings. Present a brief history of rugs and carpets and their importance through the ages. Discuss the demand for carpets during the past few decades. Review both the functional and decorative values of carpets and show examples of interiors where these values have been successful. (Many carpet stores or manufacturers will provide instructors with samples.)

Discuss the four ingredients of a fine quality soft floor covering, show examples of the basic fibers used for carpets, and outline the advantages and disadvantages of each fiber.

Show examples and pictures of the basic construction methods and the style characteristics of carpets. (A transparency of style characteristics is available.)

Review with the students the most popular handmade rugs and their use in residential and nonresidential settings. Show examples of each rug. Also discuss the similarity in folk rugs.

Walls and Wall Treatments. Discuss with the students the functional and decorative properties of walls in both residential and nonresidential spaces. Outline how to select the best wall materials for a particular room. Present visual materials to support this process.

Nonresilient Wall Coverings. Review with the students the most frequently used nonresilient wall coverings and their characteristics and use. Show samples of each material and pictures of interiors where these materials have been successfully used.

Paints and Finishes. Review the types of paints and finishes available on the market today and the advantages and disadvantages of each. Discuss the techniques and methods of providing unusual finishes with paint. Support each method with visual material.

Resilient Wall Coverings. With the students, briefly outline the history of wallpaper and the leading contributors to the industry. Review the most common methods producing wall coverings Help the students understand the most commonly used wallpaper terms. When applicable, show examples. Examine vinyl-coated, fabric, and other resilient wall coverings.

Discuss with the students the decorative and functional values of wall coverings and how they can completely change the atmosphere of a room. Have students give examples from their own experiences. Support each point with visual materials demonstrating how these values have been applied in a space.

Ceilings. Relate the significance of interior ceilings and their style through the centuries. Review the six basic functions of the ceiling.

Outline how ceilings can be made to give the illusion of height or to appear lower. Support these decorative illusions with pictures of interiors where these suggestions have been applied.

Examine the various types of ceilings and types of ceiling materials available and show examples of each used in either a residential or nonresidential space.

Insulating Against Noise and Heat Loss. Have students discuss the important role the designer, architect, contractor, manufacturer, and others involved in the design field play in insulating walls, floors, and ceilings against noise and heat loss.

Test Questions

Multiple Choice

__C__ 1. The three basic methods of laying wood floors include all but one:
A. Parquetry
B. Planks
C. Blocks
D. Strips

__A__ 2. Functional values of carpets include all but one of the following:
A. Can alter the apparent size of a room.
B. Insulates against drafts.
C. Provides safety.
D. Muffles noise.

__D__ 3. Decorative values of carpet include all but one of the following:
A. Can be the basis for room's decor
B. Helps bring furnishings into harmony
C. Can help express personality
D. Provides a feeling of comfort

__B__ 4. What percent of all carpet sold in the U.S. is made of synthetic fibers?
A. 60%
B. 90%
C. 30%
D. 50%

__D__ 5. Tufting accounts for about what pecentage of today's carpet construction?
A. 30%
B. 50%
C. 70%
D. 90%

__A__ 6. Oriental rugs are considered most appropriate for:
A. All interiors, regardless of style.
B. Traditional interiors
C. Formal interiors
D. Modern interiors

__C__ 7. Known as the 'father of wallpaper":
A. Baptiste Reveillon
B. John Baptiste Jackson
C. Jean Papillon
D. Plunket Fleeson

__D__ 8. The most common method of producing wall coverings today is:
A. Silk-screen printing
B. Hand blocking
C. Embossing
D. Roller printing

__B__ 9. The most common method of applying fabric to walls is the:
A. Shirring method
B. Paste method
C. Velcro method
D. Staple method

__C__ 10. To give the illusion of a lower a ceiling, all but one is applicable:
A. Extend the ceiling color down onto the wall a short distance
B. Use a predominance of horizontal lines in the room.
C. Run the wall color a short distance onto the ceiling
D. Use a wood ceiling treatment

True / False

__T__ 11. The general scheme of any room is established by its backgrounds.

__T__ 12. Nonresilient flooring is not flexible.

__F__ 13. Tile is the most widely used and versatile of all the floor materials.

__F__ 14. Today, particle board is seldom used for subflooring.

__T__ 15. History reveals that rugs were used as early as 3000 B.C. in Egypt.

__F__ 16. The first manufacturer of wallpaper on an organized basis was in England.

__F__ 17. A triple roll of wallpaper contains 72 square feet.

__T__ 18. The standard ceiling height in America is 8 feet.

Matching

Match the following synthetic fibers to the correct characteristics:

A. Nylon
B. Acrylic
C. Polyester
D. Olefin

__C__ 19. Known for having great bulk and bounce. Tendency to crush.

__D__ 20. Polypropylene is a specific type of this fiber.

__B__ 21. Outstanding characteristic is its solution dyeability.

__A__ 22. Excellent abrasion resistance. The most used of all the synthetic fibers.

Match the following types of carpet construction with the appropriate definition:

A. Tufting B. Weaving C. Needle-Punch D. Flocking

__B__ 23. Three types are Wilton, Axminster, and Velvet

__D__ 24. Produced by beater bars, spraying, and an electrostatic method.

__A__ 25. Based on the principle of the sewing machine.

__C__ 26. Until recently, almost entirely used for indoor-outdoor carpeting.

Match the following style characteristics with the correct answer:

A. (Illust. of Sculptured) B. (Illust. of Level Loop) C. (Illust. of Frieze) D. (Illust. of Random Sheer)

__C__ 27. Frieze

__A__ 28. Sculptured

__D__ 29. Random Shear

__B__ 30. Level Loop

Match the following rugs with the appropriate definition:

A. Kirman B. Sarouk C. Bokhara D. Chinese

__D__ 31. Prominent colors often blue and white. Fret designs.

__C__ 32. Distinguished by repeating "balls" or geometric shapes.

__B__ 33. A solid ground of floral motifs. Usually in deep red and blue colors.

__A__ 34. Distinguished by a medallian design in the center of the rug.

Match the following handcrafted rugs to the correct description:

A. Rya B. Savonnerie C. Aubusson D. Dhurrie

__D__ 35. Stylized animals, floral, and geometric themes. Flat tapestry rug.

__A__ 36. Shaggy. Blending of colors. Popular in Scandinavia.

__C__ 37. Pile rug with soft pastel colors and floral themes.

__B__ 38. Depicts a formal garden. Strong defined colors and patterns.

Match the following paint textures and decorative finishes to the correct answer:

A. Trompe l'oeil
B. Faux finish
C. Ragging
D. Glazing

__C__ 39. One or more colors are applied over the base coat, then partly removed by blotting or rolling to produce a marbleized effect.

__D__ 40. Layers of one or more transparent colors are applied on top of a base coat.

__B__ 41. Finishes that simulate the look of another material.

__A__ 42. "Fool the eye" surface treatment.

Match the following types of ceilings to the correct description:

A. Coved B. Shed C. Coffered D. Vaulted

__A__ 43. The ceiling and wall flow into each other by means of a curved surface.

__D__ 44. Arched ceiling structures in various forms.

__C__ 45. Constructed in a grid manner, often with moldings and sunken panels.

__B__ 46. Ceiling rises diagonally to one side in a single slope.

Essay / Short Answer

47. When deciding what type of flooring is most suitable, the designer and client need to determine a number of factors. in outline form, present these considerations:

Answer to this question is found on page 150.

48. The text outlines eight specific needs for carpets and considerations when selecting color. List and describe this criteria.

Answer to this question is found on pages 166 through 168.

49. When selecting wall materials, designers consider beauty, function, economy and character. Before deciding what wall material is appropriate, what 8 basic questions outlined in the text should be considered?

Answer to this question is found on page 176.

50. List twelve decorative and functional values of wall coverings outlined in the text.

Answer to this question is found pages 189 through 193.

Educational Resources

Publications:

Chambers, Karen S. *Trompe L'Oeil at Home: Faux Finishes & Fantasy Settings*. New York: Rizzoli International Publications, Inc., 1991.

Eiland, Murray L. *Oriental Rugs: A Comprehensive Study*. Greenwich, Conn.: New York Graphic Society, 1973.

Kopp, Jeol, and Kate Kopp. *American Hooked and Sewn Rugs* . New York: Dutton, 1975.

Lang, Donna & Robertson, Lucretia. *Decorating with Paper*. New York: Crown Publishing Group, 1993

Mead, Judson. *Walls, Floors & Ceilings*. Roundtable Press, 1984.

Riggs, Rosemary. *Materials and Components of Interior Design* . 3d ed. Reston VA: Reston, 1993.

Rupp, William, and Arnold Friedmann. *Construction Materials for Interior Design.* New York: Whitney Library of Design/Watson-Guptill Publications, 1989.

Spencer, Stuart. *Marbling: Ideas & Techniques for Creating Simulated Marble* . Crown Publishing Group, 1988.

Transparencies:

Style Characteristics of Rugs and Carpets

CHAPTER 7

WINDOWS, DOORS, STAIRWAYS, AND FIREPLACES

Chapter Focus

Chapter 7 is divided into eight sections continuing the study of Interior Materials and Components presented in Chapters 5 and 6. These sections include: Windows, Considerations in the Approach to Window Treatment, Types of Windows, Types of Window Treatments, Windows and Window Treatments That Conserve Energy, Doors, Stairways, and Fireplaces.

Text Outline

Introduction:

A. Although glass walls were known to the ancient Egyptians and Romans, historically, **windows** were merely small cutouts, known as the "***wind's eye***," to permit smoke to escape, let in fresh air, and allow glimpses of the outside. Over the years, many types of windows have been planned as an integral part of the structural design of a building.

B. **Doors** originally were purely functional, used only for necessary passage. In modern times they have assumed different forms with varying degrees of design importance and traffic control.

C. **Stairways** provide the practical function of transporting the user from floor to floor. They can also provide a striking visual experience. Their design, style, construction, and safety features are important considerations.

D. **Fireplaces** relate to the interior backgrounds as well as to the furnishings and general atmosphere. Often a fireplace functions as the room's focal point. Fireplace design, type, construction, and location are considered in this chapter.

I. WINDOWS:

A. The window is an important architectural and decorative element in a room.

B. Traditionally, windows were often symmetrically placed in the facade of the house, with small panes the norm.

C. With the development of modern architecture and technology, new types of window openings were planned.
D. Window placement and design, or ***fenestration*** , today can be either symmetrical or asymmetrical.
E. The three primary functions of windows are (1) to **admit light**, (2) to **provide ventilation**, and (3) to **enhance visual communication.**
F. The window is a conspicuous element in both the exterior and interior design of a building.
G. Window openings are not always designed with indoor function in mind. It is wise to work closely with an architect and designer to ensure good planning.

II. CONSIDERATIONS IN THE APPROACH TO WINDOW TREATMENT:

A. It is helpful to approach the location, design, and treatment of any window by studying a number of primary considerations:
1. The **architectural background.**
2. The **type of window.**
3. Is there an **outside view** to consider?
4. Does **privacy** need to be considered?
5. Is **light** excessive or insufficient?
6. The **furniture arrangement.**
7. Is there a **wind problem**?
8. Is **noise** a problem?
9. How can **energy be conserved?**
10. Is the window **stationary or movable?**

III. TYPES OF WINDOWS:

A. The three general classifications of windows are (1) **movable**, (2) **stationary**, and (3) a **combination** of movable and stationary.
1. **Movable Windows** are made to open to permit ventilation. The most common are:
a. **Double-hung windows**
b. **Corner windows**
c. **Casements**
d. **Ranch or strip windows**
e. **Horizontal sliding windows**
f. **Fixed glazing with movable end sections**
g. **Awning (or louvered) and jalousie windows**
h. **Single-pivoting sash windows**
i. **Dormer windows**
j. **Palladian windows**
k. **French doors**

2. **Stationary windows** are built as an integral part of the wall construction and require no special framing. Some common stationary windows include:
   a. Fixed glazing
   b. The **angle bay window**
   c. The **bay bow window**
   d. **Clerestory windows**
   e. **Arched windows**
   f. **Skylights**
3. **Combination of movable and stationary windows** often combine both movable and stationary sections. This window type can provide more flexibility and ventilation capacity.
4. **Other window types** include:
   a. The **single window**
   b. **Double and multiple windows**
   c. **Hexagons, circles, and other geometric shapes**
   d. **Custom-designed windows**

IV. TYPES OF WINDOW TREATMENTS:

A. Deciding on an appropriate window treatment from the almost unlimited options available can be challenging.

B. All window treatments fall into two broad categories: **soft** and **hard**.

Soft Window Treatments:

1. **Draperies** are usually made of a heavier fabric than curtains, but the terms are interchangeable.
   a. **Draw draperies** are made to draw over the window to control light, heat and cold, and provide privacy. Curtains and draperies are most often hung to one of three desirable lengths: (1) the sill, (2) the bottom of the apron, or (3) the floor.
   b. **Side draperies** are stationary at the sides of the window. **Bishop's sleeve or "puffed"** side draperies are tied back at various levels.
   c. **Glass curtains** or **sheers** are used primarily to diffuse light and provide daytime privacy.
   d. **Semisheers** or **casements** are generally made of a loosely woven fabric and are heavier than a sheer.
   e. **Drapery lining** serves several functions.
   f. **Ready-mades** are draperies and curtains made to standard lengths.
2. **Curtains.** Common types include:
   a. Priscilla curtains
   b. **Shirred curtains**
   c. **Sash curtains**

d. **Cafe curtains and tiers**
e. **Bishop's sleeve or "puffed" curtains**

3. **Fabric Shades.** Some of the most common types include:
   a. **Roman shades** come in six basic treatments (1) shirred, (2) shirred balloon, (3) flat, (4) soft-pleated, (5) balloon, and (6) accordion-pleated. Another type of balloon shade is the ***cloud.***
   b. **Austrian shades**
   c. **Pleated fabric shades (accordion) and (soft shades)** **Honeycomb shades** have smaller pleats.
   d. The **roller shade**
   e. **Window quilts or thermal shades.**
4. **Window Top Treatments: Valances**
   a. The **valance** is generally a shirred, pleated, or draped soft treatment across the window top.
   b. A **swag** is a type of valance treatment wherein fabric is draped over the top of the window and tapered at the sides.
   c. A **festoon** is a single draped member of a swag
   d. A **jabot** or **cascade** may drape down from the corners of the swag.
5. **Window Top Treatments: Cornices and Lambrequins.**
   a. **Cornices** are generally made of wood, metal, or another hard material and placed at the top of the window treatment.
   b. **Lambrequins** are similar to cornices, but they also have a rigid treatment that extends vertically down both sides of the window.
6. **Window Hardware.**
   a. **Functional hardware** is inconspicuous and includes: **sash rods, extension rods, traverse rods, spring tension rods, swinging rods, extender rods,** and **ceiling tracks.**
   b. **Decorative** hardware is functional but also decorative.
7. **Drapery and Curtain Headings.**
   a. The **heading** is the pleating or gathering at the top of curtains and draperies that forms the fold and include: **French** or **pinch pleats, ripplefolds, accordion fold, easy pleats,** and **shirred headings.**
   b. **Tiebacks** or **holdbacks** hold back stationary draperies.
   c. **Trimmings** such as fringes, braids, cords, and tassels, can give a finished look to window treatments.

Hard Window Treatments:

1. **Blinds.** Types of blinds include:
   a. **Venetian blinds**
   b. **Wooden slat blinds**

c. **Miniblinds**
d. **Microminiblinds**
e. **Vertical blinds**
f. **Woven split-wood and bamboo blinds**

2. **Shutters.** Types of shutters include:
   a. **Louvered wood shutters**
   b. **Plantation shutters**
   c. **Shutters with shirred fabric panels**
   d. **Raised panel shutters**
   e. **Vertical louvered shutters**
3. **Screens and Grills.**
   a. **Shoji screens.** The traditional Japanese window with wood mullions and muntins supporting rice paper panes.
   b. **Grills.** Usually pierced or grillwork.
4. **Glass Block, Leaded and Stained Glass**
   a. **Glass block** is a translucent block of irregular glass.
   b. **Beveled, leaded, and stained glass windows** can be used in both modern and traditional designs and in numerous ways

C. **Plants** can be used successful in lieu of other window treatments.
D. **Bare windows** are sometimes beautiful in themselves.
E. **Liquid crystal** is a new glass technology. Window glass can be changed from transparent to translucent and back again at the flick of a switch.

V. WINDOWS AND WINDOW TREATMENTS THAT CONSERVE ENERGY:

A. **Energy-efficient windows.** Today, windows are available that can save energy without being bulky and heavy.
   1. Manufacturers are making multiple-glazed windows with a special antireflective coating and tinted glass to direct the sun's heating energy inward.
   2. The most popular are windows made with low-E (low emissivity) glass.

B. **Energy-efficient window treatments.** A window's treatment may also cut down on heating and cooling costs.

VI. DOORS:

A. Although similar in function to windows, doors have distinctive qualities. For example, doors:
   1. Are an essential part of a room's **architectural background.**
   2. **Allow passage** into the house and from one room to another.
   3. By their location, **control the flow of traffic.**
   4. Provide **privacy** or a two-way view.

5. Allow **ventilation**
6. Help control **temperature**
7. Provide **sound barriers**
8. Provide **safety** and **security**
The main **entrance door** is generally the most important element and focal point in the facade.

B. **Types of Doors.** The three basic types of doors are:
1. Swinging
2. Folding
3. Sliding

C. **Placement of Doors.** If doors are well placed to preserve all space and direct traffic efficiently, they present no problem. But if a room has a surplus of doors, it may be necessary to camouflage them.

D. **Treatment of Doors.** The treatment of doors depends on the design and style of the room.
1. Doors are often painted to blend with the walls, or wood doors may be stained or left natural.
2. If a door has a particularly good design, painting it a contrasting color may augment the room's decoration.
3. When walls are paneled, doors may conform to the walls or be painted in a contrasting color.
4. Many of today's doors are dramatically tall, sometimes fitting into arched openings.

VII. STAIRWAYS:

A. Stairways may be free-standing or attached to one or two walls.

B. Basically, stairways consist of the ***tread*** (horizontal member of the step), the ***riser*** (the vertical support), and a protective ***railing***.

C. Not only are stairways visually important, but the designer needs to consider safety and functional aspects as well.
1. The depth of a tread should accommodate the entire length of the foot, and a measurement of 11 in. is generally used.
2. The vertical distance between each tread is the riser, which should be no more than 8 in. high for comfort.
3. A ***handrail*** is a necessary feature for occupants. Often a stairway has upright supports for the handrail (or banister) called balusters.
4. **Headroom clearance** should be planned for the top and bottom of the staircase; 6 ft. 8 in. is considered a minimum clearance.
5. Tread and risers should be consistent in size.
6. The basic shapes or types of stairs include **straight, L-shape, winder, U-**

shape, curved or circular, and **spiral.**

7. Stairways in nonresidential settings can be bold and dramatic, introducing the adjoining offices, shops, or other public spaces. Often the stairway functions as a focal point and can be aesthetically stimulating as well as serviceable.

VIII. FIREPLACES:

A. Fireplaces have served important functional roles through the centuries as a source of warmth and a place to cook meals.
B. In today's homes the fireplace is generally a visual luxury and may serve primarily as a room's focal point.
C. Fireplaces are expensive and hard to clean after use, and require space for fuel storage.
D. The fireplace, in spite of drawbacks, remains a symbol of "hearth and home.
E. Fireplaces in public settings can be particularly inviting.
F. Considerations when planning the fireplace include:
   1. The **location** of a fireplace requires functional and visual planning. Most homes today have one fireplace, usually located either in the living or family room.
   2. **Placement** varies in the contemporary home, whether traditional or modern in design. A fireplace may be centered on a wall, placed in a corner, situated asymmetrically, or made a freestanding unit. Regardless of style, fireplaces have a basic placement and opening in relationship to the wall.
   3. The **size** of the fireplace within a living space is flexible. It is usually determined after considering the scale and proportion of a space.
   4. The **style** of a fireplace generally falls into two categories: traditional or modern.
G. **Wood-Burning Stoves.** With the high cost of heating, the wood-burning stove has become popular and is available in a large range of styles. Faced with deterioration air quality as well as wood burning restrictions, however, many designers are choosing alternatives.
H. **Wood-burning Heaters.** In 1988, the Environmental Protection Agency (EPA) established strict codes for wood-burning heaters or stoves. Today, only certified wood heaters that meet the emission limits may be sold.
I. **Gas Fireplaces.** Natural gas log sets, fireplaces, and fireplace inserts provide the ambience of wood-burning fireplaces with none of the inconveniences. It is also cleaner burning, simple to start, easy to keep clean and costs a fraction of the price of wood to operate.
J. **Tile Stoves** descended from the beautiful alpine Kachelofen heaters of Europe and provide economical ceramic radiant heat.

K. **Fireplace Construction.**
   1. **Materials.** The most common materials for fireplace construction include:
      a. **Brick**
      b. **Stone**
      c. **Wood**
      d. **Plaster or Stucco**
      e. **Concrete**
      f. **Tile**
   2. Fireplace design often includes combinations of these materials.
   3. **Construction.** Fireplaces should be constructed with adequate safety, functional, and maintenance features. It should draw properly, incorporate fireproof materials.
      a. The concern for **energy conservation** has prompted new fireplace construction, allowing more efficient use of fuel and heat output.
      b. Construction may incorporate the fireplace as part of the total wall composition.
      c. Consideration of the scale and proportion of the room, the style, the materials to be employed, and the effect and function desired can help to determine the most appropriate construction for a particular living space.

Learning Enhancement Options

Windows: Introduce the history of windows. Simple sketches on the board can be effective. Also, visual material showing various windows designed for structures through the centuries can help the student understand the importance of windows to mankind.

Considerations in the Approach to Window Treatment: Briefly outline helpful criteria when considering what window treatment will be most appropriate. If there are windows in the classroom, they could be used to illustrate the suggestions. Show visual material to help demonstrate each point.

Types of Windows: Show the transparency of Types of Windows and slides or other visual materials demonstrating these types used in residential and nonresidential settings.

Types of Window Treatments: Show the transparency of Types of Window Treatments and slides or other visual materials demonstrating each window treatment in both residential and nonresidential settings.

Windows and Window Treatments That Conserve Energy: Discuss the latest developments in windows and window treatments that conserve energy and are available to the consumer and designer.

Doors: Review the distinctive qualities and functions of doors. Discuss and show examples of types, placement and treatment of doors.

Stairways: Discuss the basic functions of stairways. Show the transparency of the Stairway Terminology. Show examples of the various styles of stairways and how they have been used in a residential and nonresidential space.

Fireplaces: Review with the students the important functional and decorative roles of fireplaces throughout history. Ask the students to share their experiences with the advantages and disadvantages of having a fireplace in both a private and public setting. Discuss the considerations of location, placement, size and style when planning the fireplace. Review the advantages and disadvantages of wood-burning stoves and heaters, gas fireplaces, and tile stoves. Consider fireplace construction and energy conservation.

Test Questions

Multiple Choice

__C__ 1. The definition of "fenestration" is:
A. Ventilation
B. Visual communication
C. Window placement and design
D. The amount of light admission into a space

__A__ 2. The 3 primary functions of windows include all but one of the following:
A. To enhance the room's style
B. To admit light
C. To enhance visual communication
D. To provide ventilation

__D__ 3. In window construction, mullions are:
A. The wide molding covering the casing and framing
B. The part of the frame beneath the sill
C. The part of the window fitting into the wall
D. The horizontal bars separating the glass panes.

__C__ 4. The most common type of drapery heading is:
A. Shirred headings
B. Ripplefold
C. French or pinch pleats
D. Accordion folds

__A__ 5. The valance is generally a:
A. Soft window treatment
B. Hard window treatment
C. A combination of soft and hard window treatments

__B__ 6. A lambrequin is a:
A. Hard treatment at the top of the window only
B. Hard treatment on both the sides and top of the window
C. Soft treatment at the sides of the window
D. Soft treatment that surrounds the entire window

__C__ 7. A cafe curtain is a soft treatment:
A. At the top of the curtains
B. At the sides of the window
C. That straddles the mid-section of the window
D. That draws from both sides of the window

__B__ 8. A cornice window treatment is a:
A. Soft treatment at the top of the window
B. Hard treatment at the top of the window
C. Hard treatment that surrounds the entire window
D. Soft treatment that surrounds the entire window

__A__ 9. The 3 basic door types include <u>all but one</u> of the following:

A. French B. Swinging C. Sliding D. Folding

__B__ 10. A stairway tread is:
A. The vertical support
B. The horizontal support

__C__ 11. The most generally used measurement for a tread is:

A. 9 in. B. 10 in. C. 11 in. D. 12 in.

__B__ 12. The style of a fireplace falls into 2 general categories:
A. Masonry and wood
B. Traditional and modern
C. Formal or informal
D. Wood-burning or gas-burning

True / False

__F__ 13. The location of a window should not affect the way it is treated.

__T__ 14. A valance treatment is used solely for appearance; it does not change the function of the drapery.

__T__ 15. Glass block was a popular treatment of the Art Deco style.

__T__ 16. Venetian blinds were used in ancient times.

__F__ 17. Coated low-E glass prevents short-wave heat energy to enter the room.

__T__ 18. If doors are well placed to preserve wall space and direct traffic efficiently, they generally present no problem.

__F__ 19. Today, an individual may install or operate a wood-heater without following EPA instructions.

__T__ 20. Compared to wood-burning, natural gas fireplace equipment is cleaner burning.

Matching:

Match the following illustrations with the correct window type:

A. (Bay) B. (Bow) C. (Clerestory) D. (Double-hung Casement)

__D__ 21. Double-hung casement window

__B__ 22. Bow window

__C__ 23. Clerestory window

__A__ 24. Bay window

A. (Jalousie) B. (Dormer) C. (Palladian) D. (Louvred)

__A__ 25. Jalousie

__D__ 26. Louvred

__C__ 27. Palladian

__B__ 28. Dormer

Match the following illustrations of window treatments with the correct answer:

A. (One-way traverse) B. (Priscilla) C. (Sash) D. (Shirred)

__D__ 29. Shirred curtains

__B__ 30. Priscilla curtains

__A__ 31. One-way traverse curtains

__C__ 32. Sash curtains

A. (Balloon) B. (Austrian Shades) C. (Shirred balloon) D. (Flat Roman)

__C__ 33. Shirred balloon shades

__D__ 34. Flat Roman shades

__B__ 35. Austrian shades

__A__ 36. Balloon Romans

Match the following illustrations of window top treatments with the correct answer:

A. (Pinch-pleats) B. (Shirred) C. (Swag & jabot) D. (Austrian)

__D__ 37. Austrian

__A__ 38. Pinch-pleats

__B__ 39. Shirred

__C__ 40. Swag and jabot

Match the following illustrations of door types with the correct answer:

A. (Illust. of Dutch) B. (Illust. of Batten) C. (Illust. of Louvred) D. (Illust. of French)

__A__ 41. Dutch door

__B__ 42. Batten door

__D__ 43. French door

__C__ 44. Louvred door

Essay / Short Answer

45. Briefly outline the origin and historic importance of windows and their primary function in today's residential and nonresidential spaces.

Answer to question 45 is found on pages 202 and 203.

46. Outline the ten primary considerations in the approach to window treatment.

Answer to question 46 is found on page 203.

47. Window treatments fall into two basic categories: soft and hard. List some of the most popularly used treatments for each category.

Answer to question 47 is found on pages 206 through 220

48. Provide nine distinctive qualities of doors outlined in the text.

Answer to question 48 is found on page 221.

49. Outline and define the seven basic points concerning stairways presented in the text.

Answer to question 49 is found on pages 223 and 324.

50. Present information concerning the location, placement, size, and style of a fireplace. What are the most used materials for fireplace construction?

Answer to question 50 is found on pages 224 through 227.

Educational Resources

Publications:

De Fever, Carolyn Lee. *Window Covering Basics* . Paisley Publishers. San Antonio. 1992.
Lindahl, Judy. *The Shade Book* . Portland, Oregon: Judy Lindahl. 1992.
Nielson, Karla J. *Window Treatments* . New York: Van Nostrand Reinhold, 1990.
Rees, Yvonne. Window Style. New York: Van Nostrand Reinhold. 1990
Riggs, Rosemary. *Materials and Components of Interior Design. 3d ed.* Reston VA: Reston, 1993.
Rupp, William, and Arnold Friedmann. *Construction Materials for Interior Design. New* York: Whitney Library of Design/Watson-Guptill Publications, 1989.
Wrey, Lady Caroline. *Complete Book of Curtains & Drapes.* London: Ebury/Random Century Export. 1991.

Transparencies:

Types of Windows
Types of Window Treatments
Stairway Terminology

CHAPTER 8

FURNITURE SELECTION

Chapter Focus

Chapter 8 introduces Part 4: Furniture, and emphasizes helpful material that is essential for the designer when selecting furniture. This chapter is divided into four sections and includes: Considering the Human Factor, Types of Furniture, Quality and Craftsmanship and Upholstered Furniture.

Text Outline

Introduction:

A. Planning furniture for a space is an important part of the design process that ultimately must satisfy the needs of the end user.
B. Furniture for residential and nonresidential spaces is often interchangeable.
C. Careful study and planning enable the design and consumer to make wise decisions.
D. If a piece of furniture is well design initially, it will always be good.

I. CONSIDERING THE HUMAN FACTOR:

Most interiors require furniture that will satisfy specific functions within a space. Today the market abounds with furniture of many types, styles, materials, and prices, to satisfy particular lifestyles and fulfill particular needs. Wise furniture selections depends on:

A. **Function:** Furniture should serve a useful purpose. (1) What furniture is needed? (2) Will the furniture be used in a residential or nonresidential setting? (3) Who will use it? (4) Where will the furniture be placed? (5) What purpose will it serve?
   1. ***Space Allocation and Function.***
      a. How much space is available to accommodate the furniture? The size of the furniture is determined by the space available.
      b. What furniture types will be required to satisfy the functional needs of a particular project?
      c. How many of each, what specific type, what finishes, materials, and fabrics will best suit the activities that will take place?

d. Each furniture type is designed to fulfill certain functions.

2. ***Comfort and Convenience.*** To function adequately, furniture should be comfortable for the users and convenient for the various activities it must serve.
   a. The study of human dimensions, called ***anthropometrics***, is a science that measures such criteria as a person's height, weight, and shape.
   b. Anthropometrics is closely related to ***ergonomics***, a science whose goal is to provide a comfortable relationship between human beings and their environment through the study of body mechanics and sensory performance.
3. ***Physically Challenged*** . Suitable furniture may be required to meet the functional needs of users who are physically challenged. This task is particularly relevant to many nonresidential projects.

B. **Aesthetics:**
1. Often the initial impression of a furniture piece is a matter of subjective personal taste.
2. An acquaintance with the principles of design helps provide a knowledgeable background.
3. The ability to discriminate between fine furniture and faddish, furniture involves training the eye.
4. In a nonresidential space furniture generally reflects the tastes of the owners, the designer, or the company image.
5. The design or style of furniture should be compatible with the intended function and complement the overall theme and architectural background.
6. Individuality and character are the unique aspects that draw the user to a particular piece or style.

C. **Quality:**
1. How a piece of furniture is made and the quality of the materials used are of vital concern.
2. The quality of construction, materials, and finishes ranges from poor to excellent.
3. A good manufacturer takes great pride in the skilled workmanship that goes into the product.

D. **Budget:**
1. The client's budget is a necessary consideration when planning and furnishing a space.
2. What is the cost of the furniture in relation to the budget allocation?
3. Almost all design projects have a certain budget limit.
4. In addition to the initial cost of furniture, the lifetime costs must also be considered.
5. Fine quality and good design are always wise investments.

II. TYPES OF FURNITURE:

A. Human beings first created crude but somewhat functional pieces of furniture.
B. As time passed the process was refined, and furniture became an important art form.
C. After the development of early cultures, various styles evolved that proved to have a lasting influence on following generations, especially from England and France.
D. Basic furniture types have remained fairly constant with the exception of built-ins and modular units.
   1. **Chairs.** For centuries people have been fascinated by the design potential of the seating unit. Human beings use chairs every day for a variety of functions. Considerations when selecting chairs include:
      (1) The height, depth, and width should accommodate the human form.
      (2) An adjustable chair can give flexible service.
      (3) Ergonomic designs can provide maximum comfort.
      (4) Chairs of varying sizes are available.
      (5) Materials used.
      (6) Style from all periods are available.
      (7) There are chairs to satisfy every function.
   2. **Sofas.** Sofas are long upholstered seating units accommodating two or more persons. Through the ages particular terms have been associated with certain designs. ***Lawson*** is a popular type with armrests lower than the back support. The most common sofas include:
      (1) ***Couch:*** Long upholstered unit with a low back and one endpiece.
      (2) ***Davenport:*** Often used to define a convertible sofa.
      (3) ***Tuxedo:*** A completely upholstered piece with armrests the same height as the back.
      (4) ***Chesterfield:*** Upholstered sofa with upholstered ends.
      (5) ***Divan:*** A low couch without arms or back units.
      (6) ***Loveseat:*** A small sofa for two persons.
      (7) ***Settee:*** A lightly scaled piece, often with some upholstered sections.
      (8) ***Settles:*** Completely constructed of wood with very high backs.
      (9) ***Dual-purpose:*** Can be used for both sleeping and seating.
      (10) ***Modular and sectional sofas:*** Standardized series of sofa units planned to integrate with other similar units.
   3. **Tables.**
      (1) ***Dining and kitchen tables.***
      (2) ***Coffee tables.***
      (3) ***End or occasional tables.***
      (4) ***Game tables.***
      (5) ***Desks***

a. Tables should be sturdy, strong, and durable and of a usable size and shape.
b. The height should be adequate and comfortable for the intended function.

4. **Beds.** A bed may be:
(1) ***built-in,***
(2) ***composed of modular units,***
(3) ***freestanding,***
(4) ***a dual-purpose piece,***
(5) ***a fold-down-from-the wall type,***
(6) ***a bunk bed,***
(7) ***a water bed,***
(8) ***or a trundle bed.***

5. **Storage.**
a. Many innovative pieces designed for functional storage are available to help alleviate the problems of small living spaces.
b. Convenient and efficient storage can be provided in many rooms of the house with ***chests, cupboards, hutches, china cabinets, shelves,*** and ***armoires.***

6. **Built-in Wall and Modular Units.**
a. ***Built-in furnishings*** may function as seating, tables, beds, and storage space and are an integral part of the wall construction.
b. They have the advantage of providing architectural unity and a more spacious feeling.
c. A drawback can be the inability to move the components.
d. ***Modular units*** can be arranged in a variety of compositions, providing great flexibility.

7. **Systems Furniture.**
a. ***Systems furniture*** are modular pieces used for office design projects.
b. They consist of ***work surfaces, storage units, and vertical panels*** that make up a ***workstation.***
c. These flexible pieces can be set up in a variety of configurations to fit the space available.
d. They can serve the needs of ***executive, management, secretarial, clerical*** and ***work processing workstations.***

III. QUALITY AND CRAFTSMANSHIP:

The quality of construction and craftsmanship of a piece of furniture are often readily apparent. Following are some construction features to look for:

A. All sections must be ***firmly joined and secure.***

B. Furniture should be ***well proportioned and comfortable.***
C. A well-constructed chest, chair, or table remains ***rigid and sturdy*** when one tries to rock it.
D. A fine-quality ***finish*** is smooth and evenly applied, with no spotting, sticky areas, running, or buildup of coats.
E. ***Back panels*** should be recessed and smoothly finished.
F. ***Movable units*** must be durable and easily operated.
G. ***Leg and base supports*** should be particularly sturdy with a durable finish
H. Furniture with ***flat areas*** should be constructed of durable material.
I. The ***edges*** of tables and other pieces are especially susceptible to damage and wear. Rounded edges, reinforced strips and edges made of solid hardwood are more practical.
   1. **Wood.** Wood is the major material used for furniture construction.
      a. A piece of furniture marked ***solid*** is made from solid hardwood.
      b The label ***genuine*** shows that the furniture is made of a single hardwood, with veneer on flat surfaces and solid structural parts such as the legs.
      c. ***Veneer*** is a thin layer of finishing wood applied to the body of a less refined wood. Only veneering permits the beautiful effects achieved by the different methods of matching wood grains.
      d. The ***wood grain*** is determined by its natural growth. The method in which the wood is cut into lumber (sawed) produces a variety of grains.
      e. Furniture is made from both hard and soft woods. ***Hardwoods*** come from ***deciduous*** trees (those that drop their leaves). Hardwoods are more durable and dent resistant than softwoods. Hardwoods are more costly and generally more attractive.
      f. ***Softwoods*** come from ***coniferous*** trees (those with needles). Softwoods are used for less expensive furniture.
      g. ***Labels*** describing the finish refer to the color only, not to the species of wood used.
      h. Each wood has its own special ***properties*** .
      i. Wood selected for a particular furniture piece should be properly dried, well suited for its intended construction, purpose, finish, size, and style; and resistant to warping, splitting, swelling, and shrinking.
      j. ***Considering the Environment.*** Currently, a strong feeling of responsibility exists among designers, manufacturers, and consumers to preserve the environment. Many furniture companies have strict policies regarding environmental issues and the use of wood from threatened or endangered species of trees, especially from rain forests. In some cases the use of certain woods for furniture construction is restricted by federal and state laws.

k. **Construction Methods.** The quality and type of wood joinings indicates the durability and aesthetic quality of a piece. The most common construction methods for joining wood are:
   (1) ***Mortise and tenon***
   (2) ***Dowel***
   (3) ***Miter***
   (4) ***Dovetail***
   (5)***Tongue and groove***
   (6) ***Rabbeted or rebated***
   (7) ***Butt***

l. **Types of finishings:** Principal types of finishes applied to wood furniture include: ***staining, paint, oil, varnish, shellac, lacquer, and polyurethane.*** Special or unusual finishes include: ***stenciling, faux, spattering, stippling, glazing, sponging, and hand painted designs.***

2. **Metal.** Metal was used as a material for furniture in ***ancient civilizations.*** During the ***Middle Ages and Renaissance***, exquisitely wrought iron and other metals were used for many furnishings. In the ***eighteenth century*** , metals were especially employed for accenting fine furniture. By the ***Victorian***

   and ***Industrial Revolution*** periods, iron and brass bed and iron furniture of all types were produced.With the advent of the ***Bauhaus*** and other modern movements, new methods of working metal have been developed, like tubular steel, sheet metal, wire, steel, etc.
   a. Metal can be shaped in many forms.
   b. The most common metals used for furniture construction include: ***brass, bronze, iron, steel, and aluminum.***
   c. A wide range of finishes are available today.
   d. Metal is relatively inexpensive, strong, durable, and cool to the touch.
   e. Be sure that the metal is rustproof. If damaged, repairs are costly.

3. **Synthetic Materials:** Man-made products for furniture construction have revolutionized the design field. Now synthetic materials, such as acrylics, vinyl, polyurethane, and laminates, are used for almost all furniture types and in numerous ways. Basically, synthetic materials are employed in six ways:
   (1)***Lamination and bonding agents.***
   (2)***Molded furniture.***
   (3)***Functional hardwood parts decorative accent pieces.***
   (4)***Finishes.***
   (5)***Upholstery fabrics.***
   (6)***Upholstery fillers.***
   a. Synthetics can be molded, sprayed, foamed, blown, or rolled into many sizes and forms, and their use for residential and contract furnishings is unlimited.

b. Synthetic materials are available in a wide range of colors, textures, and patterns.
c. Synthetics are durable and easy to keep clean. However, some synthetics may dull over time, break, or scratch and are very difficult to repair. Also some synthetic materials are flammable.
d. When well designed, synthetics mix well with other furnishings.

4. **Rattan, Cane, Rush, and Wicker** are materials that come from natural sources such as palms and grasses. Because of their nature, they are compatible in an informal setting, in an eclectic formal room, they can add interest. These materials can be used effectively in both inside and outside spaces.
   a. ***Rattan poles*** are cut from the rattan palm.
   b. ***Cane*** is split rattan from the rattan palm and is interwoven (known as mesh).
   c. ***Rush*** is tightly twisted long grass (often paper is used) made into a cord.
   d. ***Wicker (or basketwork)*** is more accurately a method (rather than a specific material) of furniture construction using rushes, twigs, and reeds.

IV. UPHOLSTERED FURNITURE:

A. Upholstered furniture was known in ***ancient civilizations***.
B. During the ***Renaissance*** simple padding or cushions were placed on top of the stretched fabric.
C. Later, fabrics were used to cover the cushion and stretched fabric.
D. By the ***sixteenth century*** padding made of horsehair, feathers, wool, and down made cushions even deeper and more comfortable.
E. In the ***eighteenth century*** springs were introduced and modern upholstery had arrived.
F. Little change occurred in upholstery construction until the introduction of synthetics during the ***1930s***.
G. Upholstered furniture today is basically of two types (1) ***overstuffed*** and (2) an ***exposed frame with partially exposed sections***.

1. **Frame.** A good frame is constructed of ***kiln-dried hardwood***. It should be firmly assembled and usually joined by ***double dowels*** that are spiral grooved and then glued. ***Reinforcement braces*** of metal or wood blocks should be glued and screwed to the corners.
2. **Webbing.** Generally of linen, jute, plastic, or rubber, the webbing is arranged in a ***basketweave*** and used on the frame to provide support for the springs and cushioning. Good quality webbing measures ***3 to 4 in. width***..
3. **Springs.** The spring construction may be of either ***sinuous wire*** or ***coils***.

a. The ***sinuous wire*** is simpler and by some criteria better.
b. The ***cone coil*** comes in both ***single and double cone***. The ***single cone coil*** is a prefabricated unit for standard styles. ***Double-cone coils*** are mounted and affixed on a resilient base such as strips of webbing or metal, and are hand tied at the top.
c. Fine-quality springs have ***individual coil springs*** contained in muslin. ***Burlap*** is used to protect and cover springs.

4. **Filling, Stuffing, and Padding** materials of various types and qualities are used for cushioning, either alone or in combination. These materials - but not the qualities - are listed on the label. Today, the most commonly used fillings include:
   a. ***Polyester*** is lightweight, resilient, and odorless. Often wrapped in Dacron.
   b. ***Foam rubber or latex*** (looks like well-beaten egg whites). Durable.
   c. ***Polyurethane foam*** is more suitably used today than foam runner. Along with polyester, it is the most used filler.
   d. ***Down or feathers*** are soft but are not resilient. High cost.
   e. ***Rubberized fibers*** such as sisal. Used in moderately priced furniture.
   f. ***Shredded fibers*** from natural sources such as leave are generally used in low-priced furniture.
   g. ***Cotton*** is occasionally used for small pieces.
   i. ***Muslin*** used as covering over the filling material is always employed on fine quality furnitue. ***Cotton felt*** is used to protect springs and other filling materials.
5. **Fabric** is used to cover all the construction of the piece, and it should be professionally finished.
   a. ***Seat and back cushions and pillows***, filled with the materials just mentioned, may be added to complement the furniture's style. They may be fastened or movable.
   b. Cushioning should be ***comfortable, resilient, able to take hard usage,*** and it should ***stay in place***. Some questions are: What kind of cushioning does the piece have? Will it retain its shape? Can it be cleaned? It is odorless and nonallergenic?

H. **Upholstery Fabrics.** In the purchase of upholstered furniture, fabric is a primary consideration. In selecting the fabric, ***use*** is generally the determining factor. Selecting suitable upholstery fabric involves answering questions such as:
   1. What ***type of fiber and weave*** are employed, and how durable is the fabric?

2. Is the fabric ***attractive and comfortable*** ?(3) Is a ***pattern or plain*** fabric preferred?
3. Is the fabric ***suitable for its intended function*** ?
4. Is the fabric the best quality the ***budget*** will allow?
5. What ***maintenance process*** is necessary?
6. Does the upholstery fabric fit the ***style, mood,*** and ***character*** of the room? Additionally, the quality of upholstery construction is readily apparent. In selecting a piece of upholstered furniture, consider the following criteria:
   a. ***Precise tailoring*** is necessary.
   b. Large ***patterns*** should be carefully centered and matched.
   c. When fabrics are ***quilted,*** close, secure stitching prevents snagging.
   d. ***Cushions*** should fit snugly.
   e. If ***zippers*** are used, they must be ***sewn straight.***
   f. When fabric has a ***nap,*** it should only run in one direction.
   g. ***Fabric*** should be ***smoothly stretched over the frame.***
   h. ***Back panels*** should be ***firmly and neatly tacked or stitched.***
   i. ***Exposed wood parts*** should be of ***hardwood*** and be ***well finished***

I. **Government Labels.** Federal and state laws require labels to be attached to furnishings to provide specific information about the piece. Reputable manufactures guarantee or warranty the materials used, or that the furniture's performance will meet the specifications outlined on the label.

Learning Enhancement Options

Considering the Human Factor: Ask students how furniture can satisfy specific functions within a space. Review the basic considerations that include function, (including comfort and convenience and the physically challenged), aesthetics, quality, and budget. Present visual material to support the ideas and information discussed.

Types of Furniture: Present a short history on the evolution of various types of furniture and their importance to mankind. Outline the basic furniture types, (and selection considerations), including: chairs, sofas, tables, beds, storage, built-in wall and modular units and systems furniture. Show examples of each type.

Quality and Craftsmanship: Review with the students how to determine the quality of construction and craftsmanship of a piece of furniture. Discuss the basic materials used in the construction of a piece of furniture including: wood, (and the environment, construction methods, types of finishes), metal, synthetic materials, and rattan, cane, rush, and wicker. Discuss with the students how upholstered furniture evolved and the parts of upholstered furniture. Show visual materials to support each point.

Upholstered Furniture: Discuss with the students how upholstered furniture evolved through the centuries and the changes brought about from the 1930s to the present. Review the parts of upholstered furniture including the frame, webbing, springs, filling, stuffing, padding, and fabrics. Discuss the use of fabrics for upholstering and questions to consider when evaluating the success of an upholstered piece. Incorporate visual material and examples to support the information.

Test Questions

Multiple Choice

__B__ 1. The term "ergonomics" means:
- A. Budget considerations
- B. Furniture design based on anthropometric studies
- C. Furniture design based on comfortable materials
- D. The height, depth, and width of a seating unit

__ B__ 2. "Genuine" wood marked on a piece of furniture indicates:
- A. A piece of furniture made of solid wood
- B. Furniture is made of a single hardwood with veneer on flat surfaces
- C. Thin layer of finishing wood is applied to the body of less refined wood
- D. Furniture made of all veneered wood

__C__ 3. A tuxedo sofa is:
- A. A convertible sofa
- B. A sofa with armrests lower than the back support
- C. An upholstered piece with armrests the same height as the back
- D. A low couch without arms

__A__ 4. Metal used as a material for furniture was introduced:
- A. By ancient civilizations
- B. During the Middle Ages
- C. During the Renaissance
- D. During the Industrial Revolution

__D__ 5. An armoire is:
A. A French armchair
B. A type of French sofa with arms
C. A French desk
D. A French storage closet

__A__ 6. Modular pieces used for office design projects are known as:
A. Systems Furniture
B. Unit Furniture
C. Workstation Furniture
D. Panel Furniture

__C__ 7. A good furniture frame is constructed of:
A. A hardwood that is not kiln-dried
B. Kiln-dried softwood
C. Kiln-dried hardwood
D. A combination of kiln-dried softwood and hardwood

__C__ 8. Good quality webbing measures:
A. 1 to 2 inches in width
B. 2 to 3 inches in width
C. 3 to 4 inches in width
D. 4 to 5 inches in width

__B__ 9 Regarding sinuous wire springs, select the best answer:
A. Particularly desirable for traditional overstuffed furniture
B. Pariticularly desirable for slimline modern furniture
C. Made in a single and double cone
D. Mounted and affixed on a resilient base

__D__ 10. Currently, the most used fillings, stuffings, and paddings are:
A. Shredded fibers
B. Down or feathers
C. Rubberized fibers and foam rubber
D. Polyurethane foam and polyester

True / False:

__T__ 11. Furniture for residential and nonresidential spaces is often interchangeable.

__F__ 12. When purchasing furniture, the consumer is generally wise to have a short-range plan.

__T__ 13. The aesthetic appeal of a furniture piece is purely subjective.

__T__ 14. Settles were originally used in Early American homes to retain heat from the fireplace.

__F__ 15. Synthetic materials for furniture construction are generally difficult to clean and are not as durable as natural materials.

__F__ 16. When a fabric has a nap, it can run in either direction of a chair or sofa.

__T__ 17. An upholstery fabric will last longer if the warp and fill are the same weight and tightly woven.

__T__ 18. Polyurethane foam is more suitably used today than foam rubber.

__F__ 19. Systems furnishings consist of free-standing coordinating pieces.

__T__ 20. Federal and state laws always require labels to be attached to furniture specified for nonresidential spaces.

Matching:

Match the following illustrations with the correct answer:

A. (Wing) B. (Tub) C. (Windsor) D. (Spoonback)

__ C__ 21. Windsor

__A__ 22. Wing

__B__ 23. Tub

__D__ 24. Spoonback

A. (Harvest) B. (Butterfly) C. (Pembroke) D. (Breakfront)

__D__ 25. Breakfront

__C__ 26. Pembroke

__A__ 27. Harvest

__B__ 28. Butterfly

A. (Couch) B. (Davenport) C. (Chesterfield) D. (Divan)

__A__ 29. Couch

__D__ 30. Divan

__B__ 31. Davenport

__C__ 32. Chesterfield

Matching the following illustrations of joinings with the correct answer:

A. (Dovetail) B. (Dowel) C. (Tongue & Groove) D. (Mortise & Tenon)

__B__ 33. Dowel

__C__ 34. Tongue & Groove

__D__ 35. Mortise & Tenon

__A__ 36. Dovetail

Match the following materials with the correct answer:

A. Rattan B. Cane C. Rush D. Wicker

__C__ 37. Tightly twisted long grass into a cord

__D__ 38. Basketwork - rather than a material

__A__ 39. Poles are cut from a palm and bent to form furniture

__B__ 40. Split and interwoven (known as "mesh")

Essay / Short Answer

41. When selecting furniutre for either residential or non-residential projects, it is essential to consider the human factor. List four considerations and provide relevant information under each heading.

Answer to this question is found on pages 232 through 234.

42. What are 7 considerations when selecting chairs?

Answer to this question is found on page 235.

43. List eight basic bed types.

Answer to this question is found on pages 240 and 242.

44. What nine furniture construction features outlined in the text constitute fine quality furniture.

Answer to this question is found on pages 243 and 244.

45. What is the designer's and manufacturer's resonsibility in regards to considering the environment and how can this issue be addressed?

Answer to this question is found on page 244.

46. Synthetic materials are used for almost all furniture types and in numerous ways. Basically, synthetic materials are emplyed in six ways. List these six ways:

Answer to this question is found on page 246.

47. Outline the parts of upholstered furniture and provide important information under each heading.

Answer to this question is found on pages 249 and 250.

48. List the various types, qualities, and uses of upholstered filling, stuffing, and padding.

Answer to this question is found on pages 249 and 250.

49. In selecting fabric, use is generally the determining factor. What basic questions can be answered before selecting suitable upholstery fabric?

Answer to this question is found on page 250.

50. What nine criteria should be considered when inspecting the quality of upholstery construction.?

Answer to this question is found on page 250 and 251.

Educational Resources

Publications:

Boyce, Charles. *Dictionary of Furniture.* New York: Roundtable Press, 1985.
Franks, Beth. *Wicker, Cane, & Willow.* Grove/Atlantic Monthly Press. 1990
Hanks, David A. *Innovative Furniture in America from 1800 to the Present.* New York: Horizon, 1981.

Movies / Videos:

Furniture: A Buyer's Guide : 31 min / 1985 / Insight Media
Furnishing and Decorating Your First Home : 25 min / Learning Seed, Illinois

Transparencies:

Furniture Types
Types of Wood Joining and Upholstery Construction

CHAPTER 9

FURNITURE STYLES

Chapter Focus

Chapter 9 is divided into two general sections: Basic Furniture Styles and General Classification of Furniture Styles. These topics include: The Spanish Styles, Seventeenth and Eighteenth-Century Country Style, Early and Late Georgian, The Neoclassic Period, The French Styles in America, Victorian Furniture, Contemporary and Modern Furnishings, American Oriental Style, and Style Selection.

Text Outline

I. **BASIC FURNITURE STYLES:**

A. Throughout history, the diversity of world cultures has found expression in many directions, including the way people have lived in their homes and their furnishings.

B. Differences in designs of furniture, as well as the decorative arts, were the result of a number of factors including climate, politics, religion, and customs.

C. Furniture styles that have had the greatest impact on Americans include:

1. **The Spanish Styles.** The Spaniard colonists built private and public buildings primarily in what is now New Mexico and California during the seventeenth to nineteenth centuries. The California Mission Colonial Style (circa Eighteenth Century to the Present) . A string of Catholic missions were built along the California coast, introducing characteristics of architecture based on prototypes in Spain. Furniture reflects original Spanish designs. The Mexican influence was also incorporated.

a. **General Characteristics**: Heavily proportioned, strong, and sturdy furnishings. Influence of Spain and Mexico. Strong geometric designs. Use of spindles, finials, and grilles. Dark wood. Scrolled Spanish foot. Nails and joinings exposed. Furniture ornamented with metal.

(1) *Seating* : Heavy. Metal nailheads. Ironwork. Ladderbacks topped with hoods and finials. Tooled leather. Geometric designs, lattice, and turned spindles. Shepherd's chairs. Leather upholstered bench.

(2) *Casepieces* : ***Vargueno.*** Cupboard or ***trastero.***
(3) *Tables:* Heavily carved ***trestle*** table with iron stretchers.
(4) *Beds:* Carved spindles arrangement topped with finials typical.

b. **Fabrics**: Leather. Velvets and tapestries. Colors in strong chroma.

c. **Accessories**: Wrought-iron chandeliers, candlesticks, and sconces. Tinware. Hand-painted Mexican tile and pottery. Christian relics. Mirrors with ironwork or heavily carved wooden frames

The Southwest Adobe (circa Seventeenth to Twentieth Century) and the Santa Fe Styles (circa 1920s to present): Unique blending of Indian and Spanish cultures. In the 1920s, a fresh style based on original Southwest Adobe interiors and furnishings was developed. It has become distinctive and highly sophisticated with the addition of English and Modern furnishings.

a. **General Characteristics:** Simple and functional.
(1) *Seating* : Spindle backs, rush-bottomed seats. Lodgepole pine furniture. ***Equipale*** leather and wood. Carved colonial chairs and benches.
(2) *Casepieces* : Storage pieces with perforated tin design. Large cupboard ***trastero*** . Stars and stripes cupboard. Mexican cupboard. Geometrically carved grain chest.
(3) *Tables* : ***Equipale*** leather and wood drum table. Trestle. Simple table with carved apron.
(4) *Beds* : Carved colonial bed. Lodgepole pine.

b. **Fabrics**: Informal. Wool and cotton. Geometric designs. Indian influence. Embroidery. Warm desert colors used for Santa Fe Style.

c. **Accessories**: Handcrafted Spanish, Indian, and Mexican art. Navajo rugs. Tinware. Indian pottery and baskets. Religious relics. Candlesticks. Cactus plants. Kachina dolls. Silver and metal items. Any accessory reflecting New Mexico lifestyle. **Spanish Monterey and California Ranch Styles** have furnishings similar to those found in the Spanish Mission and Colonial style. Monterey style typically includes eighteenth-century English furniture blending with Spanish influences.

2. **Seventeenth and Eighteenth-Century Country Style (Early American Furnishings).** Is an informal provincial style during the settlement period. Furnishings reflected the colonists' English, Dutch, Swedish, and German heritage. Furnishings authentically reproduced in the new land. English colonies were dominant.

a. **General Characteristics**: Informal country look. Simple handcrafted furnishings. Utilitarian pieces.
(1) *Seating*: ***Brewster, Bannister-back, Wainscot, Ladder-back. Carver, Jacobean, William and Mary wing back, Windsor.***

and ***Hitchcock*** chairs. ***Settles*** . ***Jacobean day bed.*** Shaker chairs.

(2) *Casepieces* : ***Court cupboard. Hadley chest. Sunflower chest. Corner cupboard. Slant-top*** desk. ***William and Mary highboy*** and ***lowboy. William and Mary double-hooded desk. Dry sink.***

(3) *Tables* :***Trestle*** table. ***Gateleg*** table. ***Butterfly*** gateleg. Candle stand. Table chair.

(4) *Beds* : ***Trundle*** bed and cradles.

b. **Fabrics**: Made on looms. Homespun wood. Some cotton. Natural dyes employed. Coverlets. Needlework. Rugs from fabric strips. Quaint prints.

c. **Accessories**: Quaint pictures. Utilitarian items. Simple pottery. Wall clocks. Candles and holders. Courting mirrors.

3. **Early and Late Georgian (circa 1700-1790).** Period of prosperity. Formal and elegant style. Named after English kings George I, II, and III. Queen Anne furniture introduced around 1700. Thomas Chippendale furniture introduced on grand scale around 1745. ("Golden Age"of great cabinetmakers). Both Queen Anne and Chippendale furniture took on distinct regional differences in the colonies. **Queen Anne:**

a. **General Characteristics:** ***Queen Anne*** based on the ***cyma (S)*** curve. Graceful and dainty. Use of mahogany. Introduction of lacquering. ***Scallop-shell*** motif most typical.

(1) *Seating* : ***Fiddleback*** side chair. Use of the ***pad*** or ***club*** foot. Wing chair. ***Cabriole leg.*** Round-about chair. Sofa with high curved back.

(2) *Casepieces* : ***Highboy*** and ***lowboy.***

(3) *Tables* :***Tea*** table.***Tilt-top*** table. Dropleaf table.

b. **Fabrics**: Elegant formal damasks, velvets, taffetas, and brocades. Informal chintz, cotton and wool. Red, gold, muted green, and blue most common.

c. **Accessories**: Oriental rugs and vases. Brass or bronze chandeliers. Mirrors with S-curved top. Tall case clock.

Chippendale Furniture:

a. **General Characteristics:** Sturdy and elegant with vigorous carving in high relief. Masculine. Mahogany. Ornate metal, butterfly, stirrup, and ring hardware.

(1) *Seating* :***Yokeback*** chair. ***Pierced ladder*** chair. ***Marborough*** leg. ***Claw-and-ball*** foot. ***Cabriole leg. Camelback*** sofa.***Wing*** chair.

(2) *Casepieces* : ***Highboys, lowboys*** and ***chest-on-chest*** . ***Secretary. Breakfront. Knee-hole desk. Finials. Broken and scroll pediments. Bracket*** supports. ***Fret*** designs.

(3) *Tables* : ***Piecrust tilt-top*** table. Folding card table.

(4) *Beds* : ***Chinese Chippendale*** .

b. **Fabrics:** Formal damasks, brocades, taffetas, and velvets. Rich gold, yellow, deep red, blue, and Williamsburg green.

c. **Accessories:** Mirrors. Baroque brass or bronze chandeliers. Oriental rugs and porcelain. Wall sconces. Tall case clocks.

4. **The Neoclassic Period (circa 1790-1845).** The Neoclassic period is divided into three overlapping subperiods: (1) the ***Early Federal Period*** (ca 1790-1804); (2) the***Late Federal, Early American Empire,*** and ***Regency*** period (ca 1804-1825); and (3) the***Greek Revival*** or ***Late American Empire*** period (ca 1825-1845)

Early Federal Period: Distinguished by light forms and straight lines, with some semicircular and elliptical curves. Federal period is dominated by the styles of English cabinetmakers ***George Hepplewhite, Thomas Sheraton,*** and the ***Adam*** brothers. Emphasis on color and surface decoration rather than form. Smaller in scale. America produced its most famous cabinetmaker, ***Duncan Phyfe.***

Hepplewhite Furniture:

a. **General Characteristics:** Bridge between Chippendale style and Neoclassic style. Modified Chippendale scroll on casepieces, mirrors and camelback sofa. Leg is straight, square, tapered and either plain or fluted. Terminates with or without a spade foot. Inlay. Brass ring hardware.

(1) *Seating* : Chair backs in form of shield, hearts, or ovals. ***Martha Washington*** chair.

(2) *Casepieces* : Sideboard. ***Tambour*** secretaries. China cabinets and bookcases. Chests.

(3) *Tables* : Dining tables usually oval. ***Pembroke*** tables. ***Pier*** table and ***sewing-bag*** table.

(4) *Bed* : ***Four-poster bed.***

b. **Fabrics:** Formal and elegant damasks, velvets, brocades, and taffetas. French and classical themes in pastel colors.

c. **Accessories:** Convex mirror with eagle motif. Crystal chandeliers. Wedgwood china. Oriental or French rugs. Intricate stitchery. Tall slender clock cases.

Sheraton Furniture:

a. **General Characteristics:** Dominance of straight lines and simplicity of design. Graceful. Influence of Adam brothers, Hepplewhite, and Louis XVI. Classical motifs. Leg is straight, tapered and reeded and terminates in a thimble foot.

(1) *Seating* : Chair back square, but in a variety of designs. Sofas have carved railing across back and armrests. Opening between armrest and upholstery.
(2) *Casepieces* : Buffets. Secretaries.
(3) *Tables* : Dining and small tables. Sofa table. Dual-purpose tables.
(4) *Beds* : Four poster topped by canopy. ***Twin*** beds.

b. **Fabrics:** Same as Hepplewhite.
c. **Accessories:** Mirrors architectural in form. Some accessories similar to Hepplewhite.

Duncan Phyfe Furniture: New York based (1795-1847). Two basic periods: (1) ***early period*** and (2) ***late period.***

a. **General Characteristics:** Fine proportions. Clean, simple lines with freehand curves. Fluting, reeding and foliate carving. Motifs include lyre, palm leaves, holly, laurel, small acanthus, lion's head, medallions, wheat and swags.
(1) *Seating* : Chairs with ***lyre*** backs. Slip type seats. Legs are straight and reeded or ***saber-shaped***, ending in animal paws. ***Curule-shaped*** supports. Sofas with rail in sleigh form, often with lyre motif. ***Cornucopia*** leg. ***Recamier*** sofa.
(2) *Tables* : ***Console.*** Card, library, and dining tables. Splayed leg typical.

b. **Fabrics:** Similar to Hepplewhite and Sheraton.
c. **Accessories:** ***Cheval*** mirror best known.

Late Federal, Early American Empire, and Regency Period:
Marked by the continuing Federal period in America, the Napoleonic period in France, and the Regency period in England. Furniture dominated in America by Duncan Phyfe. Ancient motifs from Rome, Greece, and Egypt, favored by Napoleon. A renewed interest in the "Golden Age" of ancient Grecian and Roman architecture. ***Biedermeier*** furniture in Germany a simplification of the style.

a. **General Characteristics:** Generally heavy, massive, and masculine. Lion-paw feet and figural elements of swans and dolphins. Classical accents. Motifs from ancient Greece and Rome.
(1) *Seating* : Grecian ***Klismos, Roman curule*** , or X-based chairs dominant. Some chairs had heavy scrolls and ***caryatid*** supports. Boston rocker became higher. Window bench. Interpretations of the Grecian couch.

(2) Heavy sideboards. ***Wardrobe*** introduced.
(3) *Tables* : French-styled ***pier*** table. Small tables
(4) *Beds* : ***Sleigh*** bed introduced.

b. **Fabrics:** Elegant damask, brocade, and velvets. Green, yellow, red, gold, and blue in strong chroma. Black and white. Motifs from ancient Egypt, Greece, and Rome.

c. **Accessories:** ***Banjo*** clock.***"Bull's eye"*** mirror. ***Torchere*** lamps. Harp and lyre. Crystal and oil-vessel chandeliers. "***Punkah*** " ceiling fan. ***Ormolu*** decorations. ***Pier*** mirrors. Items reflecting ancient Egypt, Greece, and Rome.

The Greek Revival Period: Third phase of the Neoclassic Style in America.

a. **General Characteristics:** Bold and monumental. Heavier versions of the Empire Style. Supports became large animal-paw feet with hairy shanks and acanthus leaf carvings and cornucopias, plumes and pineapple motifs and ormolu. Swan and dolphin were favorite decorations. In the late 1830s carving more plain and simple. Darkened mahogany surfaces were lavishly gilded, painted and stenciled.
(1) *Seating* : ***Gondola***.. Heavily scrolled and carved sofas.
(2) *Casepieces* : Wardrobe.
(3) *Tables* : ***Pier*** table. ***Pedestal*** or pillar table. Card table.

b. **Fabrics:** Use of cotton. Elegant fabrics. Horsehair. Stripes. Printed bold medallions. Greek key patterns. Strong colors.

c. **Accessories:** Fine glass. Silver tea sets, porcelain and stoneware. Oil-burning lighting devices. Dolphin-shaped glass candlesticks and hurricane glass over candles. Brass fireplace and lighting fixtures.

5. **The French Styles in America (Late Eighteenth Century to Present).** Influence of king Louis XV (Rococo),Louis XVI (Neoclassic), the Empire style, and the French provinces.

Louis XV Style (1715-1774)

a. **General Characteristics:** Elegant, graceful and elaborately carved. Strong feminine influence. Dainty and lightly scaled. Freeform and asymmetrical decoration. Gilded , painted and ***chinoiserie*** surfaces. Local and imported woods. ***Marquetry***. Ormolu mounts.
(1) Seating : ***Fauteuil*** and ***bergere*** chairs. ***Cabriole*** leg. ***Dolphin nose*** foot. ***Chaise longue***. Sofas and day beds. ***Canape*** sofa. Stools.

(2) *Casepieces* : ***Commode***. Chinese themes and gilded lacquered and painted finishes. ***Armoire ,Secretaire*** and ***console.*** Lady's desk.
(3) *Tables* : Tables to meet all needs. Typical curved lines. ***Bureau plat.***
(4) *Beds* : Lavishly carved and draped ***canopy*** bed. ***Alcove*** bed.

a. **Fabrics:** Formal and elegant. Tapestries, cut velvets, brocatelles. Brocades and silks. Small patterns. Asymmetrically arranged flowers and flowing ribbons. Soft pastels.

b. **Accessories:** Aubusson, Savonnerie, or Oriental rugs. Crystal chandeliers. Asymmetrical candle holders and wall sconces. Ornate clocks and mirrors. Oil paintings in ornate frames. French and Oriental porcelains. Busts of royalty.

Louis XVI Style (1774-1793):

a. **General Characteristics:** Renewed interest in architectural forms and ornament of ancient Greece, Rome, and Pompeii. Rectangular forms. Straight lines. Feminine influence at court continues. (Marie Antoinette) Exquisite furniture. Classical motifs and forms.
(1) *Seating* : ***Fauteuil*** and ***bergere*** chairs with straight lines. ***Canapes. Confident.*** Day beds. Benches.
(2) *Casepieces*: Desks, ***commodes***, cabinets, and secretaries. ***Armoire*** with straight forms. ***Roll-top desk. Drop-leaf*** desks.
(3) *Tables* : ***Bureau plat.*** Console. Console-buffet. Dining table. ***Bouillotte. Gueridon..***
(4) *Beds* : ***Alcove beds.*** "***angel*** " bed with canopy.

b. **Fabrics:** Formal silks, damasks, velvets and tapestries. Soft pale colors. Motifs drawn from classical Greece and Rome. Bouquets and baskets of flowers and the ***love knot.*** Small floral prints and stripes. ***Toile de Jouy.***

c. **Accessories:** Elegant and formal accessories of gold gilt. Architectural mirrors. ***Trumeau*** mirror. ***Sevres*** vases. Sconces and candelabra with classical motifs. Clocks of gilt bronze. Elaborate fireplace accessories. Crystal chandeliers. ***Aubusson, Savonnerie*** and Oriental rugs. Oil paintings in ornate gold frames. Busts of royalty.

Provincial French and Country French:

a. **General Characteristics:** Influenced by the Court styles but were simpler, more affordable. Louis XV style emerged as the most prominent influence. Homemade crafted pieces for Country French style. Distressed furniture shows rustic Louis XIV feeling.
(1) *Seating* : ***Ladderback*** chair with ***salamander*** back. Simple Louis XV ***fauteuil.*** Stool with rush seat.
(2) *Casepieces* : Simplified Louis XV commode, buffet and armoire. Hutch. Cupboard with "chicken wire" grills.

(3) *Tables* : Long, end, and other functional tables in Louis XV style. Breading table.

(4) *Beds* : Closed bed or ***lit clos***.

a. **Fabrics:** Formal Provincial fabrics include velvets, tapestries, damasks, and silks. Cottons, wool, and linen used for informal Provincial French and Country French. Toil de Jouy. Plaids, checks, stripes, and small quaint prints. Colors: red, blue, white and apple green.

b. **Accessories:** For formal Provincial French, accessories similar to Louis XV and XVI. Informal accessories include decorative and utilitarian items. ***Panetiere*** and other items of metal. Primitive paintings, silhouettes, pottery, and pictures of song birds. ***Tole lamps***.

French Empire (circa 1804-1815)

a. **General Characteristics:** Massive, bisymmetrical, and rectangular. Rigid edges and right angles. Elegant and grand. Adaptations of pre-existing types. Mahogany most preferred. Furniture supports were caryatids, sphinxes and Egyptian busts. Elaborate ormolu mounts. Influence of Napoleon. Letter N motif enclosed in laurel wreath. Ancient Egyptian, Grecian and Roman themes.

(1) *Seating* : ***Gondola*** chair. Straight, ***saber***, or winged lion legs. ***Meridienne***. Reclining couch. ***X-stool***.

(2) *Casepieces* : Massive and elaborately decorated. ***Commode***. Sideboard. Bookcases. ***Fall-front secretary*** and ***roll-top desk***.

(3) *Tables* : Circular or octagonal tables. Dining tables round and massive. Bureau plat. Console. ***Tripod***. ***Lavabo***. ***Gueridon***. Pedestal tables.

(4) *Beds* : Heavy, majestic beds. ***Boat-bed***. ***Tent or field bed***.

a. **Fabrics:** Silks lavishing used. Taffetas, damasks, satins, brocades and velvets. Empire motifs. Brilliant colors. Motifs: Letter N in a laurel wreath, bees, stars, swans, and eagles. Motifs from ancient Egypt, Greece and Rome.

b. **Accessories:** Represent Napoleonic reign or items of classical or Egyptian origin. ***Psyche*** mirror. Elegant clocks. ***Sevres*** porcelain with Empire designs.

6. **Victorian Furniture (circa 1840-1900).** Imitations of furniture styles of the past interpreted in various manifestations in America. These primarily included Gothic, Rococo, and Renaissance Revival styles. Massive forms and deeply carved ornamentation. Regeneration of the Louis XVI style. Two outstanding furniture designers are John Belter (1804--1863) and Charles Eastlake (1836-1906) who wrote "*Hints on Household Taste.*"

Belter Rococo, Eastlake Gothic/Renaissance, and Classic Victorian

a. **General Characteristics:** Elaborate adaptations of French, Rococo, Second Empire, Neoclassic, Gothic, Renaissance, Oriental, Elizabethan, and Jacobean prototypes.

1. ***Belter Rococo.*** Lavish furniture adapted from the Louis XV style. Walnut, rosewood, and mahogany popular.
2. ***The Eastlake or Gothic/Renaissance.*** Furniture recalls Renaissance and Gothic forms. Lightly scaled and simplified machine-made furniture. Basically rectilinear forms with incised, carved, and turned designs. Oak most typical wood.
3. ***Regeneration of the Louix XVI or Classic Victorian*** . Simplified version of the French Louis XVI style. Next in popularity after Belter and Eastlake.
    - (1) *Seating* : Belter's ***lady's and gentleman's*** chairs. Carved high back Belter chair. ***Balloon-back*** chair. Renaissance revival sofa. Eastlake ***settee*** and chair. Gothic "***rose window*** " chair.
    - (2) *Casepieces* : ***Bureau*** (dresser). Belter console. ***Etagere. Wooten patent desk.***
    - (3) *Tables* : Rococo rosewood and Eastlake center tables. Tall Eastlake pedestal stand.
    - (4) *Beds* : Carved and laminated Belter rosewood bed. Massive and carved Eastlake Renaissance bed. Iron or brass bed with Gothic arch design.

b. **Fabrics:** Formal brocades, plush velvet, lace, and damasks. Horsehair. Large and small patterns profusely employed. Gold fringe. Colors: deep red, dark pinks, mauves, purples, golds, browns, and dark greens.

c. **Accessories:** Gilt pier mirror. Whatnot shelves laden with bric-a-brac. Small bronze statuary. Dried flowers under glass domes. Patterned rugs. Collections of all types. Electrified gasolier chandeliers. Tinted and painted glass lamps. Silhouette and charcoal portraits. Currier and Ives prints. Blackamoor statuettes. Picture viewers.

II. GENERAL CLASSIFICATION OF FURNITURE STYLES.

A. Furniture styles typically fall into two general categories: (1) ***period*** or ***traditional*** and (2) ***modern*** or ***contemporary.***

B. Terms used to describe period or traditional furniture:

a. ***Antique*** : A piece of furniture or work of art that must be at least 100 years old.

b. ***Reproduction*** : A copy of an original.

c. ***Adaptation*** : A piece in which only some elements from the original have been adapted to a contemporary design.

d. ***Period style*** : A single item or a complete interior, including the architectural background, furniture, and decorative arts prevalent in a specific country or a particular time in history. This style is often referred to as ***traditional***.

Contemporary and Modern Furnishings.

A. ***Contemporary.*** Current styles are called ***contemporary***, often referring to eclectic designs that to some degree have been adapted from historical or modern influences.

B. ***Modern*** . At any time in history when a new art form emerges that breaks all ties with previous design forms it is referred to as ***modern.***

1. Today's modern furniture design is principally an expression of the twentieth century and aptly suggests the tempo of modern Americans.
2. The roots of modernism can be traced to the***Industrial Revolution*** .
3. With the invention of new materials and technology, a fresh approach to furnishings gradually emerged.

C. A brief outline of the major design directions and constributors include:

1. ***Earliest Modern Furniture:*** As early as 1840, ***Michael Thonet*** developed a process for bending wood. His *bentwood rocker* and *Vienna cafe* chair remain classic pieces.
2. ***The Arts and Crafts Movement:*** In England and America in the latter half of the nineteenth century, the Arts and Crafts Movement revolted against machine-made products and advocated a return to handcrafted furnishings. Inspiration was drawn from medieval and Gothic prototypes. Leading furniture designers included:
   a. *England* :***William Morris*** , the founder. ***Charles Eastlake, Edward Godwin, Philip Webb, Ernest Gimson,*** and ***Charles F.A. Voysey*** created simple handcrafted furniture considered early expressions of modernism.
   b. *America* : ***Gustav Stickley, Frank Lloyd Wright, Henry Hobson Richardson*** , and ***Charles and Henry Greene*** designed handcrafted structural furniture based on their own interpretations of the movement. (Arts and Crafts furniture in America also known as ***Mission style***).
3. ***Art Nouveau (circa 1890-1910).*** Is a decorative style based on natural forms that flourished primarily in Europe and America. Art Nouveau motifs include flowers, vines, the female form, reptiles, waves of the ocean, whiplash line, and flowing forms of all types. Leading contributors include:
   a. *France* : When ***Samuel Bing*** opened his Paris studio, La Maison de l'Art Nouveau in 1895 the style was officially named. ***Hector Guimard, Emile Galle*** and ***Louis Majorelle*** were known for their exquisite furniture.

b. *Belgium* : ***Henri van de Velde*** , considered the spokesman for the style, opened his own furniture studio in Brussels. Also, ***Victor Horta*** is well known for his Art Nouveau furniture and architecture.
c. *England* : ***Arthur Heygate Mackmurdo*** and ***Charles F.A.Voysey*** created furniture in a more conservative and symmetrical manner.
d. *Spain* : ***Antonio Gaudi*** was known for his sculptural furnishings.
e. *Germany* : ***Richard Riemerschmid*** designed simple interpretations. The new style was known as ***Jugendstijl*** in Germany and Austria.
f. *Finland* : ***Eliel Saarinen*** is known for his *White Collection..*
g. *Scotland* : ***Charles Rennie Mackintosh*** in Glasgow. Extraordinary "*perpendicular* " furniture includes the *Argyle, Hill House* , and*Willow.*
h. *America* :***Louis Comfort Tiffany*** designed superb stained-glass lamps and other furnishings.

4. ***The Secession (circa 1897-1903)*** . The Secession was an artistic movement that "seceded" from historical styles. The movement's focus was primarily in Vienna, Austria. Leaders included ***Otto Wagner, Adolf Loos, Josef Maria Olbrich*** , and ***Josef Hoffmann.*** Hoffmann's classic pieces include the *Fledermaus, Prague,* and *Haus Koller* chairs. The***Wiener Werkstatte*** (studio) was an offshoot of the Secession and provided more geometric and structural design.
5. ***De Stijl (1917-circa 1932)*** . Was a radical style that emerged in Holland in 1917. The group adhered to strict design principles they called ***neoplasticism***: (1) only red, yellow, blue, white, gray, and black were used; (2) had to be abstract; (3) have smooth, shiny surfaces; and (4) be composed only of right angles. Leaders included the painter ***Piet Mondrian***; ***Theo van Doesburg***, the founder; and ***Gerrit Rietveld***, whose classic furniture pieces include the *Red/Blue* and *Zigzag* chairs.
6. ***The Bauhaus (1919-1933) and International Style*** . The focal point of modern design from 1919 to 1933 was the Bauhaus in Weimar, Germany and later at Dessau, Germany. Its philosphy was that aesthetically pleasing objects could be created by mechanical means. Two great furniture pioneers, ***Marcel Breuer*** and***Ludwig Mies van der Rohe*** , developed the cantilever and the use of tubular steel for furniture construction. Breuer's *Wassily lounge* and *Cesca* chair, and Mies' *Barcelona Collection* and *Brno* chair are classics.

   Le Corbusier, who worked in Paris, is considered a master of the International Style. His classics include the *Grand Confort* and *Pony chaise lounge*. Other designers of note in Paris were ***Eileen Gray***, who designed the *Transat* chair, and ***Robert Maillet -Stevens*** , whose *stacking chair* is particularly popular.

7. ***Art Deco (circa 1909-1940)*** .Was a decorative style that flourished in Europe and America principally between World War I and World War II. The term ***Art Deco*** was derived from the great *Paris Exposition in 1925.* Inspiration for the new style was drawn from many sources (movies, jazz music, African art, ancient Egyptian, Assyrian and Aztec Indian cultures, new technology, etc.). Motifs include the zigzag; lightning flash, pyramid; Egyptian themes, the peacock; stylized flowers and animals; and numerous geometric shapes. Many types of new materials and technology used for furniture. Outstanding designers include:
   a. *France* : ***Jacques-Emile Ruhlmann*** designed elegant and expensive furniture. Others of note include ***Jean-Michel Frank, Andre Groult, Clement Rousseau, Sue et Mare*** , and ***Jules-Emile Leleu.***
   b. *America* : ***Frank Lloyd Wright's*** *Imperial* chair,***Paul Frankl***, known for his *skyscraper* furniture, and ***Donald Deskey*** are important furniture designers. ***Eliel Saarinen*** , moved to America in 1922. His best known classics of this period include the *Cranbrook sidechair* and the *Blue Collection.*
8. ***The 1930s*** . Contribution of a number of designers from various countries whose classics are widely recognized include: (1) Spain: ***Salvador Dali's*** surrealistic *Mae West Lips* chair (2) Denmark: ***Kaare Klint's*** *Deck chair*, (3) England: ***T.H. Robsjohn-Gibbings'*** *Klismos* chair, and (4) Argentina: ***Bonet, Kurchan, and Hardoy's*** *Butterfly chair.*
9. ***Postwar Scandinavia*** : After World War II, the Scandinavian countries developed furniture of exceptional quality and design. Classic pieces and designers include:
   a. *Finland* : ***Alvar Aalto's*** lightly scaled laminated bentwood designs. ***Eero Aarnio's*** *Globe* and *Gyro* chairs.
   b. *Denmark* : ***Hans Wegner's*** *"The chair "*, *Peacock,* and *Chair 24.* ***Arne Jacobsen*** is known for his *Egg and Swan* chairs, and his *Series 7 Group.* ***Poul Kjaerholm's*** classics include Chair 22 and 20. ***Vernor Panton*** is known for his *Panton Stacking Chair.*
10. ***Postwar America*** : After World War II, America emerged as a world leader in furniture design led by ***Charles Eames*** and ***Eero Saarinen***.. Eames's classic pieces include the *Eames Lounge, DAR Shell,* and the *Aluminum Group* . Saarinen's classics include the*Tulip Pedestal Group.* Other designers and classics include: Harry Bertoia's *Wire Collection* , ***Warren Platner's*** *Wire Collection* and ***George Nelson's*** *Coconut* chair.
11. ***Italian Design*** : Influenced by the Bauhaus and International Style, Italian designers attracted world attention after World War II for their innovative use.

of materials and technology. Pioneer designer ***Gio Ponti*** created his classic *Superleggera* in 1957. ***Joe Colombo*** was noted for his plastic designs including the *Elda* and *Colombo* chairs. ***Vico Magistretti*** designed the *Selene* and *Marlunga.* Other classics from Italy include the *Plia* chair by Giancarlo Piretti; the *Soriana Collection* by ***Tobia and Afra Scarpa*** ; the *Sacco* by Design Studio and the *Cab* chair by ***Mario Bellini.***

12. ***Other Postwar Contributions:*** This period saw the development of the sculptural furniture of ***Pierre Paulin*** in France. A classic is his *Ribbon* chair. ***Pedro Freideberg*** in Mexico created a well-known example of ***Pop Furniture*** , the *Hand Chair.*
13. ***The Handcraft Revival*** : At the end of the 1970s in England and America, inspired by the ideals of William Morris and the Arts and Crafts Movement, some designers returned to the handcraft movement. A few classic pieces and designers are the *Ebony Gothic* chair by ***John Makepeace***; *Rocking Chairs* by ***Sam Maloof***, and *Bench with Horses* by ***Judy Kensley McKie*** .
14. ***Furniture of the 1980s*** : During the 1980s various design directions emerged, many of them extensions or reinterpretations of previous modern styles. Of particular note are the following:
    a. ***Handcraft revival.*** (just described)
    b. ***High-tech furniture*** employs the most advanced scientific and industrial techniques and materials.
    c. ***Post-Modern*** is distinguished by a freer spirit of expression. Primarily rejecting the austere International Style, Post-Modern designers are sensitive to new modern concepts expressed through strong form and color. Outstanding leaders and classics are ***Michael Graves*** and the *Graves armchair*, and ***Robert Venturi's*** *Venturi Collection.*
    d. ***Classic modern*** brings styles of the past into the twentieth century, adapted in elegant and simplified terms. A famous classic is the *Grande Flute* by ***Angelo Donghia*** .
    e. ***Ergonomic*** furniture is created with a concern for human comfort and efficiency. ***Niels Diffrient's*** *Jefferson chair* is a superb example.
    f. ***Memphis*** is an avant-garde group of international designers assembled in 1981 by ***Ettore Sottsass, Jr.*** Memphis design is typified by complete freedom of expression. Sottsass's *Carlton bookshelf/room divider* and ***Michele de Lucchi'*** s *First* chair are excellent examples.
    g. ***Art furniture*** is created by artists as a piece for "art's sake." Some outstanding pieces are *Queen Anne, Queen Anne* by ***Terence and Laura Main*** , and *Nothing Continues to Happen* by ***Howard Meister.***
    h. ***Individualists*** have created outstanding classic furnishings during the past decade. Outstanding invidualists and classics include ***Philippe***

Starck and his *Richard III chair,* ***Mario Botta*** and his *87 Seconda* , ***Vico Magistretti*** and his *Sindbad chair,* and ***Gaetano Pesce*** and his *Sunset in New York.*

i. ***Classics of the l990s*** . A few new creations are representative of some of the design directions of the l990s. Designers and new chair designs include: ***Massimo losa-Ghini's*** *Bolidista* chair, ***Milo Baughman's*** *Mac II,* ***Frank Gehry's*** *Cross Check* , ***Peter Danko's*** *Chairs for the Electronic Cottage* , and ***Paul Tuttle's*** *Skate Series- "Z" chair.*

2. **American Oriental Style:** The Oriental influence, particularly from China and Japan, is part of America's early tradition. Principles and elements of Japanese architecture, including the use of the horizontal line and natural materials, asymmetry, open planning, simplicity and the absence of ornamentation, were used by Frank Lloyd Wright.

The **interior** of the Japanese house is open and uncluttered; wood floors have ***tatami*** mats, ceilings are beamed or modular, walls are plain, and ***shoji*** screens, often used for both walls and windows, open onto gardens. Furniture is sparse, usually in a natural finish, and built low. Basic pieces include a low table, a chest, and ***zabuton*** (pillows) for seating.

Design influences from China have had their greatest impact for American designers in the field of furniture and accessories. Manufacturers in the America have borrowed freely from both Japan and China to create "Oriental" furniture collections. Following are some of the most recognizable features:

FROM JAPAN:

a. Simple unembellished furniture, usually in a natural finish
b. Low tables.
c. ***Zabuton*** (Pillow)
d. ***Tansu*** (Oriental chest)
e. ***Shibui*** color schemes (drawn from nature)
f. A few treasured items displayed

FROM CHINA:

a. More decorative furnishings
b. ***Finishes*** : Lacquered black, red-orange, gold and green. Tortoise shell. Painted Oriental scenes, motifs, and figures. Highly polished natural finishes.
c. ***Colors*** : Brighter. Blue, white, red, red-orange, gold, yellow-gold and jade green.

TYPICAL FORMS, MOTIFS, AND ACCESSORIES FROM JAPAN AND CHINA:

a. ***Forms*** : "monkey paw and elephant legs. Pagoda. Fret design. Chest-on-chest arrangements.

b. ***Motifs*** : Bamboo, chrysanthemum, cherry blossoms, assymmetrical pine branch; fret design, mandarin duck,heron, horse, tiger, dragon, and fish. Oriental figures, parasol and pagoda. Mt. Fuji and floating clouds.

c. ***Accessories*** : ***Bonsai*** plants, Oriental figures, ***calligraphy, coromandel*** screen, wall-hung multipanel screen, Chinese porcelain and rugs, ***temple foo dogs*** , brass hardware, statues of Oriental gods, simple flower arrangements (***Ikebana***), jade pieces, ivory, the hanging scroll, wood carvings, lacquerware.

D. **Style Selection** : Making a selection can be simplified by determining the general feeling desired. The approaches fall into five basic categories:

1. ***Informal Provincial*** : is generally a handcrafted, simple, and casual look. One ethnic style or combined furnishings from many country sources may be used, as long as the feeling is one of unpretentious homeyness. The "***country look*** " is currently a popular term for this direction.
2. ***Formal Traditional*** may refer to interior furnishings from any country if they are of the more formal styles. Many of the favorite traditional designs come from the eighteenth century.
3. ***Informal Modern*** : Numerous types and styles of "modern" furniture may fall into this category as long as the look is informal. Casual fabrics with a matte finish, simple materials and unpretentious accessories will help achieve this direction.
4. **Formal Modern** : A formal modern environlment can be created by employing elegant, sophisticated and refined architectural backgrounds, accessories, and fabrics
5. ***Eclectic or Mixing Styles*** is preferred by many designers today. Mixing modern and traditional furnishings from many periods and styles can give a highly sophisticated look. Generally, there should be a common theme with pieces that relate in scale and chosen with a final goal in mind.

Learning Enhancement Options:

Basic Furniture Styles: Review with the students the basic characteristics of furniture styles and how they can be incorporated into today's residential and nonresidential interiors. Show visual materials that supports each style.

General Classification of Furniture Styles: Examine the various contemporary and modern styles of furnishings (including American Oriental furniture) and how they can be incorporated into today's interiors. Show visual materials of these styles used in various settings.

Test Questions

Multiple Choice:

__A__ 1. The furniture piece illustrated at the right is a:
A. Vargueno
B. Trastero (Illustration of Vargueno)
C. Moorish casepiece
D. Trestle casepiece

__C__ 2. The furniture style illustrated at the right is typically used in:
A. Country English style
B. French Provincial style (Illustration of a Lodgepole pine chair)
C. Santa Fe style
D. Monterey style

__D__ 3. The chair illustrated at the right is a:
A. Hitchcock
B. Jacobean (Illustration of a Windsor Chair)
C. Brewster
D. Windsor

__A__ 4. The chair back illustrated at the right is an example of:
A. Chippendale
B. Queen Anne (Illustration of a Chippendale wing back chair)
C. Sheraton
D. Duncan Phyfe

__C__ 5. The leg design illustrated at the right is typical of:
A. Queen Anne furniture
B. Hepplewhite furniture (Illustration of a Sheraton leg)
C. Sheraton furniture

__B__ 6. The hardware design illustrated at the right is known as:
A. Urn
B. Paterae (Illustration of a paterae design)
C. Butterfly
D. Egg and Dart

Matching:

Match the following illustrations of furniture pieces with the correct answer:

A. (Illust. of Brewster)
B. (Illust. of Equipale)
C. (Illust. of Hitchcock)
D. (Illust. of Martha Washington)

__A__ 7. Brewster chair

__C__ 8. Hitchcock chair

__D__ 9. Martha Washington chair

__B__ 10. Equipale chair

A. (Illust. of William & Mary casepiece)
B. (Illust. of Court Cupboard)
C. (Illust. of Breakfront)
D. (Illust. of Armoire)

__D__ 11. Armoire

__A__ 12. William and Mary casepiece

__B__ 13. Court Cupboard

__C__ 14. Breakfront

A. (Illust. of Queen Anne Wingback)
B. (Illust. of Chippendale Wingback)

__B__ 15. Chippendale Wingback

__A__ 16. Queen Anne Wingback

(Illust. of Greek Revival) A. | (Illust. of Chippendale) B. | (Illust. of Jacobean) C.

__C__ 17. Jacobean

__B__ 18. Chippendale

__A__ 19. Greek Revival

(Illust. of Louis XVI) A. | (Illust. of Louis XV) B. | (Illust. of Sheraton) C. | (Illust. of Hepplewhite) D.

__B__ 20. Louis XV

__C__ 21. Sheraton chair

__A__ 22. Louis XVI

__D__ 23. Hepplewhite chair

(Illust. of Duncan Phyfe) A. | (Illust. of Eastlake) B. | (Illust. of Belter) C.

__C__ 24. Belter

__B__ 25. Eastlake

__A__ 26. Duncan Phyfe

Match the following modern styles with the correct definition:

A. Arts and Crafts B. Art Nouveau C. Secession D. De Stijl

__B__ 27. Early modern style based on natural forms.

__D__ 28. Modern style based on the design concept of "Neoplasticism."

__A__ 29. An early modern style that revolted against machine-made products. William Morris was the founder.

__C__ 30. Modern style that pulled away from historic styles. Josef Hoffmann is the leading furniture designer.

A. Bauhaus B. Art Deco C. Post-Modern D. Ergonomics

__A__ 31. Philosophy was that aesthetically pleasing objects could be machine-made.

__D__ 32. Modern design based on function and comfort.

__C__ 33. Primarily rejects the International Style. Freer spirit of expression.

__B__ 34. Many types of new materials employed for furniture, and old materials used in new ways.

Match the following illustrations of classic modern furniture with the correct answer:

A. (Fledermaus) B. (Barcelona) C. (Hill) D. (Red/Blue)

__C__ 35. Hill/Mackintosh

__A__ 36. Fledermaus/Hoffmann

__D__ 37. Red/Blue/Rietveld

__B__ 38. Barcelona/Mies van der Rohe

A. (Bentwood)	B. (Cesca)	C. (Grand)	D. (Soriana)

__B__ 39. Cesca / Breuer/ Bauhaus

__C__ 40. Grand Confort / Le Corbusier / International Style

__D__ 41. Soriana / Scarpas / Italian

__A__ 42. Bentwood / Thonet

A. (Cross Check)	B. (Eames Lounge)	C. (Deck Chair)	D. (Venturi Chair)

__D__ 43. Venturi / Post-Modern

__A__ 44. Cross Check / Gehry

__C__ 45. Deck / Klint / Scandinavian

__B__ 46. Eames Lounge / Eames

A. (Batting Joe)	B. (First Chair)	C. (Grande Flute)	D. (Pedestal Chair)

__C__ 47. Grande Flute / Donghia / Classic Modern

__D__ 48. Pedestal / Saarinen

__B__ 49. First / de Lucci / Memphis

__A__ 50. Batting Joe / Design Studio / Italy

Essay / Short Answer:

51. Outline the basic design influences from Japan and China and list typical forms, motifs, and finishes used for Oriental American Furniture.

Answer to this question is found on pages 292 through 294.

52. List and define the five basic categories used when determining a style direction..

Answer to this question is found on pages 294 and 295.

Educational Resources

Publications:

Battersby, Martin, et al. *History of Furniture* . New York: Morrow, 1976.
Boger, Louise Ade. *Furniture, Past and Present* . Garden City, NY: Doubleday, 1966.
Boyce, Charles. *Dictionary of Furniture* . New York: Roundtable Press, 1985.
Fitzgerald, Oscar P. *Three Centuries of American Furniture* . Englewood Cliffs, NJ: Prentice-Hall, 1982.
_______. *Twentieth-Century Furniture* . New York: Van Nostrand Reinhold, 1980.
Hanks, David A. *Innovative Furniture in America from 1800 to the Present* . New York: Horizon, 1981.
Lucie-Smith, Edward. *Furniture: A Concise History* . London: Thames & Hudson, 1985
Mang, Karl. *History of Modern Furniture* . New York: Harry N. Abrams, 1979.
Molesworth, H.D. and John Kenworthy-Browne. *Three Centuries of Furniture in Color.* New York: Viking Press, 1972.
Page, Marian. *Furniture Designed by Architects* . New York: Whitney Library of Design, 1980.
Stimpson, Miriam. *Modern Furniture Classics* . New York: Whitney Library of Design, 1987.

Movies / Videos:

Choosing Furnishings : 10 min / 1990 / Insight Media
The Story of English Furniture : 2 vols./ 105 min each / 1987 / Insight Media

Transparencies:

Illustrations of best known traditional furniture - 1
Illustrations of best known traditional furniture - 2
Illustrations of best known classic modern modern furniture - 1
Illustrations of best known classic modern furniture - 2

CHAPTER 10

FURNITURE ARRANGEMENT AND WALL COMPOSITION

Chapter Focus

Chapter 10 is divided into four major sections covering furniture arrangement and wall composition. These sections include: Designing Space with Furniture, Programming Furniture Needs, Guidelines for Furniture Arrangement, and Wall Composition.

Text Outline

Introduction:

A. Planning for furniture is an important part of the design process, from the early stages of formulating ideas to the actual placement of furniture, furnishings, and equipment (known in the profession as **FF&E**) within a space.

B. The arrangement of furnishings in a room constitutes a composition in spatial design.

C. Since a room is planned for particular people and their unique way of living, furnishing a room should be approached from a practical, commonsense point of view, employing the principles of design as guidelines.

I. DESIGNING SPACE WITH FURNITURE:

A. New economic standards, contemporary trends in architecture, changing lifestyles, new furniture styles, and a variety of functions and needs, all influence the use of space in both residential and nonresidential design.

B. With the increase in building costs, space is at a premium.

C. The key word today in furniture arrangement for both homes and public spaces is efficiency.

D. When arranging furniture in any room of a residence, first priority should be given to ***the household and its lifestyle*** .

E. Beauty and good design are important, but comfort and convenience are the most essential.

II. PROGRAMMING FURNITURE NEEDS:

A. Programming is the initial planning stage of the design process. In this phase, the designer gathers information to determine the needs of the end users. Goals are established to solve the project's particular problems.

B. A well organized plan or program aids the designer in creating a space that is efficient and successful.

C. It is essential to keep in mind the function the furniture must serve and the mood and style desired.

D. Generally, no room must adhere so rigidly to a theme or style that it is monotonous or does not allow for new expressions.

1. ***Function*** . The function or functions that will take place within a space dictate what furniture, furnishings, and equipment (FF&E) will satisfy the end users. The program indicates what pieces are needed, how many, and what types. Rarely is a piece of furniture complete in its self.
2. ***Human Comfort*** must be provided for the end users. Comfort is directly related to how effectively the human body is accommodated. Other attributes of "user-friendly" furniture are how easily it can be moved or rearranged and how efficiently it can be cleaned. Some terms related to design and human comfort include:
   a. ***Ergonomics*** is the study of human beings and their responses to various working conditions and environment. The goal is to produce furnishings that are comfortable to use for particular functions and tasks.
   b. ***Proxemics*** involves a study of the use of space by human beings in a particular culture.
   c. ***Anthropometrics*** is a study that measures the size and proportion of the human body. The average human being weighs between 100 and 200 pounds and is between 5 and 6 feet in height. These measurements are the criteria for designing and positioning furnishings for functional and comfortable interiors.
   d. ***Territoriality*** is a term used to describe human needs for personal space.
3. ***Special Need Users*** are the elderly, infants, or the physically challenged. In planning spaces for both residential and nonresidential design designers must adequately satisfy their needs for safety, convenience, comfort, and well being. **Barrier-free access** for physically challenged users is required.
4. ***Analyzing and Evaluating the Space*** . The designer should assess the room's size, shape, assets, and possibilities.
   (1) Are the dimensions of the room pleasing or will altering the apparent height, width, or length be necessary?
   (2) Are the openings well placed for balance and convenience?
   (3) Are there jogs, niches, or other features to be minimized or emphasized?

(4) Would built-in furniture be effective?
(5) Will it be necessary to redirect traffic?
(6) What is the light exposure?
(7) How much will the quality and quantity of light affect the choice of colors and furnishings?

5. ***Arranging Furniture on a Floor Plan*** .
   a. ***A floor plan drawn to scale*** can aid in determining furniture placement within a space. Generally, ***graph paper*** using a measurement of 1/4 in. equaling 1 ft is preferable for use in residential design. Commercial space planning usually requires a smaller scale.
   b. The drawn plan indicates the exact position of all architectural features and mechanical systems.
   c. ***Circulation or traffic lanes*** should be clearly marked.
   d. Experiments with different furniture arrangements can be made on the plan. ***Furniture templates*** can be moved around until the desired functional and decorative effects are achieved.
6. ***Computer-Aided Design*** .
   a. When planning furniture for particular spaces, many designers have access to computer-aided design (CAD) programs.
   b. Furniture of various types, colors, and textures can be called up on the computer screen and an infinite number of solutions for arranging the furniture for a specific project can be explored.

III. GUIDELINES FOR FURNITURE ARRANGEMENT:

A. When the programming and design process has arrived at the stage when the actual arrangement of furniture, furnishings, and equipment is to take place, consider these **guidelines**:
   a. Keep the ***functions*** and multifunctions of the room in mind.
   b. Arrange furniture to accommodate necessary major and minor ***traffic lanes***.
   c. Adequate ***clearance*** between furnishings is essential.
   d. Determine the room's ***focal point*** .
   e. ***Large furnishings*** usually work best when placed parallel to the wall.
   f. Keep furnishings in ***scale*** with the room.
   g. Arrange furnishings to give the room a sense of ***equilibrium***.
   h. A good ***balance of high and low*** and ***angular and rounded*** furniture helps establish interest.
   i. ***Architectural features*** and ***mechanical systems*** are important concerns.
   j. Create a feeling of space by placing furniture pieces with regard to the ***positive areas*** and ***negative spaces***.

k. *Avoid crowding* .

l. Since most groupings need ***lighting*** , choose appropriate lamps or fixtures to provide adequate light for the particular purpose.

m. Achieving ***rhythm*** is a worthwhile goal.

n. The placement of ***accessories*** usually comes last and can pull other furnishings together, establish the mood and style of the room, and reflect the occupant's personal taste. Planning a room that is functional, comfortable, conveniently arranged, and aesthetically appealing is the ultimate goal in spatial planning.

B. Spacial Planning for Rooms of Various Shapes.

1. The ***square or nearly square room*** is considered one of the least pleasing in proportion. Some suggestions include:
   - (1) Expand two opposite walls by using a light, receding color. Use a darker tone on the two remaining walls.
   - (2) "Extend" one wall by running bookshelves the entire length.
   - (3) Place an area rug the full length of the room.
   - (4) Arrange furniture to create a rectangular effect.
2. A well proportioned ***rectangular room*** is the easiest to arrange.
3. The ***long, narrow room*** may present a problem. The apparent proportions of the room can be modified through skillful use of the elements of design.
4. The ***L-shaped room*** lends itself naturally to a division of activities.
5. The ***room with a jog*** need not be a problem. The offset area can be used as a feature to the room.

C. **Space Planning for Specific Residential Spaces.** Each room of the house presents a unique problem according to its function:

1. *Entrance Hall* . Empty space permitting an easy flow of traffic is essential. If space permits, an entrance can accommodate a bench, a console or narrow table, a mirror, lighting, a coat rack, and accessories.
2. *Living Room* . The conversation area is the most important group in the living room and usually enhances and is combined with the focal point. The goal is to provide an intimate grouping, out of the line of traffic. The optimum distance across this area is between 8 and 10 ft. ***The Six Basic Conversation Groupings*** are:
   - (1) The ***straight-line grouping***
   - (2) The ***L-shaped grouping***
   - (3) The ***U-shaped grouping***
   - (4) The ***box-shaped grouping.***
   - (5) The ***parallel grouping***
   - (6) The ***circular grouping.***

   Low-level ***lighting*** adds a feeling of intimacy. ***Mirrors*** should be hung where they are not distracting. Provide chairs of various types and sizes. The ***use of pairs*** can enhance a living room. Find the right wall space for a piano. Provide functional ***end tables*** and ***coffee tables***. ***Console tables*** can be both decorative and functional. ***Large case or wall pieces*** are usually located to lend a feeling of balance.

3. ***Dining Room***. The ***scale of the room*** can help determine the size of the furniture. The ***table*** is usually placed in the center of the room under an architecturally fixed ***lighting source*** with a ***chest or buffet for storage*** against the longest wall and a ***small serving piece*** near the kitchen door. ***Chairs*** generally work best when not too wide across the front. Where space is limited, a round or oval table allows more room for passage. Occupants need adequate space for a pleasurable and convenient dining experience.
4. The ***Family Room*** is probably the most used room of the house. Use, convenience, and practicality are guiding principles in arranging furnishings: ***Seating*** for conversation incorporates similar solutions as the living room. When ***television viewing*** is an activity, plan seating for easy viewing. Include additional flexible seating. A number of ***tables*** can add comfort. Convenient and adequate ***lighting*** is essential. An ***audiovisual entertainment system*** is often an important addition and needs the most advantageous space. A ***game table*** can be incorporated when space is available.
5. ***Bedrooms.*** Since furniture arrangement is usually more limited, carefully planned space is especially important. Decide which ***purposes the room will serve*** in addition to sleeping. Because of its size, ***the bed*** will occupy the dominant place in the room. ***Built-in units or tables*** placed at the sides of a bed are essential. ***Lighting*** should be conveniently located next to the bed. ***Windows*** should be kept free of furnishings to facilitate ***ventilation and light.*** Space permitting, ***seating*** is a practical and comfortable addition. ***Chests, built-ins, chest of drawers*** and other casepieces are essential furnishings. A ***mirror*** is a necessary furnishing.

D. Nonresidential Furniture Planning.

1. Nonresidential projects include transportation, medical, retail, hospitality, entertainment, business, museum, government, education, and industrial facilities. Each of these public places has ***unique functions***.
2. When programming the arrangement of furniture for a nonresidential project, the designer must ***determine the activities that will take place*** and the furniture needed to adequately serve these purposes.
3. Arranging furniture may require solving ***special placement problems*** unique to the particular setting.
4. Often furnishings employed for residential spaces are suitable for use in a

nonresidential space..

5. The design process follows many of the principles outlined for residences. Organization of space, circulation, clearances, comfort, lighting, balance, rhythm, and other criteria are also considerations when placing furniture in a public space.
6. Arranging furniture for the physically challenged is an important task.
7. Arranging furniture for aesthetics and atmosphere can add to users' enjoyment of a particular nonresidential space.

D. **Making the Most of Space with Furniture.**

1. ***Making a Small Room Appear Larger.*** Examine the room carefully and define the traffic lanes. Beginning with the backgrounds, apply space-making principles to expand the room. Some suggestions include:

Background:

a. Use light walls and coordinated wall-to wall and floor-to-ceiling drapery.
b. Avoid patterned walls and full ruffled curtains.

Furniture:

a. Use ***small scaled*** furniture.
b. Use ***casepieces supported on legs.***
c. Use ***high, shallow pieces*** for storage and display.
d. Use tables and other furnishings with ***rounded corners.***
e. Use ***clear glass or plastic tops*** on tables.
f. Use chairs and other furnishings with ***see-through backs*** or backs and sides of ***caning or of clear plastic.***
g. Use ***furnishings with no arms.***
h. Cover upholstered pieces in a plain or small all-over patterned fabric.
i. Use ***neatly tailored upholstery without skirts.***
j. ***Align furniture against the walls.***
k. ***Extend shelves to the ceiling*** and use ***high storage units attached to walls.***

Lighting:

a. Cast light on ***ceilings*** or on the ***upper part of the wall or drapery.***
b. Use lamps with ***inconspicuous shades that provide indirect lighting.***
c. Use ***uplighters*** placed at key points.
d. Use lighting in the ***corners*** of the room.

Accessories:

a. ***Avoid clutter.***
b. Use a ***few bold accessories.***
c. Place ***mirrors*** at strategic points.
d. Use a ***few plants*** , preferably small-leaved ones.

(For additional space-saving techniques, see the section in Chapter 1 on Space)

2. ***Making a Large Room Appear Smaller.*** The challenge of making a big room livable is not a common one, but it does occur. Some suggestions include:
   a. The most important consideration is ***scale*** . Massive furniture, overscaled patterns, and large pictures can be chosen.
   b. All furnishings need not be massive. Lighter pieces can be used to complete the groupings.
   c. Too little furniture in a big room can result in a cold, uninviting interior, and too much furniture may give a feeling of clutter. More important than quantity, however, is the ***arrangement*** .
   d. All furniture used in the middle of a room should look attractive from all angles.
   e. A ***few empty spaces*** in a large room can be pleasant.

IV. WALL COMPOSITION:

A. A floor is a ***horizontal plane*** , and its composition is primarily one of furniture arrangement, which also affects wall elevation. The floor plan is always designed with this third dimension in mind.

B. A wall is on a ***vertical plane*** limited by ceiling, floor, corners, and other permanent ***architectural features.*** Because the wall is viewed from a different angle, ***movable items*** seen in relationship to the wall are part of the complete composition.

C. If architectural features are not well planned, a designer can ***disguise or emphasize*** whatever will enhance the total wall composition.

D. Consider wall elevation in a room individually. Each composition should present a pleasing effect suitable to the style and mood of the room.

E. Application of the ***principles and elements of design*** is helpful when selecting and arranging items for a wall composition.
   1. The ***scale relationship*** among the individual items, and between the overall composition and the room, should seem right. The ***placement*** of items against the wall and the ***proportion*** of the wall to be covered should be complementary to the complete composition.
   2. Try to achieve a feeling of ***balance*** .
   3. ***Straight lines*** are enhanced when curved lines are introduced.
   4. ***Uneven numbers*** often make a more interesting composition than even numbers.

   No specific rules of measurement are available by which to produce a perfect composition.

F. **Two- Dimensional Art.** The need to add some form of visual interest to the walls of a dwelling has existed for centuries. Considerations for selecting and arranging two-dimensional art for a wall composition include:

1. ***The frame.***
   a. A picture worth displaying is worth framing appropriately.
   b. Frames are available in many materials and may be ***structurally or decoratively*** designed.
   c. A ***frame should not dominate*** the artwork..
   d. Often traditional oil paintings are framed in heavy, ornately carved frames, and simple etchings and watercolors in lighter, narrower frames.
   e. Many two-dimensional artworks are enhanced by a ***mat*** .
2. When a picture is selected for a composition, the ***texture*** of the wall should be compatible with the art piece.
3. Pictures can be hung ***individually or in groupings*** and should relate to the sofa, chairs, tables, or other furnishings that constitute part of the ***total wall composition.***
4. ***Positive areas*** and ***negative areas*** should be pleasing.
5. When a single picture is used on a wall, it may work best when hung at ***eye level.*** Pictures may be hung at an ***unusual levels*** for a more sophisticated treatment.
6. Wall art can provide the room's ***focal point*** .
7. A picture hung above a chair or sofa should be ***placed high enough*** so the head of the seated person does not touch the frame.
8. To ***assemble*** an arrangement of a two-dimensional art composition, lay a large sheet of brown paper the size of the area to be covered and trace each object around the perimeter.
9. Pictures look best when ***hung flat*** against the wall with nails and hooks securely attached and cords and wires concealed.

G. Storage Units.

1. A storage unit partially or completely covering a wall and extending from floor to ceiling, containing both open shelves and closed units, will occupy little space, provide abundant storage, and be an ***important architectural feature*** in the room.
2. When artfully planned and arranged into a harmonious composition, the storage wall can be a masterpiece of design and color and may even form the room's ***focal point*** .
3. Since walls of a room form the background not only for furniture but for people, the final effect usually works best when not an obstructive one. With this in mind, and with an acute awareness of the importance of the ***relationship of form, space, line, texture, and color***, a successful wall composition can be achieved.

Learning Enhancement Options

Designing Space with Furniture: Discuss with the students how new economic standards, changing lifestyles, new furniture styles, and a variety of functions and needs all influence the use of space. Review the importance of arranging furnishings for efficiency, function, and aesthetics in both residential and nonresidential design.

Programming Furniture Needs: Discuss with the students the role of programming for furniture needs and what is involved in this phase of the design process. Review the importance and consideration of function, human comfort, special need users, analyzing and evaluating the space, arranging furniture on a floor plan and computer aided-design when programming furniture needs.

Guidelines for Furniture Arrangement: Demonstrate how the the principles and elements of design and guidelines for a floor composition can be applied to a residential or nonresidential project. Use the floor plans, templates, and graph paper found in the student packet. If available, a furniture arranging kit can be an effective tool in teaching the concepts of successful furniture arrangement.

Wall Composition: Help the students to analyze wall arrangements found in periodicals, studio setups, and public places. Discuss with the students how the designer can experiment with various wall compositions until a pleasing arrangment has been found. Show slides, pictures and the transparency to support the material in this chapter.

Test Questions

Multiple Choice:

__B__ 1. Which of the following are not particularly involved with analyzing a space:
A. Traffic considerations
B. Background textures
C. Light exposure
D. Window and door openings

__C__ 2. Generally graph paper uses a measurement of_____for residential design:
A. 1/16 in. equals 1 foot
B. 1/8 in. equals 1 foot
C. 1/4 in. equals 1 foot
D. 1/2 in. equals 1 foot

__B__ 3. All but one of the following could give a new dimension to a square room:
A. Use light colors on two ossosite walls.
B. Paint all walls the same color and use a darker color on the ceiling.
C. Place a rectangular area rug the full length of the room.
D. Run bookshelves the entire length of one wall.

__A__ 4. A grand piano works best when placed:
A. So the raised lid is toward the listener.
B. When the raised lid is toward the wall.

__A__ 5. All but one of the following will help provide a more spacious feeling:
A. Furnishings with squares corners.
B. Furniture with caning sections.
C. Furniture with no arms.
D. Casepieces on legs.

__C__ 6. The arrangement of furnishings in a room constitutes a composition in: (Select the best answer)
A. Floor plans
B. The principles of design
C. Spatial planning
D. The elements of design

__D__ + 7. The key word today in furniture arrangement is:
A. Aesthetics
B. Character
C. Economy
D. Efficiency

__C__ 8. Generally, major traffic lanes require:
A. 4 feet
B. 5 feet
C. 6 feet
D. 7 feet

__B__ 9. In reference to current building conditions and the availablility of residential space, space:
A. Has increased during the past decade
B. Is at a premium
C. Has remained the same during the past decade

__D__ 10. The following shape is consider the easiest to work with when arranging furnishings:
A. The square
B. The L-shape
C. The long narrow room
D. The rectangle

__B__ 11. Considered the optimum distance across a conversation area:
A. 5 to 8 feet
B. 8 to 10 feet
C. 10 to 12 feet
D. 12 to 15 feet

__C__ 12. Usually, the room's accessories are placed:
A. Before the large furnishings are arranged.
B. After each large piece is arranged.
C. After all the larger furnishings are arranged.

True / False:

__F__ 13. Aesthetic appeal is the most important factor when arranging furniture.

__T__ 14. Programming is the initial stage of the design process.

__T__ 15. Barrier-free access for the physically challenged in public places is actually required by law.

__F__ 16. CAD programs do not have practical application when arranging furniture.

__T__ 17. Large furnishings usually work; best when placed parallel to the wall.

__F__ 18. Sunlight and climate changes do not affect the placement of a piano.

__F__ 19. Furniture placed a short distance into the room will generally provide a more spacious feeling.

__T__ 20. A few bold accessories can often give a sophisticated feeling without visually eliminating space.

__T__ 21. Rarely is a piece of furniture complete in itself.

__F__ 22. It is generally pleasing to keep the height of furniture at the same level.

__T__ 23. In a wall composition, straight lines are enhanced when curved lines are introduced.

__T__ 24. Generally, there are no specific rules of measurement available by which to produce a perfect wall composition.

Multiple Choice:

Match the following terms to the correct answer:

A. Ergonomics
B. Proxemics
C. Anthropometrics
D. Territoriality

__D__ 25. Deals with human needs for personal space.

__B__ 26. A study of the use of space by human beings in a particular culture.

__C__ 27. A study that measures the size and proportion of the human body.

__A__ 28. The study of human beings and their responses to various working conditions and environments.

A. Straight-line furniture grouping
B. Parallel furniture grouping
C. Circular furniture grouping
D. Box-shaped furniture grouping

__A__ 29. Especially ideal for public places.

__D__ 30. Popular when space is ample. Needs suffficient access openings.

__B__ 31. Tends to emphasize an existing focal point.

__C__ 32. May encompass an entire room. Intimate because it provides an enveloping seating element.

Match the accessibility dimensions for the physically challenged with the correct answer:

A. 36 inch minimum
B. 32 inch minimum
C. 42 inch minimum

__B__ 33. Doorways

__A__ 34. One-way passage

__C__ 35. Corner turn

Match the following terms to the correct answers:

A. Negative Space B. Positive Areas

__A__ 36. Areas in between pieces of an art wall composition.

__B__ 37. The actual spaces filled with two-dimensional artwork.

Essay / Short Answer:

38. When designing spaces with furniture, what are some of the current criteria outlined in the text that the designer must contend with and consider?

Answer to this question is found on page 300.

39. How does programming furniture needs relate to arranging furniture within a space?

Answer to this question is found on pages 300 through 302.

40. How can the designer adequately plan furniture within a space for special need users?

Answer to this question is found on page 303.

41. What 7 steps outlined in the text are involved in analyzing and evaluating the space?

Answer to this question is found on page 303.

42. How can a floor plan drawn to scale aid in determining furniture placement within a space?

Answer to this question is found on page 303.

43. What are the advantages of Computer-Aided Design when planning furniture arrangment within a space?

Answer to this question is found on page 303.

44. Discuss 10 of the 14 Guidelines for Furniture Arrangement outlined in the text.

Answer to this question is found on pages 303 through 307.

45. List the six basic conversation groups and briefly discuss the advantages and disadvantages of each.

Answer to this question is found on pages 310 and 311.

46. Provide information on successfully arranging furniture for the (1) Dining Room, (2) Family Room, and (3) Bedroom.

Answer to this question is found on pages 313 through 315.

47. Briefly discuss the designer's task when planning and arranging furnishings for a nonresidential project.

Answer to this questions is found on page 315.

48. Through the adroit use of the principles and elements of design, small rooms can be made to appear larger. What are some specific ideas that can be used when planning the (1) Backgrounds, (2) Furniture, (3) Lighting, and (4) Accessories?

Answer to this question is found on pages 315 through 318.

49. What are some of the basic considerations when planning a wall composition?

Answer to this question is found on pages 319 and 320.

50. What 9 points may be considered for selecting and arranging two-dimensional art for a wall composition?

Answer to this question is found on pages 320 through 322.

Educational Resources

Publications:

American National Standard for Buildings and Facilities - Providing Accessibility and Usability for Physically Handicapped People . Washington, D.C.: U.S. Department of Housing and Urban Development, 1986.

Faulkner, Sarah. *Planning a Home* . New York: Holt, Rinehart and Winston, 1979.

Furniture Arranging Templates - A.S.I.D., Washington, D.C., 1993.

Gilliatt, Mary. *The Decorating Book* . New York: Pantheon, 1981.

Panero, Julius. *Anatomy for Interior Designers* . New York: Whitney Library of Design, 1981.

Panero, Julius, and Martin Zelnik. *Human Dimension and Interior Space* . New York: Whitney Library of Design, 1979.

Reznikoff, S.C. *Interior Graphic and Design Standards* . New York: Whitney Library of Design, 1986.

St. Marie, Satenig S. *Homes Are For People* . New York: Wiley, 1973.

Transparencies:

Arrangement of Furniture on Graph Paper
Wall Composition

CHAPTER 11

ACCESSORIES

Chapter Focus

Chapter 11 is divided into five major sections that focus on accessories and their use in both residential and nonresidential design. These sections include: Functional Accessories, Decorative Accessories, Accessory Checklist, Selecting and Placing Accessories, and Nonresidential Accessories

Text Outline

Introduction:

A. When a project is successfully completed, accessories will most certainly ***enhance*** the setting.
B. Accessories may be described as a ***wide variety of objects,*** usually smaller in scale than other basic furnishings.
C. Accessories add the ***finishing touches*** to a room, more surely reflecting the ***personal taste and individuality*** of the user than any other element.
D. Accessories can establish the ***design theme.***
E. Accessories can be ***supportive of the architectural background.***
F. Accessories are highly ***flexible*** in terms of their use in the environment.
G. A ***focal point*** may be established through the use of accessories.

I. FUNCTIONAL ACCESSORIES:

A. Functional accessories serve a ***utilitarian purpose*** but may also become an interesting display item.
B. The ***purpose or use*** of the room should be the prime consideration when selecting functional accessories.

II. DECORATIVE ACCESSORIES:

A. Generally provide no other value than the pleasure derived from their aesthetic qualities.
B. Decorative items abound in furniture and antique stores, galleries, design studios, art and craft exhibitions, and numerous other sources.

C. Accessories are available in every traditional or modern style and may be handcrafted or machine-made - old or new.

D. An outline of the basic accessories that complete a room:

1. ***Art.***
   a. Paintings. Original paintings in ***oil, acrylic, watercolor***, or ***tempera*** are usually the most expensive type of art.
   b. **Drawings**. Original drawings are usually executed in ***ink, charcoal, pencil*** , or ***crayons***.
   c. **Prints and Photographs.** Include ***etchings, lithographs, woodcuts*** , ***steel engravings*** , and ***drypoint***. They are designed by an artist and usually produced by the artist or under his or her supervision. ***Limited edition*** prints are numbered and signed by the artist.
   Posters are available at minimal cost and are usually considered a low-budget accessory. Family or artistic ***photographs*** add variety and interest as accessories.
   d. **Importance of Frames and Mats**. Displaying two-dimensional art is a sure way to express individual taste and personality. Naturally the art itself is important, but the way it is framed also attracts attention. The frame and mat can either enhance or detract from the art. Considerations for determining how to frame and mat art work include:
      (1) Consider the ***colors*** in the art piece and the room where it will be displayed.
      (2) Consider the ***style*** of the room.
      (3) The architectural background ***textures***.
      (4) Will the picture be enhanced with a ***decorative or structural frame?***
      (5) Consider the ***frame materials*** available.
      (6) Consider ***line and form*** .
      (7) Consider the ***size*** of the frame.
      (8) Drawings, etchings, watercolors, and prints are usually complemented by including a ***mat*** .
      (9) ***Glass*** is usually used over prints, watercolors, and etchings.
   e. **Sculpture**. Three-dimensional works of art can be fashioned in many media. Placement often depends on the size of the piece. If the sculpture is large, it can be used as a focal point.
   f. **Other Types of Art and Crafts.**
      (1) ***Ceramics*** including porcelain, china, earthenware, and stoneware.
      (2) ***Mosaics*** are made up of small usually square pieces of ceramic, stone, or glass and arranged in an artistic design and set in cement.
      (3) ***Glass Art*** includes vases, dishes, bowls, and sculpture. Glass can be

etched, colored, enameled, pressed, gilded, cut, and engraved. Leaded stained glass can also be an artistic accessory.

(4) ***Weaving and Textile Art*** has been known in almost every country of the world, and each has developed distinctive cultural designs.

(5) ***Tapestry*** is an intricate (usually pictorial) multicolored handwoven textile design with a ribbed surface.

(6) ***Pillows and Cushions*** add a touch of warmth and human comfort, helping to soften the straight lines of architecture and furnishings.

(7) ***Rugs and Blankets*** . Handcrafted and custom-designed rugs are widely used as accessories, often as a focal point in a room or as the basis for a room's color scheme.

(8) ***Baskets*** . The art of basket weaving has changed little since ancient times. Today's designers have further developed this art by introducing new approaches in color, form, pattern, and style.

(9) ***Wood Crafts*** . Wood carving is another art that has survived through the ages. Items include sculpture and statuary, bowls, vases, picture and mirror frames, lamp bases, clocks, kitchen utensils, and candle holders.

(10) ***Metal Works*** . Bronze, brass, gold, silver, pewter, iron, aluminum, steel, stainless steel, chromium, tin and copper are some popular metals employed for such items as sculpture, statuary, pots, bowls, vases, plates, planters, candle holders, fire tools, decorative and functional hardware,

(11) ***Candles*** were originally used for purely functional purposes. Handcrafted candles today are a highly intricate art form. Candles provide a warm, inviting element in the private or public environment.

2. ***Screens.*** A wide variety of screens in numerous styles and materials are on the market. In addition to its decorative values, a screen may serve many functional purposes. It can (1) set of an entrance where the front door opens directly into the living area, (2) act as a room divider, (3) close of a kitchen, (4) set off a private area by making a room within a room, (5) redirect traffic, (6) extend the apparent size of a room, (7) control the flow of air and the direction of light, (8) camouflage an old fashioned radiator or air-conditioning unit, and (9) conceal storage.
3. ***Lamps.*** The lamp is an important element of beauty and purpose both during the daytime and at night. A lighting fixture that is carefully chosen for a specific room, style, mood, location or purpose can be an important contributing element. When selecting lamps for the interior, (l) select lamps that are well proportioned and are in scale with other furnishings, (2) make

sure the colors and materials of the lamp are compatible with other colors and textures in the room, (3) select lamps that complement the room's decor, (4) consider the functional as well as the decorative requirements the lamp must serve.

4. ***Books.*** can do more than anything - except people - to add friendliness to a home. Usually no room has a mood that would preclude books nor a color scheme so complete it cannot benefit from the warm tones and textures of books. Additionally, books can add a decorative quality to a room. They also mix well with other accessories.
5. ***Mirrors.*** Since the fourteenth century, mirrors have been a decorative and functional object in homes and public places. Mirrors can (1) add beauty, (2) multiply space, (3) conceal unattractive structural features, (4) distribute and double light, (5) brighten dark areas, and (6) bring life into an otherwise drab room.
6. ***Clocks*** have long been important accessories in the home and public place. They not only serve a necessary function but also add an important decorative touch. Clocks are available in numerous styles and sizes and in a variety of textures. Style preference, available space, and function are important considerations when selecting a clock.
7. ***Flowers, Foliage, and Plants.***

   Fresh Flowers. Of all accessories making up the final touches of a residence or commercial space, almost nothing can duplicate the effect of fresh flowers. Whatever the season, flowers and foliage of some type are available. Three popular flower arranging styles are (1) Oriental (***ikebana***), (2) traditional, and (3) contemporary free style. The flowers' container also contributes to the total success of the arrangement.

   Living plants generously placed around living spaces contribute to the total design scheme and help to bring something of the outdoors into the interior. Personal preference for texture, form, color, and size is a consideration in selecting plants, as well as special care requirements for light, water, and temperature.

   Dried arrangements . Dried flowers, weeds, branches, pods, and other foliage types are often arranged as alternatives to fresh plants and flowers. They have the advantage of being permanent and require no upkeep.

   Silk Flowers and Foliage. Today there is a growing demand for flowers, foliage, and plants made of silk and other fibers. They are permanent and require only occasional dusting.
8. ***Finishing Touches.*** The finishing touches to an interior give a personal stamp.

   a. ***Hardware*** . A contemporary room can be made strikingly modern and a traditional room can take on an authentic feeling through the discriminating use of small details such as door knockers, doorknobs, switch plates, curtain rods, and tiebacks, drawer pulls, escutcheons, and hinges.

III. ACCESSORY CHECKLIST:

A. When determining what accessories are suitable for a particular space, it is helpful to consider a wide range of possibilities.

B. Reviewing an outline of numerous items often sparks an idea of the accessory or accessories that tie an entire grouping together. (See Table 11.1)

IV. SELECTING AND PLACING ACCESSORIES:

A. ***Selecting Accessories*** .

1. A first step is to determine what functional and decorative accessories are required to ***meet the needs*** of the owner.
2. Always keep in mind the ***principles and elements of design*** .
3. Some of the most common ***sources*** for decorative functional accessories are art galleries, auction houses, museums, antique dealers, specialty shops, art and craft shows, exhibitions, greenhouses, flower shops, design studios, retail stores, and tourist shops.
4. The process of selecting accessories is often more rewarding when they are collected over a long period of time and accumulated from a variety of sources.

B. ***Placing Accessories*** .

1. The desire to display prized possessions is universal; the challenge is to arrange these treasured objects into an appealing composition.
2. Successful placement of accessories lies in training the eye to see beauty in color, texture, form, and spatial relationships. Application of the principles and elements of design are helpful when planning the best location for each item.

C. ***Grouping Accessories.***

1. Grouping items in an artistic arrangement can be an effective means of creating an interesting display in the room.
2. By themselves small things may be insignificant, but through skillful arrangement even the simplest items can take on special meaning.
3. When grouping small objects, keep in mind that they are seen against a background of walls and furniture.
4. Perhaps a grouping of round objects of varying sizes is pleasing, but adding a rectangle can provide a different perspective.
5. A common color subtly running through each element can add unity and

interest.

D. *Experiment* .

1. Experimentation with accesories can help create the desired outcome.
2. Items for functional or decorative use in all areas of the home add visual pleasure when displayed alone or grouped with an aesthetic eye.
3. Experimenting with combinations of accessories and their placement is a valuable learning process.

V. Nonresidential Accessories.

A. Designers often play an important role in selecting accessories for commercial and institutional spaces.

B. Art and accessories should be placed so as not to interfere with the function of the facility, but still contribute an aesthetic quality to the interior.

C. Most often, nonresidential spaces do not incorporate personal items except in private offices.

D. Adding accessories to a nonresidential setting can provide an inviting, warm character in an otherwise sparse setting.

E. Often the designer is limited in purchasing fine quality items for the nonresidential setting because of budget restrictions.

F. The challenge is to obtain accessories that project an aesthetic appeal that will last through the years.

G. Accessories that relate to the function of the facility itself can add character to the space.

H. Whatever accessories are selected for the nonresidential setting, the result should be an enhancement of the environment and the addition of a humanizing element.

Learing Enhancement Options:

Functional Accessories: Discuss with the students what accessories found in a residential or nonresidential setting are functional and how they contribute to the space.

Decorative Accessories: Discuss with the students what accesories are decorative and how they contribute personality and aesthetic appeal in a space. Present visual material that shows both functional and decorative accessories in both residential and nonresidential design.

Accessory Checklist: Show the Accessory Checklist transparency and help the students understand the advantages of scanning this list for possible accessory selections.

Selecting and Placing Accessories: Discuss with the students how selecting accessories can enrich the total design of a room and outline the steps involved in this process. Ask students where most accessories can be obtained. Review with the students how to successfully place accessories in various functional spaces. Present the idea of experimenting with accessories as a valuable learning experience.

Nonresidential Accessories: Discuss the role of the designer in selecting accessories for commercial and institutional spaces. Outline the considerations when selecting and placing accessories for particular nonresidential settings such as restaurants, health care facilities, educational facilities, and retail stores.

Test Questions

Multiple Choice:

__B__ 1. Generally, accessories do all but one of the following:
- A. Reflect individuality
- B. Generally perform only one function
- C. Can create a focal point
- D. Support the architectural background

__A__ 2. Usually, doorknobs, towel racks, and drapery rods are considered:
- A. Functional accessories
- B. Decorative accessories

__C__ 3. The following is a two-dimensional accessory:
- A. A piece of sculpture
- B. A vase
- C. An oil painting
- D. A decorative candle

__D__ 4. Mirrors have been in general use as decorative and functional objects since:
- A. 300 B.C.
- B. 300 A.D.
- C. The 8th century A.D.
- D. The 14th century A.D.

__A__ 5. Three popular flower arrangements outlined in the text include all but one of the following:
A. Scandinavian style
B. Ikebana
C. Traditional
D. Contemporary free style

True / False:

__F__ 6. An accessory may be either decorative or functional, but generally not both.

__T__ 7. Mixing styles of accessories is often considered more creative.

__T__ 8. Decorative accessories generally provide no other value than the pleasure derived from their aesthetic qualities.

__F__ 9. The art of basket weaving has greatly changed since ancient times.

__T__ 10. Usually no room has a mood that would preclude books.

__F__ 11. The process of selecting accessories is often more rewarding when selected over a short period of time.

__T__ 12. A room may often have a certain charm when there is an empty space.

__F__ 13. Glass is usually placed over an oil painting to preserve the art.

__T__ 14. Generally, displaying family or artistic photographs is considered poor taste.

__T__ 15. Tapestry usually has a pictorial design.

__F__ 16. Tesserae refers to a type of textile art.

__T__ 17. Pillows are often used to soften the straight lines of architecture.

__T__ 18. Originally, candles were meant to be only functional.

__F__ 19. Generally, traffic flow cannot be regulated by the use of a screen.

__T__ 20. Most designers feel almost nothing can duplicate the effect of fresh flowers.

__T__ 21. The desire of human beings to display possessions is universal.

__F__ 22. When grouping accessories, the walls and furniture are not considered a part of the arrangement.

__T__ 23. Most often, nonresidential spaces do not incorporate personal items.

__F__ 24. In a nonresidential project, the designer usually has very little budget restriction.

Matching:

Match the following accessories to the correct definition:

A. Posters
B. Limited editions
C. Drawings
D. Paintings

__C__ 25. Usually executed in ink, charcoal or pencil.

__D__ 26. Mediums include tempera and acrylics.

__A__ 27. Originally called "poor man's art."

__B__ 28. Numbered and signed by the artist.

A. Mosaics
B. Glass art
C. Tapestry
D. Screens

__A__ 29. Made up of tesserae.

__C__ 30. Usually depicts intricate pictorial designs

__B__ 31. Treatments often include etching, gilding, engraving, and enameling.

__D__ 32. Serves numerous functions in addition to being decorative.

Essay / Short Answer

33. Describe the term "accessories" and relate their importance in both residential and nonresidential projects.

Answer to this question is found on page 326.

34. Define and list some functional accessories. How are functional accessories effectively used in an interior?

Answer to this question is found on pages 326 and 327.

35. Define and list some decorative accessories. How are decorative accessories effectively used in an interior?

Answer to this question is found on page 328.

36. Outline information regarding paintings as decorative accessories.

Answer to this question is found on pages 328 and 329.

37. List information regarding (a) drawings, (b) prints and (c) photographs as decorative accessories.

Answer to this question is found on page 329.

38. List some basic considerations for determining how to frame and mat an art work.

Answer to this question is found on page 329.

39. Briefly outline information on sculpture and its' effective use as an accessory.

Answer to this question is found on page 329.

40. Provide information on (a) ceramics, (b) mosaics, and (c) glass art as accessories in an interior setting.

Answer to this question is found on pages 329 through 331.

41. Provide information on (a) weaving and textile art, (b) pillows and cushions, and

(c) rugs and blankets and successfully using these items as accessories.

Answer to this question is found on pages 331 and 332.

42. Provide information on (a) baskets, (b) wood crafts, (c) candles and (d) metal works and how they may be effectively used as accessories in a space.

Answer to this question is found on pages 332 and 333.

43. In addition to its decorative values, a screen may serve many functional purposes. List 8 of these functions outlined in the text.

Answer to this question is found on page 335.

44. Briefly discuss the importance of lamps as decorative and functional accessories in residential or nonresidential settings.

Answer to this question is found on page 335.

45. Provide information on books, mirrors and clocks and their use as accessories.

Answer to this question is found on pages 335 and 336.

46. Discuss the use of (a) fresh flowers, (2) plants, (3) dried arrangements, and (4) silk flowers and foliage as accessories in residential and nonresidential projects.

Answer to this question is found on pages 336 through 338.

47. What is hardware as it relates to interior design? How can these items add to the success of an interior design project?

Answer to these questions are found on page 338.

48. Discuss the advantages of reviewing an accessory checklist. What are some general suggestions when selecting accessories for the home? Where are good places to find accessories?

Answer to these questions are found on page 338.

49. Briefly outline some of the suggestions presented in the text for placing and grouping

accessories. What is the advantage of experimenting with accessory placement and grouping?

Answer to this question is found on pages 339 through 341.

50. What is the role often played by the designer in a nonresidential project? What are some considerations and suggestions for selecting and placing accessories in this environment?

Answers to these questions are found on pages 441 and 442.

Educational Resources

Publications:

Better Homes and Gardens. *Better Homes and Gardens New Decorating Book.* Des Moines: Merideth, 1981.
Gilliatt, Mary. *Decorating With Mary Gilliatt* . Little, Brown, 1992.
Hicks, David. *Style and Design* . Boston: Little, Brown, 1987.
Hilliard, Elizabeth. *Finishing Touches* . Outlet Book Company, Inc. 1988.
Kilmer, Rosemary, and W. Otie Kilmer. *Designing Interiors* . New York: Harcourt Brace Jovanovich, 1992.
Knobler, Nathan. *The Visual Dialogue* . New York: Holt, Reinhart and Winsotn, 1981.
Mount, Charles Morris. *Residential Interiors* . Glen Cove, New York: P.B.C. International 1992.

Movies / Videos

Design for Living : 33 min / 1988 / Insight Media.

Transparencies:

Accessory Checklist

CHAPTER 12

HISTORIC HERITAGE OF ARCHITECTURE AND DESIGN

Chapter Focus

Chapter 12 is divided into nine sections that present the major historic influences on American architecture and interior design. These sections include: Classic Influences, The Spanish Influence, The English Heritage - Medieval and Renaissance Influence, New England Saltbox, Garrison, Gambrel, and Cape Cod, The English Heritage - The Georgian Period, Neoclassicism in America, Other International Influences, The Victorian Era, and Preserving Our Architectural Heritage.

Text Outline

Introduction.

A. The history of American architecture is the history of our nation.

B. The dwellings of the earliest colonists were merely crude shelters against the elements.

C. An understanding of the traditional styles of American architecture is necessary to the interior designer.

   a. This knowledge can deepen an appreciation of our architectural heritage.

   b. Many individual elements are often used today to give a feeling of a historical style.

   c. Provides a basis for making an intelligent style selection.

   d. Exteriors of a particular period may be adapted to fit today's floor plans.

   e. Well-designed historical styles, for either residential or nonresidential structures, are always appreciated.

D. Of equal necessity to the interior designer is an appreciation for the background of modern architecture. (See Chapter 13)

I. CLASSIC INFLUENCES:

A. The ancient Greeks made significant contributions in art and architecture, especially during the ***Golden Age*** .

B. **The Classic Orders of Architecture:** The Greeks developed a system of coding the design and details of columns, capitals, and ***architraves*** . The coding system is known as the three classic orders of architecture:
   1. The ***Doric order***
   2. The ***Ionic order***
   3 The ***Corinthian order***

C. The Romans adapted the Greek orders and added two more, the ***Tuscan*** and ***Composite*** .

D. In architecture, the ***Roman arch*** , in combination with the ***barrel vault*** or arched roof, allowed ***domed*** construction. The ***Pantheon*** is one of the world's most important examples.

E. Other influential early periods in interior design and architecture include the ***Romanesque, Gothic, Renaissance,*** and ***Baroque*** periods. (See Table 12.1)

II. THE SPANISH INFLUENCE (circa 1565 - twentieth century):

A. The Spaniards established the first permanent European settlement in the U.S. in St. Augustine, Florida.
   1. ***Oldest House*** is claimed, by some to be the oldest in the United States.

B. The Spanish tradition further spread when explorers, politicians, the Catholic clergy, and others settled in what is now New Mexico, Texas, Arizona, and California.

C. The Spanish home as we know it today falls into four distinct categories: The ***Spanish Colonial/Mission, Southwest Adobe, California Ranch, and Monterey*** styles.
   1. **Spanish Colonial / Mission Style**: In the sixteenth century Cortez introduced the Spanish influence into Mexico, where it took on a colonial atmosphere unique to the area. General **exterior characteristics** include:
      - Blending of the Mexican, Indian, and Spanish cultures
      - Stucco-covered walls, whitewashed or tinted, often with a crude finish.
      - Low-pitched tile roof with broad overhang
      - Heavily carved doors in geometric patterns
      - Arcaded porches surrounding an inner courtyard
      - Intricate wrought-iron designs employed for interior and exterior
      - ***Reja,*** or wooden grating, typical on windows of original houses
      - Balconies and terraces occasionally built

Interior:
      - Floors of plain wood or paved with Mexican tile or brick
      - Whitewashed stucco walls, often with a crude finish
      - Colorful painted tile trim around doors and on stair risers
      - Chandeliers of hand wrought black iron

- O Heavy masculine furnishings with deep geometric carvings
- O Accessories and artifacts depicting religious themes, especially in Catholic and Indian relics (See Chapter 9 - Furniture Styles)

2. **Southwestern Style:** In 1605 Southern colonists traveled to the area that is now New Mexico, where they found Indians living in ***pueblos*** . ***Taos Pueblo*** is considered the oldest occupied apartment dwelling in the United States. Dominated for about 300 years by Spain or Spanish Mexico, a unique vernacular architecture evolved incorporating elements of the native Indian, Spanish, and Mexican cultures. In 1610 Santa Fe became the capital for Spain and the ***Palace of the Governors*** , (oldest public building in the United States) was built. General **exterior characteristics** include:
   - O Thick adobe brick construction
   - O Flat roof and deeply set windows and door, often painted blue
   - O Exterior finished with a thin coating of mud
   - O Sculptured contoured exterior and interior corners
   - O Rough-hewn pole beams called ***vigas*** projecting through walls
   - O Rectangular plan with one or more stories
   - O Pole ladders on exterior in place of interior stairs
   - O A courtyard-centered arrangement surrounded by a Greek Revival ***colonnade*** (row of columns) was a typical later feature, posts have a carved ***corbel*** or bracket top called a ***zapata***

Interior:

- O Informal feeling
- O Backgrounds of plastered surfaces with exposed ceiling beams (***vigas***) and brackets (***zapatas***)
- O ***Latillas*** , or sticks, arranged on ceiling between viga
- O Rounded, molded plastered fireplace, often in corner, with a round arched opening, often a long seating ledge flanking fireplace
- O Tile or wood plank floors
- O Small recessed niche in wall, often used for displaying religious artifacts
- O Furniture and accessories are a blend of Spanish, Indian and Mexican pieces, Santa Fe style furnishings are eclectic (See Chapter 9)
- O Colors reflect the desert landscape

3. **California Ranch House** is a mixture of the Spanish style and the old western farmhouse built circa 1800 to the present. The low, rambling structure was suited to an informal lifestyle. An authentic California ranch house has several identifying **exterior characteristics**:
   - O Structure hugging a relatively flat terrain
   - O Long, low roofline; roof originally of tar, then tile. Shingles used later
   - O Wide low overhangs supported by posts cover a porch

- O Indigenous material used for construction (adobe, brick, wood stucco)
- O Wing-sheltered patio easily accessible from most rooms

Interior:

- O Similar to interior details of Spanish Colonial (today, great freedom of style is incorporated)

4. **Monterey House** is a blending of the Spanish, French, and New England architecture that had its birth in Monterey, California. ***Thomas Larkin*** , of Boston, Massachusetts, contributed significantly to the original Monterey style when he combined various cultural details in his home completed in 1837 He introduced the use of wallpaper in the area. **Exterior characteristics** include:

- O Adobe, stucco, or whitewashed brick walls, sometimes tinted
- O Flat-pitched tile roofs. (Spanish influence)
- O Wide overhangs to shade windows
- O Long second-story balcony supported with posts (French galerie influence)
- O Woodwork showing New England influence

Interior:

- O Walls, floors, and other backgrounds incorporate English and Spanish influences, as does the exterior
- O Furnishings and accessories are either elegant or simple English, Spanish, or a combination (See Chapter 9)

III. THE ENGLISH HERITAGE - Medieval and Renaissance Influence (1607-eighteenth century):

A. The mainstream of American culture began at Jamestown, Virginia, and Plymouth, Massachusetts in the seventeenth century.

B. Technically, American houses built during the seventeenth century and based on historic English prototypes fall under the category of English Medieval. However, styles that have merged from this period are quite distinctive.

1. **Early Half-Timber, Brick, and Stone Houses.** The first permanent dwellings constructed by English settlers who landed in ***Jamestown*** in 1607. Early structures were patterned after the half-timbered one-room tudor and Elizabethan "hall." **Exterior characteristics** include:

- O Two to three stories
- O Rambling Design
- O Half-timber most common construction with ***wattle and daub*** or ***nogging***
- O Use of the ***Tudor arch*** over doorways and fireplaces
- O Second-story overhang or ***jetty*** frequently used
- O Sharp ***gables***
- O ***Clustered*** or columned chimneys, buttressed, stone-end or simple

- O *Bay* windows (optional)
- O Small-paned leaded windows, often diamond shaped casement windows
- O Projecting porch or doorway (optional)

2. **Elizabethan Manor House.** During the reign of Elizabeth I, the Gothic and Medieval English design merged with the new Dutch influence, resulting in the great ornate-gabled house known as the ***Elizabethan*** . The English manor house built in the colonies follows the same general style as its prototype in England. **Exterior characteristics:**

- O Rambling design, often E-shaped
- O Large house with two or three stories
- O Stone or brick structures most typical (also carryover of half-timber)
- O ***Flemish gables*** and ***parapets*** reflecting Dutch influence
- O ***Balustrades*** often used
- O Bay and oriel windows with small leaded panes
- O Doorways recessed, round or Tudor arch framing, Gothic arch optional
- O Numerous clustered chimneys and exterior chimneys

Interior:

- O Simple Tudor homes: plain plastered walls, sometimes with vertical wood paneling, half-timbering often exposed inside
- O Large fireplace with heavy wood mantel or Tudor arch
- O Wide plank wood floors, Tudor arch over doorways optional
- O Heavy wood-beam ceilings
- O Furniture often handcrafted
- O Simple informal fabrics
- O Elizabethan and Jacobean manor homes: more elegant interior details.
- O Wood or stone fireplaces with Tudor arch
- O Gothic detailing (optional)
- O Fabrics: tapestry, crewel embroidery, chintz, leather; rich colors.

3. **Cotswold House.** These stone houses are often characterized by a front attached chimney, an asymmetrical arrangement, dormer windows, and a low cottage look. The Cotswold house is a simplified interpretation of the Tudor and Elizabethan styles.

IV. NEW ENGLAND SALTBOX, GARRISON, GAMBREL, AND CAPE COD

A. The pilgrims at Massachusetts Bay found heavily wooded land and built their houses of wood construction in a simple manner. They were derived from English folk architecture of the late Medieval and Elizabethan periods. The strong Tudor and Elizabethan influences in early New England architecture can be seen in many of the seventeenth century houses that are still standing.

1. Half-House. The first houses were but a single room (half-house) with the

chimney to the side wall.

2. **Two-Room or Double House.** Soon a second room was added on the other side and the fireplace became the central core of the house.
3. **Saltbox.** To provide additional space, a ***lean-to*** that usually became the kitchen was added to the two-room house. It was called a ***saltbox*** because the shape resembled the boxes in which settlers stored their salt.
4. **Garrison (Jetty).** In many houses the second story extended beyond the first floor, a carryover from medieval England. The over-hang or ***jetty*** , had end brackets with hand-carved ***pendants*** .
5. **Gambrel.** Another modification had a double-pitched roof made of two sections or rafters. This roof style was inexpensive to build and permitted more headroom in the attic.
6. **Cape Cod (Transitional).** During the final decade of the seventeenth century one of America's best-loved houses made its appearance. This style was an outgrowth of the half-house and the two-room or double house. What has come to be known as the ***Cape Cod*** was a humble cottage that retained much medieval character. Covered with clapboards or shingles, the structure had a central chimney, a simple plank doorway, and small-paned windows. Early in the eighteenth century, the Cape Cod house took on some of the features of early Georgian architecture.

Along with their own distinguishing characteristics **the four seventeenth - century New England houses share a number of features:**

O Rectangular plan
O Wood or shingle construction
O Central chimney
O Small casement windows
O Asymmetrical and symmetrical arrangement
O Simple English medieval character

Interior:

O Plain plaster walls or ***palisade*** wood paneling. ***Wainscoting***
O Exposed beamed ceiling
O Small-paned sash windows with diamond panes or double-hung sash type
O Wide plank floors (later, Oriental rugs)
O Large brick fireplace with cooking utensils
O Furniture often homemade (See Chapter 9)
O Fabrics similar to those in Elizabethan and Jacobean manor home

V. ENGLISH HERITAGE - THE GEORGIAN PERIOD (circa 1700-1790):

A. The period when England was ruled by the Stuarts is divided into three subperiods: (1) ***Jacobean*** (1603-1689), (2) ***William & Mary*** (1689-1702) and (3) ***Queen Anne***

(1702-1714).

B. For the first forty years in the seventeenth century there was little change in English architecture - inside or out.

C. Then ***Inigo Jones*** revolutionized English architecture when he introduced the ***Renaissance*** and ***Palladian*** influence to England.

   a. ***Sir Christopher Wren*** became its foremost exponent. In Wren's capable hands, the ideas of Inigo Jones developed into a gracious architecture style called ***Georgian***. (Named after the English kings: George I, II, and III).

   b. By the second decade of the eighteenth century, the colonies had grown and the people prospered. English craftspeople and builders, laden with tools and architectural drawings, arrived in the colonies.

   c. At the time of the American Revolution, the new style had become familiar in American cities from Jamestown to Portsmouth.

1. **Early Georgian or Wren-Georgian Style (circa 1720-1750).** The Early Georgian house in America retained the basic elements, fine proportions and symmetry of its English ***prototype*** , but it took on local differences. **Exterior**:

   - Influence of English Baroque and Sir Christopher Wren
   - Symmetrical facade with a feeling of dignity and formality
   - Two to three stories - rectangular block
   - Symmetrically placed double-hung (sash) windows with small panes
   - Central doorway flanked by pilasters and crowned by one of the four pediments
   - Hipped roof, often with a balustrade protecting a captain's or widow's walk, dormer windows typical, often with shutters.

   d. As the new style spread, great brick and wood mansions were built in the new Georgian manner, but with regional differences. In ***New England*** the gambrel roof and ***wood construction*** was favored.

2. **Late Georgian or Gibbs-Palladian Style (circa 1750-1790)**

   a. The Roman Palladian style (developed by ***Andrea Palladio*** , an Italian Renaissance architect), became popular with English aristocracy in the early eighteenth century and was introduced to America near the middle of that century, primarily through books. One of the most important was ***James Gibbs' A Book of Architecture*** (1728).

   b. **Exterior** characteristics of the late Georgian Palladian style in America include:

   - Features of basic structure essentially Wren-Georgian
   - Classical details such as pilasters and pediments
   - Central section of facade emphasized by pedimented ***pavilion*** or ***breakfront*** extending above the roofline
   - Pavilion sometimes flat, sometimes projecting portico form

- O Side dependencies or wings connected to the main block, often by open ***colonnades***
- O ***Palladian window prevalent***
- O ***Quoining*** on corners (optional)
- O Pilasters on corners (optional)

Interiors:

- O Cornices with dentil trim
- O Pediments over doorways and mantels
- O Painted wood paneling or plaster; stained wood paneling; late Georgian featured more Palladian interior details
- O Wallpaper above a dado; late Georgian favored continental or Chinese wallpaper
- O Wood plank floors with Oriental rugs
- O Fireplaces with wood panels and classic details; late Georgian fireplace often has pediment mantel; fireplace has ears or square projections at top corners
- O Brass or bronze baroque chandeliers
- O William and Mary, Queen Anne, and Chippendale furniture; Chippendale especially popular in late Georgian interior (See Chapter 9)
- O Elegant and formal fabrics; damasks, velvets, brocades, etc.
- O Prominent colors: rich golds and reds, Williamsburg green, deep gray-blue.

VI. NEOCLASSICISM IN AMERICA (circa 1790-1845)

A. Neoclassicism in America is made up of two periods: ***Federal*** and ***Greek Revival*** and no clear lines of demarcation exist. Much neoclassicism was communicated to the colonies through books, but also young men were encouraged to go abroad and study classical architecture. Englishman, ***Benjamin Latrobe*** was one of the first architects to infuse European ideas into American architecture.

1. **Federal Period (circa 1790-1825).** The decades following the revolutionary war, there was a tendency to break with anything reflecting English dominance, and interest in French modes grew.
   a. Consequently, when the excavation of ***Pompeii*** the new classical style rapidly superseded the Georgian.
   b. Although America was reluctant to adopt this style from England, the neoclassic designs of English architects and cabinetmakers (especially the ***Adam brothers***), exerted the most influence - especially in the North. Later the designs of ***Thomas Jefferson*** , dominated in the South.
   c Two main factors brought about this change in America: (1) the need for an official architecture and (2) Thomas Jefferson's enthusiasm for the new

classicism. His designs established the columned portico as the essential motif of American official architecture. His home, ***Monticello*** , inspired by the ancient ***Pantheon*** in Rome influenced the design of domestic buildings.

d. In residential work, four names stand out: ***Samuel McIntire*** of Salem, ***Charles Bulfinch*** of Boston, ***John McComb*** of New York, and ***Benjamin Latrobe*** in the South.

e. **Exterior - Federal-English Influence:**
- **O** Influence of Robert Adam and English Georgian architecture
- **O** Influence of Samuel McIntire and Charles Bulfinch
- **O** Influence of ancient Grecian and Roman architecture
- **O** Three stories high, with smaller third story
- **O** A columned portico in front
- **O** Doorway ***sidelights***; entrance topped by ***elliptical fanlight***
- **O** Delicate classical detail
- **O** Windows crowned by pediments or ***jack arch lintels*** (optional)
- **O** Flattened hipped roof with balustrade above cornice (optional)

f. **Exterior - Federal-Roman Influence:**
- **O** A rejection of the delicacy of the Adam style
- **O** Expresses qualities of strength based on architecture of Republican Rome
- **O** Influence of Andrea Palladio and Thomas Jefferson

g. **Interiors for both influences include:**
- **O** Classical detailing from ancient Greece, Rome, and Pompeii
- **O** Woodwork usually painted white, wallpaper, often scenic, above a dado
- **O** Adam mantels
- **O** Crystal chandeliers
- **O** Parquet or wood plank floors, Oriental rugs
- **O** Hepplewhite and Sheraton furniture (See Chapter 9)
- **O** Fabrics: formal and elegant; motifs from classical Greece and Rome
- **O** Colors: muted blues, greens and other soft pastel colors

2. **Greek Revival Period (circa 1825-1845)**

a. Although the Neoclassic style reached the South later than the North, the style of the Greek Revival period became more predominant in the South than anywhere else.

b. The size and elegance of the plantation mansion and luxurious manner of living lent themselves well to the new style.

c. The architects in the South adapted the classic style to meet the needs of the hot climate.

d. The magnificent columns were replicas of the classic orders of architecture.

e. **Exterior:** The Greek Revival house is characterized by the following features:

- Continued use of Georgian, Federal and French forms
- Precise adherence to Greek proportions, orders, and ornaments
- Isolated temple form
- Profuse use of two-story columns on more pretentious houses; columns continue on all sides, second story balcony (optional)
- White exterior typical
- Many or a few steps leading up to the veranda or porch
- House often built with gable end to street
- In absence of a portico, placement of pilasters, frieze and classically framed doorway
- French doors and shutters often used, especially in South
- Sidelights and fanlights continue

Interiors:

- Grand treatment of classic orders (columns and pilasters)
- Elegant crystal or oil-vessel-type chandeliers; ceiling fan (punkah) used in the South.
- Fireplace of black or white marble
- Continuation of scenic wallpaper above a dado
- Bold patterned rugs
- Dominant masculine feeling, Empire (especially Napoleonic designs) and Duncan Phyfe furniture; harp a favorite piece, some use of English Regency (See Chapter 9)
- White plaster walls
- White ivory button on newel post
- Colors: Empire green, gold, black and white, rich reds and blues; colors and motifs popular with Napoleon copied
- Fabrics: elegant and formal

VII. OTHER INTERNATIONAL INFLUENCES.

A. French Style (1714-1789)

1. **Rococo Style, Louis XV (1714-1774).** Rococo is a style of art, architecture, and decoration that developed mainly in France during the reign of Louis XV then spread to the palaces, churches, and residences of the wealthy in Europe.
   a. The new style was a reaction against the excesses of baroque and classicism in interior decoration more than in architecture.
   b. The Rococo style reflected the tastes of women at the French court.
   c. Human comfort and convenience were a concern.
   d. **Characteristics** include:
      - Formal, elegant, intimate, comfortable, visually charming, graceful, feminine, and somewhat frivolous.

- Use of delicate decorative details; many surfaces decorated, profuse use of curves, scrolls, and foliage asymmetrically arranged
- Prominent motifs: the shell and Venus, fireplace with shell motif
- Wooden panels with curved moldings, classical orders used sparingly
- Compared to baroque, lightly scaled furnishings and ornamentation
- Chinese motifs and wallpapers popular
- Pastel colors prevalent
- Rectangular parquet floors with French Aubusson or Savonnerie rugs or Oriental rugs
- Long French doors

2. **French Neoclassic Style, Louis XVI (1760-1789).** Flourished during the reign of Louis XVI and Marie Antoinette.
   a. The principle design influences were ancient Greece, Pompeii and the work of Robert Adam.
   b. The design principles of classical Greece and Rome were revived; but applied in more delicate forms.
   c. Various rooms at the palace of Versailles are best examples.
   d. **Characteristics** of the French neoclassic style include:
      - Formal, delicate and elegant
      - More restraint in ornamentation of the Rococo style
      - Use of straight lines and rectangular forms; curves when used, precisely formed by the compass; rectangular wood paneled walls often painted with gold or silver finishes.
      - Classical details and motifs particularly influenced by the decorations of the ancient city of Pompeii and the works of Robert Adam
      - Symmetrical balance dominates
      - Parquet wood floors and French rugs typical
      - Use of pastel colors
      - Carved marble fireplace most common
      - Tall French windows and double doors
3. **Provincial French or Country French (eighteenth century-present)** throughout France the lesser nobility and wealthy merchants copied or adopted the styles of Louis XV and XVI; but in an effort to economize, simplified the interiors and furnishings. The emphasis of the country French style focused on comfort, livability, and family life.
4. **The French House in America.** The heartland of America was controlled by France for over a hundred years.
   a. **The Norman Cottage**. French colonists in the north built houses that often had high hipped roofs and rounded corner towers with whitewashed exteriors reminiscent of the ***chateaux*** and manor houses they had known in France.

but greatly simplified.

b. **The French Plantation**. In the South the basic structure of the northern cottage retained and adapted to the climate by the addition of an encircling ***galerie*** or porch covered by a broad ***bonnet roof.***

With the passage of time, new architectural influences could be seen in the evolution of the French house.

During the prosperous decade that preceded the Civil War, the Greek Revival period reached its zenith in the great plantation mansions of the South.

c. **The Gallery House**. The tiny French Cajun cottage, with its front porch protected by an overhanging roof, was the original gallery house.

d. **The French Town House**. The galleries of the French town house faced away from the street onto a private courtyard. ***Lacy cast-iron balconies*** facing the street were added in the nineteenth century, which gave the ***Old French Quarter*** of New Orleans a flavor of French architecture.

e. Over the years, houses recalling original French city houses, manors, and cottages have been built in America. Four general French exterior styles have emerged and are known under the following names:

(1) **Louisiana French**
(2) **French City House**
(3) **French Manor House**
(4) **French Cottage**

(Some interior treatment characteristics that are typical of the various French styles are known in America as French provincial, provincial French, or country French).

f. <u>**Interiors**</u> **- Country or Provincial French Styles:**

- Adaptation of Court French, but in simpler terms
- Painted or wood paneling for wall treatment; plain paster walls for a typical country feeling.
- French doors
- Fireplace similar to Court French (Rococo) or a hooded fireplace
- Floor treatment same as Court French; also terra-cotta tile and braided rugs typical for a country look
- Use of simplified Louis XV furniture, wood finishes, armoire an important piece; ladderback chairs (See Chapter 9)
- Cotton, linen, and informal textiles; motifs associated with French themes; checks and stripes, small quaint prints, toile de Jouy.

(Currently there is great ***flexibility*** and freedom in designing American homes employing French styles.)

B. **Dutch Influence.** In 1650 Dutch settlements were well established throughout the regions of Manhattan Island, New Jersey, and Delaware. A few houses still reflect the Flemish influence with ***stepped gables, Flemish gables*** and ***patterned brickwork.*** Dutch houses were usually constructed of fieldstone, shingle, or clapboard and typically had high gable ends with a long sweeping roofline extending over a full-length porch (***the flowing eave***). Use of the early***Dutch or Bell gambrel*** was typical.

C. **German Style**. German colonists who settled in Pennsylvania built a variety of homes reflecting medieval features, ranging from simple log cabins to half-timbered homes (called ***Fachwerkbau)*** , to large stone manors. Most typical are homes built of ***local fieldstone*** with a steeply pitched roof (sometimes a gambrel used), and the use of the ***pent roof.***

D. **Swedish Style.** Swedish colonists who settled in the Delaware Valley in 1638 introduced the ***log cabin*** to America.

a. **Interiors of Dutch, German, and Swedish Houses:**
Craft contributions perhaps more influential than the various homes built. Handcrafted furniture was often painted with delightful and colorful motifs from their homeland. Popular crafts include: ***tole painting, quilts, stenciling, glass design,*** and ***pottery.***

VIII. THE VICTORIAN ERA (circa 1837-1900):

A. Architecture of the ***Industrial Age*** coincided with the reign of ***Queen Victoria.***

B. Many authorities have regarded Victorian architecture as inventive, full of vigor and diversity, and representative of a coherent and unified course of development.

C. During the second half of the nineteenth century four major architectural styles emerged:

1. **Gothic Revival (1840s-1880s).** ***Andrew Jackson Downing*** is considered the father of the Gothic Revival in America. Since stone was costly, Downing translated the English stone Gothic into wood, and the style became known as ***Carpenter Gothic*** . Following are **exterior characeristics** of the Gothic Revival and Carpenter Gothic styles:
   - O Use of Gothic arch; Tudor arch (optional)
   - O Broken, picturesque exterior
   - O Steep gables; finials on roof (optional)
   - O Porches leading to informal gardens
   - O Lofty windows, often pointed; leaded windows
   - O Carpenter Gothic wood sheathing, often ***board and batten***
   - O Carpenter Gothic: ***bargeboard*** or ***vergeboard*** under gables
   - O Carpenter Gothic: "***gingerbread*** " decoration in gables

2. **Italianate Style (1830-1890s/1920s).** In the 1930s America's admiration for the Italian arts resulted in the popularity for the modified Italian ***villa*** . Used for both urban and suburban dwellings, including townhouses. General **exterior characteristics** of the Italianate style include:
   - O Stately structures with vertical emphasis
   - O Low-pitched or low-hipped overhanging roof supported with large decorative brackets
   - O Free arrangement of bold square or rectangular blocks; structure topped by a square tower (belvedere or cupola)
   - O Easy access to outdoor terraces
   - O Windows topped with pediments, fanciful crowns, hoods, or "eyebrows"
   - O Small entry porches (optional)
   - O Use of the Italian arch and columns
   - O Bay windows
3. **Mansard or General Grant Style (1850s-1880s).** The ***mansard*** roof, which Francois Mansart introduced in the 1600s was the answer to many architectural problems. The style is also known as the General Grant style after President U.S. Grant. The following **exterior characteristics** include:
   - O Stately structure, rectangular or square form, tower (optional)
   - O Tall French windows opening onto deep porches; windows often topped with decorative pediments or crowns
   - O Dormer windows break the roofline (optional)
   - O Crowned by a steep sloping mansard roof; massive cornices with brackets smaller than Italianate; roofline frequently topped by iron cresting and finials, colored tile patterns (optional)
   - O Quoining on corners and stringcourse typical
4. **Queen Anne Style (1870s-1880s).** The most whimsical of the Victorian era's eclectic styles was the so-called Queen Anne. It was a deliberate imitation of many defunct architectural styles. **Exterior characteristics** include:
   - O All manner of decorative wood and plaster detailings; including gingerbread, festoons, spindles, brackets, vergeboards, patterned shingles, and belt courses.
   - O Variable heights and shapes; sometimes built on grand a scale
   - O ***Fish-scale shingles*** common.
   - O Numerous steps leading up to a porch; porches often circular with colonnettes and turned railings.
   - O Windows grouped in banks, with upper panes often colored.
   - O Most distinctive feature is circular or square tower extending from ground level to all floors, topped with a cone-shaped roof; many other projections including bay windows, balconies, porches, and turrets.

5. In addition to the four major Victorian styles, another five design directions were prevalent: (1) ***Octagonal*** , (2) ***Exotic Revival*** , (3) ***Stick Style*** , (4) ***Romanesque Revival*** , and (5) ***Shingle Style*** .
6. <u>**Victorian Interiors:**</u> Interiors during the Victorian period varied from region to region, but generally the feeling was similar and included the following:
   - O A variety and profusion of pattern
   - O Window treatments included lace casements; elegant tied-back side draperies, topped with an ornate metal crown or valance
   - O Fireplaces ornately designed; marble and round-headed; mirrors with gilded or large carved wooden frames over fireplace
   - O Furniture massive and heavily carved, drawing themes from many styles
   - O Accessories everywhere; personal collections of all kinds displayed
   - O Lighting: heavy chandeliers of crystal, brass, colorful tinted glass, and white opaline glass balls; electrified gasolier in many designs

D. **Beaux Arts Mansions.** Beginning in the early 1800s, a revival of Old World styles left a legacy of Victorian extravagance. ***William Kissam Vanderbilt's*** elegant chateau on Fifth Avenue in New York City, built in 1881 triggered the building of extravagant architecture by a few powerful, wealthy American families.

1. The name ***Beaux Arts*** was applied to this style after the world-famous design school ***L'Ecole des Beaux Arts*** in Paris.
2. ***Richard Morris Hunt*** , one of the first American arhictects to train there, was the most prominent designer of this opulent style.
3. The architectural firm of ***McKim, Mead & White*** were also well known.
4. The style remained popular during the jazz age, but generally died out with the stock market crash and Great Depression of the 1930s.
5. A few of the best-known Beaux Arts palaces are: (1), ***The Breakers*** , (2) ***Marble House*** , (3) ***Elms*** , (4) ***Viz-Caya*** , (5) ***Ringling Mansion*** , (6) ***Biltmore House*** , and ((7) ***Hearst Castle*** .

E. **Traditional Styles Revived.** Although the palatial Beaux Arts homes were suitable for the very wealthy, they were hardly affordable for the rest of America.

1. Many beautiful traditionally styled homes were also built during the Beaux Arts period capturing styles of the past interpreted in simpler terms.
2. When confronted with designing contemporary traditional homes, the architect today is generally influenced by features of original prototypes but will often reinterpret and adapt a style.

IX. PRESERVING OUR ARCHITECTURAL HERITAGE:

A. Only during the past 20 to 30 years has the preservation of our architectural heritage generated widespread interest.

1. Some earlier reconstructed villages have for some Americans created a nostalgic curiosity about the legacy of our nation.
2. Many houses have been authentically restored and opened to the public.
3. The ***National Trust for Historic Preservation*** in Washington, D.C., founded in 1949, is the largest organization in the country devoted to the preservation of historic buildings, districts, and neighborhoods.

Learning Resource Options

Introduction: Discuss with the students the first shelters built by European settlers in America. Ask why is it important for the interior designer to have an understanding of the traditional styles of American architecture.

The Classic Influence: Discuss with the students the contributions of the ancient Greeks and Romans. Review the three classic orders of architecture and their influence through the centuries. (If a part of the curriculum, also review with the students the other early periods of the Romanesque, Gothic, Renaissance and Baroque periods). Show visual examples of architecture, furnishings and details prevalent during these periods.

The **Spanish, English, French, Dutch, German, Swedish, Victorian and Beaux Arts styles:** Discuss with the students each of the architectural styles presented in the text. Illustrate the various terms and details of each style on the board and support the information with visual material showing both exterior and interior applications. If available, display books for each period and subject. Ask the students to relate personal experiences in relationship to the various architectural styles in reference to climate, geographic location, budget, function, comfort, personal style preferences and other related criteria.

Test Questions:

Multiple Choice:

__D__ 1. The illustration at the right is an example of:
A. The Roman Tuscan Order
B. The Doric Order of Architecture (Illustration of Ionic Order)
C. The Corinthian Order of Architecture
D. The Ionic Order of Architecture

__B__ 2. The illustration at the right is an example of:
A. The loggia
B. A reja (Illustration of a reja)
C. Risers
D. Vargueno

__A__ 3. The illustration at the right is an example of a:
A. Zapata
B. Latilla (Illustration of a Zapata)
C. Viga
D. Pueblo support

__C__ 4. Historians consider the mainstream of American culture began at:
A. Santa Fe, New Mexico
B. Portsmouth, New Hampshire
C. Jamestown, Virginia
D. St. Augustine, Florida

__B__ 5. The arch illustrated at the right is an example of what style?
A. Spanish Colonial
B. Tudor (Illustration of a Tudor arch)
C. Dutch
D. Georgian

__D__ 6. Wattle and daub is:
A. Mud applied to the pueblo dwelling
B. Boards used on 17th century New England houses
C. Exterior finish on Spanish Mission style structures
D. Filling material used for early English houses

__A__ 7. A pendant is most typically found on what style of architecture?
A. Garrison
B. Gambrel
C. Cape Cod
D. Saltbox

__C__ 8. This architect is known for introducing the Renaissance to England.
A. Sir Christopher Wren
B. Andrea Palladio
C. Inigo Jones
D. James Gibbs

__B__ 9. The form illustrated at the right is:
A. A pilaster
B. A pediment (Illustration of a pediment)
C. An architrave
D. A cornice

__D__ 10. Late Georgian architecture is most associated with:
A. Sir Christopher Wren
B. Samuel McIntire
C. Robert Adam
D. James Gibbs

__A__ 11. Which of the following are not associated with the Federal style:
A. Reign of Louis XV
B. Excavation of Pompeii
C. Classical Rome
D. Democratic Greece

__C__ 12. Which of the following is not associated with the French Rococo style?
A. Madame du Pompadour
B. Rocks and shells
C. Louis XVI
D. Profuse use of foliage

__B__ 13. The roof type illustrated at the right is a:
A. Hipped roof
B. Bonnet roof (Illustration of a bonnet roof)
C. Bell gambrel
D. Pent roof

__D__ 14. Andrew Jackson Downing is associated with what Victorian style?
A. Queen Anne
B. Mansard
C. Italianate
D. Gothic Revival

__C__ 15. Richard Morris Hunt is well known for designing homes in what style?
A. Neoclassic
B. English Tudor
C. Beaux Arts
D. Victoria

Matching:

Match the following architectural and interior styles with the appropriate answers:

A. Spanish Colonial/Mission style
B. Southwest Adobe
C. Monterey
D. California Ranch

__B__ 16. Exposed pole beams, flat roof and molded round edges. Use of lodgepole pine and equipale furniture.

__A__ 17. Courtyards and arcades. Use of hand painted tile. Wrought iron designs.

__C__ 18. Influence of the French, Spanish, English and Indian cultures.

__D__ 19. The long low "rambler."

A. Ancient Greece
B. English Tudor
C. Early Georgian
D. Late Georgian

__C__ 20. Governor's Palace, Williamsburg, Virginia. Influence of Wren.

__A__ 21. The Parthenon

__D__ 22. Breakfront exterior. Pediment often breaks the roofline. Influence of Gibbs.

__B__ 23. Half-timber construction. Brick nogging. The "flattened" arch.

A. Cape Cod
B. Salt Box
C. Garrison
D. Gambrel

__D__ 24. Distinguished by a double-pitched roof.

__A__ 25. An outgrowth of the half-house and the double house. A "cottage" look.

__B__ 26. A "lean to" added to the house.

__C__ 27. Distinguished by a jetty and pendants.

A. Federal Style B. Greek Revival Style C. French Style

__C__ 28. Dovecote, bonnet and high hipped roofs. Lacy wrought iron. Quoining.

__A__ 29. Influenced by Pompeii, Thomas Jefferson and Samuel McIntire.

__B__ 30. Also known as Empire style. "Grand" use of Greek orders of architecture.

A. Dutch B. Swedish C. German

__A__ 31. Stepped gable and bell gambrel roof typical.

__C__ 32. Pent roof typical. General use of field stone as a building material.

__B__ 33. Introduced log construction to the colonies in 1654.

A. Gothic Revival
B. Italianate
C. Mansard
D. Queen Anne

__D__ 34. Fish scale shingles. Whimsical. Colonnettes. Very decorative. Towers.

__B__ 35. Often topped with a belvedere. Decorative bracket supports. Bay windows.

__C__ 36. Wrought iron cresting and finials. Also known as General Grant style.

__A__ 37. Wood or stone tracery. Board and batten. Andrew Jackson Downing.

A. Chippendale and Queen Anne furniture
B. Sheraton and Hepplewhite furniture
C. Furniture inspired by the French Emperor Napoleon
D. Eastlake and Belter furniture

__D__ 38. Primarily used during the Victorian Period.
__A__ 39. Primarily used during the Georgian Period.
__C__ 40. Primarily used during the Greek Revival Period.
__B__ 41. Primarily used during the Federal Period.

A. Georgian interior
B. Federal Interior
C. Greek Revival interior
D. Provincial French interior

__B__ 42. Urn motif. Adamesque mantels. Paterae design. Woodwork usually white.

__A__ 43. Brass chandelier. Dentil molding. Shell cupboard. Rich reds and golds.

__D__ 44. Carved shell motif on mantels. Aubusson rugs on parquet floors.

__C__ 45. Bold rugs. Empire green. Black or white marble fireplace. Punkah fan.

Essay / Short Answer

46. Briefly trace the contributions made by the English settlers to American architecture and interior design. Provide information concerning the Tudor, 17th century houses in New England, Georgian, and Federal styles.

Answers to these questions are found on pages 353 through 367.

47. Trace the contributions made by the French settlers in America to architecture and interior design. Provide information on the most typical french styles. Include characteristics of the Court French, Provincial French and Country French interiors.

Answers to these questions are found on pages 370 through 375.

48. Outline the contributions made by the Spanish settlers in America. Provide information on each regional style and typical interiors.

Answers to these questions are found on pages 347 through 358.

49. How did the uniquely American Victorian home evolve? Outline the four most popular Victorian Styles in America and list the characteristics of each. Provide information on typical Victorian interiors including backgrounds, fireplaces, window treatment, lighting, furniture, and accessories.

Answers to these questions are found on pages 377 through 380.

50. Briefly outline how the Beaux Arts mansion evolved and list typical characteristics of these palaces. Include the names of five famous Beaux Arts mansions currently opened to the public.

Answers to these questions are found on pages 380 through 382.

Educational Resources

Publications:

Foley, Mary Mix. *The American House* . New York: Harper & Row, 1980.
Gowans, Alan. *Styles and Types of North American Archhitecture* . New York: Harper Collins, 1992.
Hepburn, Andrew. *Great Houses of American History* . New York: Bramhall House, 1972.
Kidder-Smith, G.E. *A Pictorial History of Architecture in America* . New York: American Heritage, 1976.
Kostof, Spiro. *History of Architecture* . New York: Oxford University Press, 1985.
Maass, John. *The Victorian Home in America* . New York: Hawthorne, 1972.
Mather, Christine, and Sharon Woods. *Santa Fe Style* . New York: Rizzoli Int., 1986.
Miller, Judith and Martin Miller. *Miller's Victorian Style: Creating Period Interiors for Contemporary Living* . Viking Studio, 1993.
Norwich, John Julius, ed. *Great Architecture of the World* . New York: Bonanza, 1982.
Pierson, Willialm H., Jr. *American Buildings and Their Architects* . Garden City: Doubleday, 1970.
Rifkind, Carole. *A Field Guide to American Architecture* . New York: Plume, 1980.
Russell, Beverly. *Architecture and Design* . New York: Harry N. Abrams, 1989.
Sinclair, Peg B. *Victorious Victorians* . New York: Holt, Rinehart & Winston, 1985.
Whiton, Sherrill. *Interior Design and Decoration..* Philadelphia: J.B. Lippincott, 1974.
Wiffen, Marcus, and Frederick Koeper. *American Architecture* . 1607-1976. 2 vols. Cambridge, Mass.: MIT PRess, 1981.

Movies / Videos:

American Houses - A Guide to Architectural Styles : 23 min / Learning Seed, Illinois

Transparencies:

Ancient classical Greece and Classic Greek orders.
Pediment forms
The Parthenon
Table 12.1

CHAPTER 13

MODERN ARCHITECTURE AND DESIGN

Chapter Focus

Chapter 13 surveys the heritage of modern architecture and design and is divided into seven sections. These sections include: Beginnings of Modernism, Principal Early Modern Movements,(Latter Half of Nineteenth Century), Principal Modern Movements (Early Twentieth Century),Current Trends, Options for Prospective Home Owners in the 1990s, The Energy-Efficient House, and Looking to the Future.

Text Outline

I. **BEGINNINGS OF MODERNISM:** During the 1880s, many designers in the United States rebelled against nineteenth-century eclecticism and enslavement to the past - a reaction first seen in Europe, and completely new structures evolved. The Shakers, a religious order in America felt decoration was wicked. Their structurally simple houses and furnishings reflected this philosophy.

A. ***The Industrial Revolution and the Beginnings of Modernism.***

1. The influential roots of modernism in the United States and Europe can primarily be traced to the ***Industrial Revolution*** .
   a. This era introduced the ***use of the machine*** for manufacturing furniture and other essentials for living, helping to change the way people lived.
   b. New ***advancements in technology*** and the development of ***new materials*** led to extraordinary architectural innovations.

B. *Michael Thonet.*

1. An early as 1830, Austrian designer ***Michael Thonet*** developed a process for bending thin strips of wood into fanciful curved forms for furniture construction.
   a. Thonet also conceived a method of ***mass producing*** these designs.
   b. The pieces he designed became immensely popular throughout Europe and the United States.
   c. One of his most famous designs is the *bentwood rocker.*
   d. The study of the modern movement in Europe and America is extensive and many significant contributions were made on both continents.

II. PRINCIPAL EARLY MODERN MOVEMENTS (Latter Half of Nineteenth Century):

A. The ***Arts and Crafts Movement*** founded by ***William Morris*** in England rejected the machine and modern society.
   1. The design group found the handcrafted ideals of the Middle Ages a perfect model for their own handcrafted furniture and decorative objects.
   2. This philosophy was reflected in simple unadorned architecture and furnishings that ironically are considered early beginnings of modernism.
   3. Other Arts and Crafts leaders included ***Charles Francis Annesley Voysey*** and ***Philip Webb***.

B. The ***Arts and Crafts Movement in America*** was the counterpart of the English movement.
   1. The foremost exponents were ***Gustav Stickley*** in New Jersey, and the brothers ***Charles Greene*** and ***Henry Greene*** in Pasadena, California.
      a. Stickley published his advanced design ideas in a periodical called ***The Craftsman*** at the turn of the nineteenth century.
      b. Greene and Greene designed handsome handcrafted furnishings for their new residential architecture.
      c. Greene and Greene helped develop the ***bungalow*** and ***shingle-styled*** homes in America.
         (1) These homes featured wood construction with handcrafted finishing, wide overhanging roofs, short thick columns, stained glass, shutters, and low horizontal lines.
         (2) Greene and Greene's masterpiece is the ***Gamble House***.
   2. Boston-based designer ***Henry Hobson Richardson***, is considered America's ***father of modern architecture***.
      a. He looked to the ***Romanesque*** churches of the Middle Ages for inspiration, using heavy rusticated stone, round arches, towers, and horizontal lines in his work.
      b. The structural and simple aspects of his architecture were combined with the latest advancements in technology.
      c. Richardson is also responsible for designing ***shingle-styled*** houses.

C. ***Art Nouveau*** **(circa 1890-1910)**, was a completely new decorative style considered modern at the time.
   1. It was based on nature and employed organic and animal motifs of all types.
   2. In 1893 in Brussels, Belgian architect ***Victor Horta*** built his exquisite ***Tassel House***, which has become a symbol of Art Nouveau architecture.
   3. The style was popular throughout Europe and America, with various designers interpreting the style in their own manner.
   4. Other important contributors were:

a. French architect and furniture designer ***Hector Guimard.***
b. The whimsical and imaginative designer ***Antonio Gaudi*** in Spain.
c. ***Charles Rennie Mackintosh*** in Scotland who combined aspects of Art Nouveau with a new direction he developed called the ***perpendicular style.***
d. ***Louis Sullivan*** of the Chicago School in America who employed organic motifs for architectural detailing on his buildings.
e. ***Louis Comfort Tiffany***, who is considered one of America's greatest designers in the Art Nouveau style is especially known for his exquisite stain-glass windows, lamps and vases.

D. ***The Chicago School*** claimed as its principal members early modern architects ***Louis Sullivan*** and ***Frank Lloyd Wright***, two leaders who introduced new ideas for home and commercial design.

III. PRINCIPAL MODERN MOVEMENTS (Twentieth Century)

A. ***Organic Architecture (Circa 1894 to present)*** In 1892, ***Frank Lloyd*** Wright broke with Sullivan and set up his own practice in Oak Park, Illinois, where he designed over 35 homes in his ***Prairie style*** employing organic architecture.

1. ***Falling Water*** (1936), is considered his greatest residential masterpiece.
2. The fundamental principles of organic architecture continue to be a prominent modern design direction and include the following characteristics:
   - O House and site coexist harmoniously; ***"a house should grow out of the*** land ", natural materials compatible with site are used.
   - O Frankly revealed structural members, simple geometric ornamentation, if any.
   - O Planning arranged from inside to outside with spatial flexibility (open planning); fireplace functions as heart of home.
   - O Large spacious balconies and terraces with wide overhanging eaves
   - O Horizontal emphasis and asymmetrical composition

B. ***The International Style (Turn of Century to Present)*** :

1. At the turn of the century, roots of the International Style - a style entirely contrary to Wright's organic architecture - were evidenced primarily through the efforts of a few major design groups in Europe:
   a. ***The Secession (circa 1897-1903)*** was a radical design movement founded by ***Otto Wagner, Josef Maria Olbrich, Josef Hoffmann*** and others in Vienna, Munich, and Berlin.
      (1) Their motto was ***"to each time its art, and to each art its freedom."***
      (2) In 1903, Hoffmann and others set up a more formal workshop named

the ***Wiener Werkstatte*** in Vienna.

(3) The structural and geometrical architecture and furnishings of this group highly influenced the International Style.

b. ***De Stijl (1917-1931)*** in Holland was a group of extremists who felt all design should be reduced to basic design elements:

(1) the use of only red, blue, yellow, black, gray, and white
(2) total abstraction
(3) smooth shiny surfaces
(4) compositions at right angles

Leaders included ***Theo van Doesburg*** , (founder), ***Piet Mondrian*** , and ***Gerrit Rietveld.***

c. *The Bauhaus (1919-1933),* was an experimental design school founded by architect and designer, ***Walter Gropius*** in Weimar, Germany, for the purpose of unifying art and technology.

(1) The Bauhaus concentrated on applying practical artisanship to solve industrial problems characterized by an economy of design and geometric proportion.
(2) Leaders include: ***Marcel Breuer*** and ***Ludwig Mies van der Rohe***

d. ***Le Corbusier*** who worked out of his Paris studio, is considered a giant of modern architecture in the International Style.

e. ***Features of the International Style*** . The International Style, a term coined by ***Philip Johnson*** and ***Henry Russell Hitchcock*** in the 1930s, firmly established a discipline based on functionalism and purity of line. Major features include:

- Basically simple design; ornamentation, if employed, generally geometric or abstract.
- Flat roof, emphasis on the horizontal line, today, vertical, curved , and diagonal lines often used.
- Common materials: reinforced concrete, stucco, steel, and glass; exterior and interior walls usually have stark white finish.
- House designed to contrast with nature rather than blend with surroundings.
- Asymmetrical composition usually dominant.
- Continuous wall surfaces, often combined with large openings and panes of glass.
- Open floor plan.
- Clearly expressed function.

f. ***Art Deco (circa 1920s-1940)*** : During the 1920s and 1930s, a new decorative style flourished based on numerous design influences.

(1) The Art Deco style was introduced on a grand scale at the Paris

Exhibition in 1925.

(2) Outstanding architects and furniture designers include: ***Eliel Saarinen Paul Frankl, Jacques-Emile Ruhlmann*** and ***Donald Deskey***

(3) Major features of the Art Deco style include:

- O Romantic, glamorous, sleek, exotic, and whimsical in expression, with strong contrasts; sophisticated, yet naive
- O Unusual and luxurious materials, often with shiny surfaces
- O Influence of industry, technology, and International Style
- O Use of red, black, gray, white, silver, pink, mauve, and many grayed colors
- O Strong geometric forms including the pyramid, ziggurat, zigzag, and sunburst motifs
- O Palm tree, Egyptian figures, motifs borrowed from ancient cultures
- O Influence of the glamorous cinema and Broadway theater
- O Men and women wearing the latest fashions used as motifs

C. ***Post-World War II Modernism.*** After World War II, although the Organic and International Styles continued to be popular, new architecture directions emerged as a number of individualists in America and Europe inspired new designs. Some primary directions and current expression include:

1. The work of ***Charles and Ray Eames*** include their revolutionary innovations in chair forms.
   a. They pioneered chairs constructed of molded plywood. The ***Eames lounge*** is most notable.
   b. They also developed structures using industrial components made of steel that are considered early examples of what is now known as ***High Tech*** architecture.
2. ***Eero Saarinen*** quickly gained an international reputation after World War II for his sculptural furniture and structures
   a. Outstanding designs include the ***Womb chair, Pedestal chair, TWA Terminal, The St. Louis Memorial Arch*** , and ***Dulles Airport.***
3. ***Richard Buckminster Fuller*** was an important engineer, architect, and educator who contributed revolutionary theories to modern design.
   a. Fuller developed a type of construction he called the ***geodesic dome.***
4. ***Brutalism*** developed during the 50s and 60s as a reaction to the International Style.
   a. It is characterized by massive structures that are often sculptural, with raw concrete surfaces.
   b. Leading designers include ***Paul Rudolph*** and ***Louis Kahn.***
5. ***Classic Modernism*** is a style that incorporates simplified and elegant structural designs influenced by ancient Greece and Rome and interpreted in

modern terms.
   a. Delicate and "pretty" architecture, often with lacy concrete blocks, slender columns, and a white finish.
   b. Architect ***Edward Durell Stone*** spearheaded this direction. His ***John F. Kennedy Center*** is an excellent example.
6. ***Scandinavian Style***. ***Alvar Aalto***, Finland's master architect and furniture designer, was particularly influential in spreading modern ideas from Scandinavia to the United States
   a. This style is a compatible blend of Organic and International styles. Simple structural white surfaces complemented with the use of natural materials are typical.
7. ***Post-Modern Style***. By the late 1960s, Post-Modern architecture began to borrow from the early modernists, whose principles were combined with new creative designs and modern technology.
   a. Post-Modern architecture often rejects the International Style and borrows freely from the past, but in extreme contemporary terms.
   b. Some leading architects include ***Michael Graves, Robert Stern***, and ***Philip Johnson.***
8. ***Freestyle Movement (1980s to present)*** emerged in California. Architects with diverse - and often contradictory-approaches - are involved. The basic elements of Freestyle seek (1) to combine American and European architectural styles with local California design to create a livable environment and (2) to enrich the routine of daily living through various textures, colors, and expressive form. An outstanding leader is ***Frank Gehry.***
9. ***High Tech Style (1970s to present)*** became popular during the 1970s.
   a. The High Tech approach utilizes frankly exposed industrial units, construction elements, and mechanical systems.
   b. Architectural structures are often punctuated with bright primary colors.
   c. Utility and function are evident in the use of the latest materials and technology.
   d. ***Richard Rodgers*** and ***Renzo Piano's Pompidou Center*** in Paris is an important example.
10. ***Modern Italian Design***. After World War II, Italy emerged as a world leader in the field of modern design, bringing fresh new ideas and uses of materials and technology.
   a. The Italians are particularly noted for exploring the potential of plastics for furniture design coupled with creative and imaginative use of form, color, and texture.
   b. ***Gio Ponti, Luigi Nervi, Joe Columbo,*** and ***Vico Magistretti*** are

a few of the outstanding Italian designers.

11. ***Crafts Revival (1970s to present)*** is a movement based on the Arts and Crafts ideals of the late nineteenth century and demonstrates the revitalization of handcraft skills.
    a. ***John Makepeace, Wendell Castle***, and ***Sam Maloof*** are major contributors.
12. ***Memphis Style (1981 to present)*** arose primarily in Italy, and was spearheaded by ***Ettore Sottsass***.
    a. Complete freedom in the use of color, texture, and form.
13. ***Deconstructivism*** is an architectural direction that emerged in the late 1980s to express an extreme reaction to the negative aspects of current society.
    a. Architecture and design are depicted with irregular, unpredictable, and even partly demolished forms.
14. ***Looking to the Future***. Currently, architects are exploring new concepts and philosophies in an attempt to design buildings that meet the needs of a changing society.

D. ***The Traditional Japanese House.*** The traditional Japanese house has contributed much to the modern style of architecture, especially to the mass-produced prefabricated house.

1. ***Frank Lloyd Wright*** was instrumental in introducing this style to the United States. **General characteristics** include:
    - Simplicity of line and form
    - Most often constructed of wood and other natural materials
    - Close connection to outdoors
    - Open planning with ***fusuma*** screen partitions
    - Materials left in natural state, little, if any, ornamentation
    - Predominance of horizontal lines
    - Unpretentious facade with frequent retaining walls
    - Sloping, protective overhangs with hipped and gabled roof
    - Natural stone foundation supporting post and roof
    - Avoidance of symmetry
    - Honest expression of basic structure
    - Feeling of serenity and refinement
    - Universal use of a uniform module and the ***tatami mat***
    - ***Tokonoma*** functions as a focal point
    - Window treatment is the ***shoji*** screen
    - Both house and garden elements symbolic

E. ***Chinese Influence in Western Interiors***. Many western designers have drawn inspiration from Chinese motifs, colors, furnishings, and accessories to

create interiors that reflect aspects of China's unique style and culture.
Outstanding features include:

- Motifs such as fret designs, exotic flowers and birds, pagodas, dragons, and human figures.
- Accessories such as the coromandel screen, porcelain, jade, brass, ivory, and religious statues.
- Colors: black, gold, red-orange, jade, and peacock blue
- Shiny lacquered finishes.
- Brass hardware with distinctively Chinese designs.

IV. CURRENT TRENDS:

A. Because of inflation, high interest rates, the need for energy conservation, smaller families, and changes in lifestyles, a number of significant changes in the demands of the building market have occurred.

- Buyers are better educated.
- Buyers want optimum balance of value and cost.
- Buyers are interested in saving energy.
- Buyers place a high value on prestigious locations.
- Living units must suit a variety of lifestyles
- Buyers place a high priority on security
- Buyers want homes with low maintenance

B. ***Trends in Residential and Nonresidential Design***

1. ***Environmentally Responsible Interior Spaces*** - the materials and furnishings of an interior can have an immediate effect on the health and welfare of the occupants.
2. ***Greening of Interiors*** - concerns include air quality, waste management, recycling, and the use of nontropical woods.
3. ***The Smart House*** - is "intelligent" because of its electronic devices that are capable of serving a myriad of needs.
4. **Housing Forecasts:**
   - Fewer single-family homes with be built in subdivisions
   - Living spaces will be smaller
   - Enclosed architectural volume will be utilized to make spaces flexible
   - Although rooms will be fewer, some will be larger
   - Floor plans will be influenced by changing lifestyles
   - More utilization of factory-made components
   - Buyers will have more building options
   - Security will be given a high priority
   - New product advances will be used to save labor, energy, maintenance, etc.

V. OPTIONS FOR PROSPECTIVE HOME OWNERS IN THE 1990s

A. A wide variety of options are available for the prospective home owner today:
1. ***The Custom Designed House***
2. ***The Predesigned Home Plan***
3. ***The Factory-Built (Prefabricated) House***
4. ***Shell Framing***
5. ***The Tract House***
6. ***The Condominium***
7. ***Remodeling and Restoring a House***

VI. THE ENERGY - EFFICIENT HOUSE:

A. The principal challenge that architects and builders will continue to face in the 1990s is the conservation of energy.
1. ***The Solar House*** is built to capture the sun's energy and conserve conventional fuel. Two major systems are:
   a. ***The Passive Solar Energy System***
   b. ***The Active Solar Energy System***

B. The idea of an ***Earth - Sheltered House*** dates back to prehistoric times.
1. The house type has some advantages and many disadvantages. Because of the disadvantages the earth-sheltered house has not been significantly developed during the 1990s.

VII. LOOKING TO THE FUTURE:

A. 1. A continuing preference for authentic historical styles
2. New materials, technology, and adaptations incorporated into period styles
3. A demand for homes with more open and livable space
4. A decrease in the popularity of solar houses
5. New expressions of the modern style in form, color, and materials
6. An increase in home restoration and renovation
7. A challenge to design more affordable houses
8. Smaller but more efficiently planned homes
9. Incorporation of better insulation elements
10. More two-, three-, and four-plex houses massed together
11. A larger condominium market
12. A strong move to suburban areas
13. A challenge to design "environmentally friendly" structures

LEARNING ENHANCEMENT OPTIONS

Beginnings of Modernism: Discuss with students the contribution made by designers who rebelled against nineteenth-century eclecticism. What contributions were made by the Shakers later helped shape the philosophy of modernism. Review the significance of the Industrial Revolution and its impact on modern design movements. Discuss the developments in furniture design made by Michael Thonet. Demonstrate these contributions through the use of visual materials.

Principal Early Modern Movements (Latter Half of Nineteenth Century): Discuss with the students the concepts of the Arts and Crafts Movement in England and America, Art Nouveau, and The Chicago School. Who were the important leaders of these movements? What are typical design approaches used? Support these principal early modern movements with visual material.

Principal Modern Movements (Twentieth Century): Discuss the concepts, leaders, and design features of ***Organic Architecture*** and the ***International Style*** (The Seccession, De Stijl, the Bauhaus, and Le Corbusier contributions). Show examples of both Organic and International Style exteriors and interiors. Compare the design philosophies of each architectural approach. Review the ***Art Deco style*** and show visual examples of this popular 1920s and 1930s style and how it has been modified for today's residential and nonresidential design. Show examples of restored movie houses and other Art Deco structures found throughout the United States.

Discuss the contributions to modern design by ***Charles and Ray Eames, Eero Saarinen,*** and ***Buckminster Fuller.*** Ask the students to define "***brutalism***" and who the leading designers are who promoted this approach.

Review the features of ***Classic Modernism, the Scandinavian Style, the Post-Modern Style, the Freestyle Movement, High Tech Style, Modern Italian Design, the Crafts Revival, Memphis Style,*** and ***Deconstructivism.*** Show a number of examples showing exterior and interior design for each style.

Discuss the ***Traditional Japanese House*** and its adaptation in the Western world. Help students to appreciate the ***Chinese Influence*** in Western Interiors. Show visual material to demonstrate Oriental influences in American residential and nonresidential interiors.

Current Trends: Discuss significant changes in the current demands of the building market. Review the seven points indicated in the text. Discuss what is meant by "environmentally responsible" interior spaces. How can this be achieved? Ask students to relate the meaning of "greening of interiors" and the "smart house." What are some of the housing forecasts for the 1990s?

Options for Prospective Home Owners in the 1990s: List the basic options available for those considering home ownership. Discuss the advantages and disadvantages of each option.

The Energy-Efficient House: Discuss with the students the principal challenge that architects and builders face regarding conservation of energy. What are some of the most efficient building solutions and the advantages and disadvantages of each option?

Looking to the Future: Ask the students to list and consider housing alternatives for the next decade. What are some new design expressions, building materials, technological advances and creative solutions to housing requirements?

Test Questions

Multiple Choice:

__C__ 1. During the 1880s, many designers rebelled against eclecticism and enslavement to the past - a reaction first seen in:
A. The United States
B. Chicago
C. Europe
D. Paris

__D__ 2. This designer developed a process for bending thin strips of wood into fanciful curved forms for furniture construction:
A. Gustav Stickley
B. Philip Webb
C. Charles Francis Annesley Voysey
D. Michael Thonet

__A__ 3. The founder of the Arts and Crafts Movement was:
A. William Morris
B. Henry Greene
C. Michael Thonet
D. Victor Horta

__C__ 4. The Bungalow and Shingle styles were made popular by:
A. Henri van de Velde
B. Charles F.A. Vosey
C. Greene & Greene
D. William Morris

__B__ 5. He used rough blocks of stone, round arches and Romanesque features:
A. Charles Rennie Mackintosh
B. Henry Hobson Richardson
C. William Morris
D. Philip Webb

__D__ 6. He published *The Craftsman* at the turn of the nineteenth century:
A. Henry Greene
B. Victor Horta
C. Charles Rennie Mackintosh
D. Gustav Stickley

__A__ 7. He designed the Tassel House, a symbol of Art Nouveau architecture:
A. Victor Horta
B. Henri van de Velde
C. Hector Guimard
D. Samuel Bing

__C__ 8. This designer combined aspects of Art Nouveau with the perpendicular style:
A. Henri van de Velde
B. Frank Lloyd Wright
C. Charles Rennie Mackintosh
D. Antoni Gaudi

__D__ 9. His philosophy was: "A house should grow out of the land."
A. Le Corbusier
B. Mies van der Rohe
C. Louis Sullivan
D. Frank Lloyd Wright

__B__ 10. This member of the Secession designed the famous Palais Stoclet in Brussels:
A. Otto Wagner
B. Josef Hoffmann
C. Josef Maria Olbrich
D. Gerrit Rietveld

__A__ 11. The founder and leader of the De Stijl group in Holland was:
A. Theo van Doesburg
B. Piet Mondrian
C. Gerrit Rietveld
D. Mies van der Rohe

__D__ 12. The Bauhaus was founded in Weimar, Germany by:
A. Marcel Breuer
B. Le Corbusier
C. Mies van der Rohe
D. Walter Gropius

__B__ 13. This Art Deco designer was known for his skyscraper furniture:
A. Jacques-Emile Ruhlmann
B. Paul Frankl
C. Eliel Saarinen
D. Donald Deskey

__C__ 14. Designed the Case Study House and pioneered innovations in chair forms:
A. Eero Saarinen
B. Eliel Saarinen
C. Charles and Ray Eames
D. Paul Rudolph

__A__ 15. He is known for designing a type of construction called the geodesic dome.
A. Buckminster Fuller
B. Paul Rudolph
C. Eero Saarinen
D. Louis Kahn

__B__ 16. Foremost exponent of the Classical Modern style. Designed the JFK Center:
A. Buckminster Fuller
B. Edward Durell Stone
C. Louis Kahn
D. Eero Saarinen

__C__ 17. Famous Post-Modern architect. Designed the Swan and Dolphin hotels at Disneyworld.
A. Paul Rudolph
B. Robert Stern
C. Michael Graves
D. Frank Gehry

__B__ 18. An outstanding leader of the Freestyle design direction is:
A. Charles Eames C. Robert Stern
B. Frank Gehry D. Gio Ponti

__D__ 19. The founder of the Memphis Style was spearheaded by:
A. Luigi Nervi
B. Vico Magistretti
C. Joe Columbo
D. Ettore Sottsass

__A__ 20. Famous Finnish architect and furniture designer who combined the Organic and International Style:
A. Alvar Aalto C. Yuro Kukkapuro
B. Eero Aarnio D. Lars Sonck

True / False:

__F__ 21. The Arts and Crafts Movement sought to create good design for mass production.

__F__ 22. Frank Lloyd Wright is known as "the father of modern American architecture."

__T__ 23. "Less is More" is a famous quote coined by Mies van der Rohe.

__T__ 24. Deconstructivism expresses an extreme reaction to the negative aspects of society.

__F__ 25. The "traditional" Japanese house has not particularly influenced modern architecture in America.

A. Arts and Crafts Movement C. Secession
B. Art Nouveau D. De Stijl

__C__ 26. Radical design movement in Vienna. "To each time its art, and to each art its freedom," was their motto.

__B__ 27. Decorative style based on nature - especially the lines in nature.

__A__ 28. Rejected modern society. Found inspiration in the Middle Ages.

__D__ 29. All design efforts reduced to basic design elements. "Neoplasticism."

A. Bauhaus
B. Art Deco
C. Classic Modern
D. Scandinavian Design

__D__ 30. A compatible blend of Organic and International Style. (White painted surfaces and wood detailing)

__A__ 31. Experimental design school that helped promote the International Style.

__C__ 32. Simplified and "pretty" design influenced by ancient Greece.

__B__ 33. Glamorous cinema, jazz age, and ancient Egypt were major inspirations.

A. Post-Modern
B. Freestyle
C. High Tech
D. Brutalism
E. Memphis

__A__ 34. May borrow from earlier modern styles. Borrows freely from the past.

__B__ 35. Emerged in Claifornia. Diverse and often contradictory approaches.

__D__ 36. Paul Rudolph and Louis Kahn are leading exponents. Exposed concrete.

__C__ 37. Frankly exposed industrial components, punctuated with bright colors.

__E__ 38. Radical design approach from Italy emerged in 1981.

A. Shoji
B. Tokonoma
C. Fusuma
D. Tatami

__B__ 39. A sacred niche and focal point in the Japanese home.

__C__ 40. Interior sliding partitions in the Japanese home or public setting.

__A__ 41. Modular designed rice paper windows used for Japanese structures.

__D__ 42. The 3 ft. by 6 ft. grass mat used in the Japanese environment.

Essay / Short Answer:

43. Discuss the beginnings of modernism during the nineteenth century. What were the major developments. Who were the leading contributors and what was their design approach?

Answer to this question is found on pages 388 to 393.

44. Compare the characteristics of Frank Lloyd Wright's Organic architecture with the characteristics of the International Style. What conclusions can be made? Discuss the Art Deco style as a major decorative approach during the 1920s and 1930s and its relationship to the International Style.

Answers to these questions are found on pages 393 to 400.

45. Outline and define ten primary directions or current expressions of design developed since the end of World War II (ca. 1945 to the 1990s).

Answer to this question is found on pages 400 through 405.

46. Briefly discuss the Japanese traditional house and its impact on Western design. List the general characteristics of the Japanese house and interior.

Answer to these questions are found on pages 405 and 406.

47. Briefly discuss Chinese influences in Western Interiors. What are a few features and items of Chinese design that are particularly favored by Western designers?

Answer to this question is found on page 407.

48. Outline the seven basic options for prospective home owners in the 1990s. Provide relavant information under each option.

Answer to this question is found on pages 409 through 413.

49. Discuss the challenge of energy-efficient structures that architects and builders continue to face in the 1990s. What are some solutions?

Answer to this question is found on page 413.

50. Housing alternatives during the past few decades have encompassed many new design expressions, materials, technological advances, and creative solutions. What trends for the future are outlined in the text?

Answer to this question is found on page 413.

EDUCATIONAL RESOURCES

Publications:

Anscombe, Isabelle. *Arts and Crafts Style.* New York: Rizzoli, 1991.
Bangert, Albrecht. *Eighties Style: Designs of the Decade.* Abeeville Press, Inc., 1990.
Bush, Donald J. *The Streamlined Decade.* New York: George Braziller, 1975.
Clark, Robert Judson (ed.). *Arts and Crafts Movement in America, 1876-1916.* Princeton, NJ.: Princeton University Press, 1972.
Duncan, Alastair. *American Art Deco.* N.Y.: Harry M Abrams, Inc., 1986.
________*New House Book.* New York: Random House, Villard Books, 1985.
Emery, Marc. *Furniture by Architects.* New York: Harry N. Abrams, 1983.
Fehrman, Cherie, and Kenneth Fehrman. *Post-War Interior Design. 1945-1960.* New York: Van Nostrand Reinhold, 1986.
Gaynor, Elizabeth. *Scandinavia Living Design.* N.Y.: Stewart, Tabori & Chang, 1987.
Hitchcock, Henry-Russell, and Philip Johnson. *The International Style.* (1932 Reprint). New York: Norton, 1966.
Horn, Richard. *Memphis: Objects, Furniture, and Patterns.* Phil.: Rushing Press, 1985.
Jaffe, Hans L.C. *De Stijl.* New York: Harry N. Abrams, 1967.
Jencks, Charles. *Architecture Today.* N.Y.: Harry N. Abrams, 1982.
Kron, Joan, and Suzanne Slesin. *High Tech: The Industrial Style and Source Book* for the Home. New York: Clarkson N. Potter, 1978.
Lindahl, Judy. *Energy Saving Decorating.* Judy Lindahl. 1981.
Marinelli, Janet. *The Naturally Elegant Home: Environmental Style.*
McFadden, David. *Scandinavian Modern Design.* New York: Harry N. Abrams, 1982.
Naylor, Gillian. *The Bauhaus.* New York: Dutton, 1968.
Neuhart, John, *Eames Design.* New York: Harry Abrams, Inc. 1989.
Page, Marian. *Furniture Designed by Architects.* NY.: Whitney Library of Design, 1980.
Pevsner, Nikolaus. *Pioneers of Modern Design from William Morris to Walter Gropius.* New York: Museum of Modern Art, 1975.
Radice, Barbara. *Memphis.* New York: Rizzoli Int. 1984.
Reed, Ronald J. *The Craftmanship Revival in Interior Design.* Outlet Book Company, Inc. 1991.
Scully, Vincent. *Modern Architecture.* New York: Braziller, 1974.
Russell, Frank, Ed. *Art Nouveau Architecture.* New York: Rizzoli, 1989.

Street-Porter, Tim. *Freestyle: The New Architecture & Interior Design from Los Angeles.* New York: Stewart, Tabori & Chang, Inc. 1986.
_______*Twentieth Century Architecture.* N.Y.: Facts on File, 1991.
Warren, Geoffrey. *Art Nouveau Style.* London: Octopus, 1972.
Wright, David. *Natural Solar Architecture.* N.Y.: Van Nostrand Reinhold, 1984.
Twonmbly, Robert C. *Frank Lloyd Wright.* N.Y.: Wiley, 1979.
Vale, Brenda and Robert. *Green Architecture: Design for the Engery Conscious Future.*
Wharton, Edith & Codman, Ogden, Jr. *The Decoration of Houses.* New York: Norton, W.W., & Co., Inc., 1978

Movies / Videos:

Frank Lloyd Wright : Public Broadcasting Production

CHAPTER 14

INTERIOR DESIGN AS A CAREER

Chapter Focus

Chapter 14 is divided into ten sections that relate to the profession of interior design. These sections include: History of the Interior Design Profession, Responsibilities of an Interior Designer, Working Procedures for the Professional Interior Designer, Preparing for a Career in Interior Design, Opportunities for Interior Designers, Computer Applications for Interior Design, Professional Interior Design Societies, Getting That First Job, Attaining Visibility, and The Interior Designer's Challenge for the Future.

Text Outline

Introduction.

A. ***Definition*** of an interior designer formulated by the NCIDQ:
The professional interior designer is a person qualified by education, experience, and examination, who:
1. Identifies, researches, and creatively solves problems pertaining to the function and quality of the interior environment,
2. performs services relative to interior spaces, including programming, design analysis, space planning, and aesthetics using specialized knowledge of interior construction, building codes, equipment, materials, and furnishings, and
3. prepares all drawings and documents relative to the design of interior spaces in order to enhance and protect the health, safety, and welfare of the public.

I. HISTORY OF THE INTERIOR DESIGN PROFESSION:
The profession interior design is a relatively new profession that evolved primarily during the latter half of the nineteenth century and the early decades of the twenties century, then fully emerge din the decades following World War II.

A. **Early Development of Interior Design.**
1. Authors, moralists, and other early advocates of good design were deeply interested in the relationship of human comfort and well-being incorporated with the effective use of sound principles of design and include:

a. **William Morris** and the Arts and Crafts Movement
b. **Charles Eastlake** who wrote ***Hints on Household Taste.***
c. **Gustav Stickley** who published ***The Craftsman.***
d. Publications: ***Godey's Lady's Book, Harper"s New Monthly, Harper's Bazaar, and Ladies Home Journal.***
e. **Edith Wharton** and **Ogden Codman** wrote ***The Decoration of Houses*** in 1907.
f. **Candace Wheeler** published numerous articles on interior decoration.
g. **W.C. Gannet** wrote articles called ***"The House Beautiful."***
h. Design contributions made by **Frank Lloyd Wright, Greene and Greene** and others.

B. Elsie de Wolfe.

1. One of the most famous individuals to offer interior decorating services to the public in New York at the turn of the century.
2. In 1901, Elsie de Wolfe set herself up in business as "America's first interior decorator."
3. Through her efforts, along with the work of other including **Nancy McClelland, Syrie Maugham, Dorothy Draper, Rose Cummings; and later Billy Baldwin** (known as the ***"Dean of Decorators."***) the profession of interior decorating was firmly established.
4. The female interior decorators became known as ***"the ladies of good taste."***
5. The establishment of professional ***interior design societies*** began in the 1930s.
6. Today there are many prominent professional interior designers.

II. RESPONSIBILITIES OF AN INTERIOR DESIGNER:

A. The professional interior designer is:

1. Required to be proficient in the planning, designing, and implementing of residential and nonresidential design.
2. Qualified to coordinate all elements of design to create functional and aesthetically pleasing living and working environments that fulfil the total needs of the client or user.
3. Trained to make the most of space.
4. Qualified to work with an architect from the initial planning stages to completion.
5. Knowledgeable about and able to appropriately integrate period and contemporary styles of architecture, furniture, and decorative arts.
6. Knowledgeable about furniture, materials and construction.
7. Concerned not only with the immediate effect but also with the construction, durability, and maintenance of fabrics and finishes. Well qualified to select and employ fabrics and textiles for the best performance and appearance as applied

to all aspects of an interior.
8. Knowledgeable about lighting and its effect.
9. Familiar with a broad range of products, and services, and have a good working relationship with those professionals who provide the products and services.
10. Able to draw upon reliable sources to complete a design project.
11. Responsible for the completed project.
12. A good visual and oral communicator.
13. Able to incorporate artistry and expertise with the client's purposes and objectives within the bounds of good taste.
14. An effective salesperson.
15. A person with attributes including enthusiasm, imagination, curiosity, perceptual skills, sociability, keen insight, respect for time commitments, and organizational and record-keeping skills.

III. WORKING PROCEDURES FOR THE PROFESSIONAL INTERIOR DESIGNER:

A. Outline of the **basic elements involved**:
1. Workspace
2. Contract of agreement.
3. Programming.
4. Presentation to the client.
5. First-step drawings.
6. Final detailed drawings.
7. Presentation to the client for final approval.
8. Blueprints or "construction drawings."
9. Estimates and bids.
10. Scheduling the project.
11. Purchase the necessary materials.
12. Supervision of all major aspects of the design project.
13. Supervision of the final details.
14. Evaluation.

B. **Fee Systems.** Interior designers are compensated for their services in a number of ways:
1. Flat or fixed fee.
2. Hourly fee.
3. Cost plus fee.
4. A fee based on the total square feet of the project.
5. Percentage of the total project expenditure.

IV. PREPARING FOR A CAREER IN INTERIOR DESIGN:

A. One of the initial steps toward becoming a professional interior designer is to successfully complete an interior design program. Education includes training in such areas as:

1. Visual, written, verbal, and graphic communication skills, as well as drafting skills and preparation of a portfolio.
2. Theory, elements, and principles of design.
3. Development of knowledge about building and interior support systems and building codes, textiles, lighting, materials, and barrier-free design.
4. Programming and planning, interior component selection, furniture layout, space planning, and cost estimates.
5 History of art, architecture, interiors, and furnishings.
6. Business practices and principles.
7. Human factors and ergonomics.
8. Product design and construction.

Internship experience is invaluable to the student. Students:

1. Experience operational procedures, policies, and various phases of design.
2. Learn to be open to new and different attitudes and perspectives in all aspects of design.
3. Learn more about themselves in terms of potential future desires and goals as a professional interior designer.
4. Acquire valuable experience that can be entered on a job resume for use after graduation.

A. Licensing and Registering.

1. Basically, there are two types of licensing acts:
   a. A ***title act*** protects those who are competent to use particular "titles" that pertain to the profession of interior design.
   b. A ***practice act*** requires those who qualify as professional interior designers and plan to practice this occupation to register with a state board.

B. National Council for Interior Design Qualifications.

1. ***NCIDQ*** organization was formed in 1972 to establish a professional level of competence for interior designers.
2. Level of competence is determined through an examination.
3. Another purpose of NCIDQ is to investigate the advantages and disadvantages of pursing legal registration or certification of the profession.
4. The examination, offered twice a year at various location around the country, consists of two parts given on two consecutive days: the (1) ***academic section*** and a (2) ***conceptual solution to a realistic design problem***

V. OPPORTUNITIES FOR INTERIOR DESIGNERS:

Career opportunities open to professional interior designers fall into two general categories:

A. **Residential Design:**
   1. Involves the designing of **private living quarters or homes**, including detached houses, apartments, condominiums, town houses, dormitories, and mobile homes.

B. **Nonresidential Design:**
   1. Nonresidential design, also known as contract or commercial design, is not related to private living spaces. General categories include:
      a. **Office design.**
      b. **Government and public buildings.**
      c. **Retail design.**
      d. **Health care.**
      e. **Entertainment design.**
      f. **Hospitality design.**
      g. **Financial institutions.**
      h. **Recreation.**
      i. **Industrial design.**
      j. **Institutional design.**
      k. **Transportation.**

C. **Specialized Design:**
   1. A designer may focus on specific design-related projects:
      a. **Rendering designer.**
      b. **Set designer.**
      c. **Adaptive reuse designer.**
      d. **Historic preservation and restoration designer.**
      e. **Kitchen designer.**
      f. **Lighting specialist.**
      g. **Color consultant.**
      h. **Interior design educator.**
      i. **Design journalist or photographer.**
      j. **Drafting designer.**
      k. **Buyer.**
   2. There are also additional design specialists areas such as storage, cabinet, and closet design; window treatments; hard floor materials; exhibition design; marketing consultant or representative; wholesale representative; communication design; textile design; design specialist for physically challenged users; model home design; energy conservation; solar home design; and environmental safety design.

VI. COMPUTER APPLICATIONS FOR INTERIOR DESIGN:

A. Some **major tasks** computers are capable of handling include:
   1. **Expediting routine office tasks.**
   2. **Drafting and perspective drawing. (CAD)**
   3. **Aiding in the planning process** with data banks of information readily available.
   4. **Estimating costs.**
   5. **Preparing specifications.**
   6. **Communicating.**
   7. **Ordering.**

B. Computer programs typically come to the user with a basic working capacity.

C. As the computer becomes more adapted to usage in the design world, many innovations are being developed to make the work of the designer and architect more efficient.

D. Being relatively new to the design realm, computers have both pros and cons for use in architecture and interior design.

E. With constant advancements in computer equipment and techniques, training design students is an ongoing process, and it is often necessary for the new employee to receive updated training for the first few weeks on the job.

VII. PROFESSIONAL INTERIOR DESIGN SOCIETIES:

A. **American Society of Interior Designers.**
   1. Is a professional international organization established to enact and maintain standards of excellence to enhance the growing recognition of interior design as a profession.

B. **Institute of Business Designers.** IIDA
   1. IBD is an internationally established organization dedicated to the professional designer those major field is commercial and institutional interiors and products.

C. **Interior Design Society.**
   1. IDS, organized in 1973, is an arm of the ***National Home Furnishings Association*** and provides its members with a variety of sales aids and educational programs.

D. **Interior Design Educators Council.**
   1. IDEC, incorporated in 1967, is dedicated to the development of interior design education.Its purpose is to strive to improve the teaching of interior design.

E. **National Council for Interior Design Qualifications (NCIDQ)**
   (See material presented on page 229)

F. **Other Professional Organizations.**
   (See reference list outlined in text on pages 432 and 433)

VIII. GETTING THAT FIRST JOB:

A. How is that important first job obtained? Possibilities include:
1. Read trade journals, newsletters, and periodicals dealing with the field of interior design.
2. Explore every available source of information, including visits to design offices, agencies and profession organizations
3. Examine personal needs, assets, and weaknesses. Is the **resume** a full and honest representation? Is the **portfolio** a true reflection of the best professional and creative work?
4. Examine your personal appearance carefully and objectively.
5. Approach the potential employer in a positive state of mind. Be polite, articulate, straight-forward, honest, and self-confident, but without arrogance.
6. Point out training, skills, and a genuine desire to be of service to the company.

IX. ATTAINING VISIBILITY:

A. 1. Be proud of and enthusiastic about the profession. Believe in yourself.
2. Put your profession within reach of everyone in the community.
3. Write articles for local newspapers. Express stimulating ideas.
4. Contact local radio stations. They might be interested in presenting a series of daytime lectures on practical interior design problems.
5. Show courtesy and concern for every client encountered, regardless of whether or not a contract is secured.
6. Become involved in preservation and restoration efforts.
7. Participate in national and local professional interior design or related organizations.

X. THE INTERIOR DESIGNER'S CHALLENGE FOR THE FUTURE:

A. In light of the impact professional design and designers have on the economic, social, cultural, and environmental life of our nation, the challenge for the interior designer as a protector of the human environment is significant.
1. Perhaps the first challenge and major responsibility is: ***to design for people*** People take precedence over buildings and interior design.
   a. The most important obligation is to improve the quality of life for everyone.
2. In today's cost-inflated work, profound ***social and economic changes*** are occurring that present new challenges.
3. Designers today and in the future will be challenged with addressing crucial environmental issues. A considerable amount of time during the design process is spent evaluating ***responsible solutions to environmental issues.***
4. ***Technology*** is rapidly making inroads in residential designs. The ***computer market*** and its corresponding technologies are making a direct impact on the

interior design industry.
5. Another challenge to the interior designer is ***preservation and restoration***
6. As design has become more demanding and technical, ***specialists have emerged*** to take over in areas where the interior designer requires particular expertise, such as in lighting, drafting, and computer design.
7. As a practicing professional, the interior designer is compelled to keep abreast of the field through a ***continuing educational process*** in order to serve clients adequately.
8. The future will present many new conditions demanding ***innovative design solutions.*** Constant recycling and renovation of the environment are necessary to meet changing human needs. ***Designers must be masters of change.*** The future can be built on the appreciation of and dedication to preserving the best of the past and combining it with the finest of the present.
9. The challenge for the designers of the future is to ***meet the demands of current and future technological advances while addressing functional and aesthetic needs of society.*** In view of current and future challenges, the services of interior designers are invaluable now and will be in demand even more in the future.

LEARNING ENHANCEMENT OPTIONS:

History of the Interior Design Profession: Discuss with the students how interior design emerged as a separate and distinctive career direction. Review the major developments and contributions made by various individuals who helped establish the profession.

Responsibilities of an Interior Designer: Outline and discuss the fifteen basic responsibilities of a professional interior designer.

Working Procedures for the Professional Interior Designer: Discuss with the students how to establish a successful working procedure combined with creative design solutions and the importance of satisfying the client. Show examples of completed drawings by students or professional interior designers. Discuss fee systems. If possible, schedule a guest interior designer in your area to share “on the job” experiences.

Preparing for a Career in Interior Design: Discuss the initial steps toward becoming a professional interior designer. Outline what areas of training the student can expect in their education. Discuss the two basic types of licensing and provide information about the NCIDQ exams.

Opportunities for Interior Designers: Discuss with the students the career opportunities open to interior designers and outline the two general categories of residential and nonresidential design and types of projects involved with both areas of design. Support this information with visual material. For example, show examples of hotel design, office design and health care facilities as well as examples of private dwelling places.

Computer Applications for Interior Design: Discuss with the students some of the tasks computers are capable of when used for interior design projects. Show examples of computer generated projects.

Professional Interior Design Societies: Discuss with the students importance and function of interior design societies. Outline some of the major societies and the benefits of becoming affiliated with these organizations.

Getting That First Job: Discuss with the students some of the plans and strategies to consider when pursing that first job.

Attaining Visibility: Outline some of the points brought out in the text for attaining visibility. Ask students to present additional ideas.

The Interior Designer's Challenge for the Future: Discuss with the students the impact professional interior designers have on the economic, social, cultural, and environmental life of our nation. Provide personal experiences and have the students relate their ideas regarding this topic.

Test Questions:

(Note to Instructor: Since Chapter 14 is generally used as a reference for students interesting in pursing interior design as a profession, a few essay questions are included here for instructors who test their students regarding this material.)

Essay / Short Answer:

1. Outline the important designers and basic events that have contributed to the evolution of interior design as a separate profession.

Answer to this question is found on pages 418 to 421.

2. What are the principle responsibilities of an interior designer? Discuss the 15 points

7, #5

presented in the text.

Answer to this question is found on pages 421 to 422.

3. What are 14 general working procedures for the professional interior designer?

Answer to this question is found on pages 422 to 425.

4. What steps are necessary when preparing for a career in interior design? What areas of training can a student expect? What are the values of an internship experience?

Answer to this question is found on page 426.

5. List the opportunities for interior designers in both residential and nonresidential design projects. List the general categories for each design type.

Answer to this question is found on page 427.

6. Discuss the 7 points outlined in the text regarding the major tasks computers are capable of handling for the interior designer.

Answer to this question is found on page 429.

7. What is the importance and function of interior design societies? What are some major interior design societies?

Answer to this question if found on page 431 to 433.

8. Briefly discuss some of the planning strategies for "getting that first job."

Answer to this question is found on page 433.

9. What are some of the suggestions outlined in the text an interior designer might consider to attain visibility?

Answer to this question is found on page 433.

10. Discuss the interior designer's challenge for the future. What are some of the points outlined in the text?

Answer to this question if sound on page 434.

Educational Resources

Publications:

Brown, Erica. *Sixty Years of Interior Design* . New York: Viking Press, 1982.

Burdon, Ernest E. *Design Presentation: Techniques for Marketing & Project Presentation.* New York: McGraw-Hill, Inc., 1983.

Burstein, David. *Project Management for the Design Professional.* New York: Watson-Guptill Publishers., Inc., 1991.

Farren, Carol E. *Planning and Managing Interior Projects* . Kingston, Mass., R.S. Means, 1988.

Ferebee, Ann. *A History of Design from the Victorian Era to the Present* . New York: Van Nostrand Reinhold, 1970.

Jones, Frederic H. *The Concise Dictionary of Interior Design* . Crisp Publications, Inc., 1991.

Kirkpatrick, Beverly and James Kirkpatrick. *Autocad for Interior Design and Space Planning*. New York: Macmillan Publishing Co., 1993.

Kleman, Walter B. *The Challenge of Interior Design* . New York: Van Nostrand Reinhold, 1981.

Knackstedt, Mary V. *The Interior Design Business Handbook.* New York: Whitney Library of Design, 1992.

Massey, Anne. *Interior Design of the 20th Century.* New York: Thames and Hudson, 1990.

McCorquodale, Charles. *A History of Interior Decoration* . New York: Vendome Press, 1983.

McLain-Kark, Joan. *The Designer's AutoCAD Tutor*. New York: Van Nostrand Reinhold. 1990.

_______*Means Interior Cost Data* . Mean, R.S., Co., Inc., 1993.

Murphy, Dennis Grant. *The Business Management of Interior Design* . North Hollywood, CA: Stratford House Publishing Company, 1988.

National Council for Interior Design Qualification. *NCIDQ Examination Guide* . NewYork: National Council for Interior Design Qualification, 1989.

Pegram, Kay L. *Marketing & Promotion from A to Z: For Home Fashions Retailers & Interior Designers* . Kaymar Books, 1992.

Pile, John. *Dictionary of 20th Century Design* . New York: Facts on File, 1990.

Piotrowski, Christine. *Interior Design Management: A Handbook for Owners and Managers*. New York: Van Nostrand Reinhold, 1992.

________*Professional Practice for Interior Designers.* New York: Harper & Row, 1987.

Reznikoff, S.C. *Specification for Commercial Interiors* . New York: Whitney Library of Design-Watson Guptill Publications, Inc., 1989.
Siegel, Harry, and Alan Siegel *A Guide to Business Principles and Practices for Interior Designers.* Rev. ed. New York: Whitney Library of Design, 1982.
Smith, S. Jane. *Elsie de Wolfe: A Life in the High Style.* New York: Atheneum, 1982.
Smith, C. Ray. *A History of Interior Design in 20th Century America* . New York: Harper & Row, 1987.
Veitch, Ronald, et al. *Professional Practice* . Winnipeg, Canada: Peguis, 1990.
Wharton, Edith & Codman, Ogden. *The Decoration of Houses* . New York: Norton, W.W., & Co., 1978.
Whitney, Patrick. *Computers in Design* . New York: Random House, Inc., 1985.
Zandi, Martin. *Computer-Aided Design & Drafting* . Delmar Publishers, Inc., 1985.

Movies / Videos:
Careers in Interior Design : 24 min / 1990 / Insight Media
Computer Aided Design : 20 min. / 1986 / Stanfield House

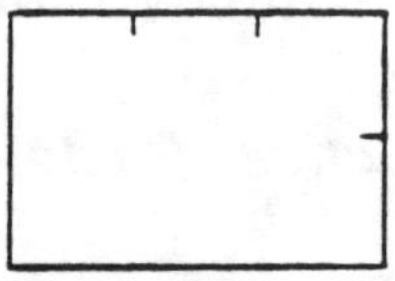

The golden rectangle. The Greek standard for good proportion is a rectangle with its sides in a ratio of 2:3.

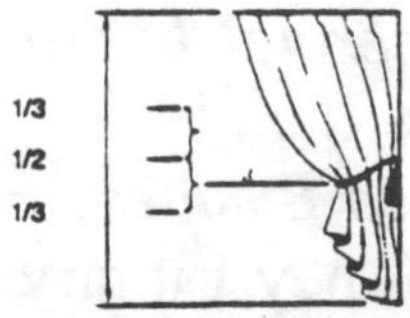

The golden mean. The division of a line somewhere between one half and one third is the most pleasing.

The Parthenon at Athens—based on a mathematical ratio of 1:1.6—fits almost precisely into a golden rectangle. Because of the frequency with which it occurs in the arts, the golden rectangle has mystified experts for centuries.

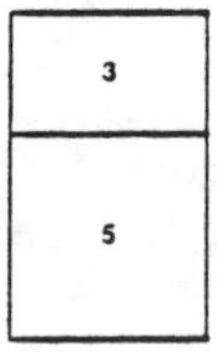

The golden section. 3:5 is roughly the same ratio as 5:8

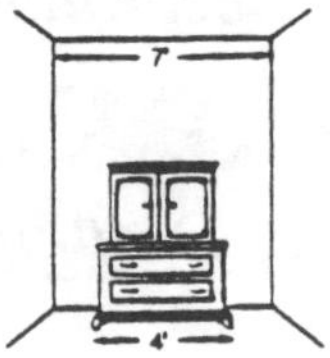

4:7 is a pleasing proportion.

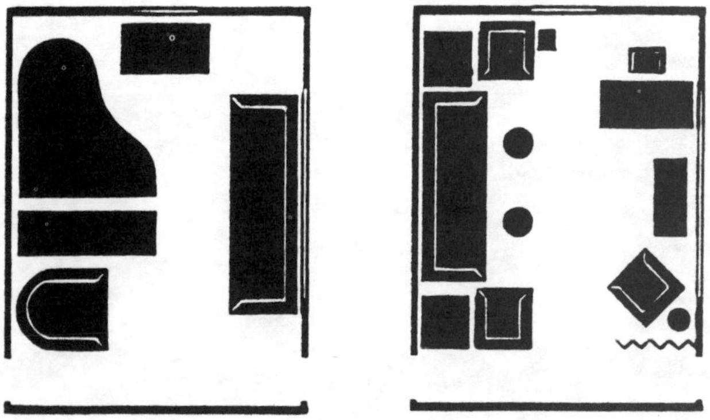

Poor

Better

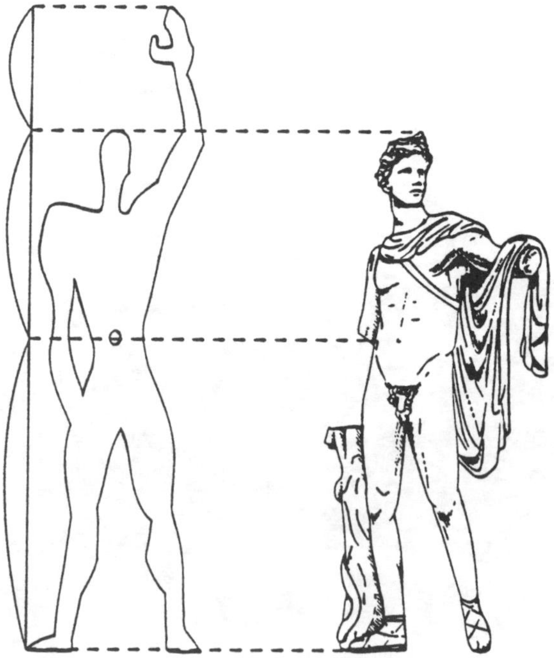

Proportions Discovered by the Ancient Greeks and Applications

ASSIGNMENT

The following assignment is aimed at promoting awareness of the many principles and elements involved in the complete design of a room.

Select a *clear, colored* picture of a living room. The view should be complete, not just a corner of the room. Mount the picture on white paper, allowing a margin sufficiently wide for answering question 1. Write the answers to the remaining questions below the picture.

1. Point out the following by drawing a line from the correct object or objects in the picture to the explanation in the margin:

   An example of structural design

   An example of decorative design

   The use of the golden mean (explain briefly)

   A vertical line

   A horizontal line

   A curved line

   A diagonal line

   An example of bisymmetrical balance (explain briefly)

   An example of asymmetrical balance (explain briefly)

   Rhythm by repetition

   Rhythm by gradation

   Rhythm by opposition

   Rhythm by transition

   Rhythm by radiation

   Rhythm by contrast

2. Is there a predominance of one line, or are lines pleasingly distributed?
3. Are the elements of the room more strong or more delicate, or is neither effect predominant?
4. What kinds of designs are used in the fabrics in the room (e.g., naturalistic, conventional, abstract, geometric)? If the fabrics have no design, point out two specific textures used.
5. What is the focal point of the room? Point out four ways through which elements were used to bring this area into focus (see the section on emphasis).
6. Does the room have a feeling of unity and harmony? Examine the room carefully: backgrounds, furniture, fabrics, and accessories. Point out six specific elements of the room that contribute to the overall feeling of unity (see the section on harmony).
7. Does the lighting appear to be adequate? Are lighting fixtures and lamps artfully and conveniently located?

Make comments specifically related to the picture submitted. Selection and presentation will be considered in evaluating this project.

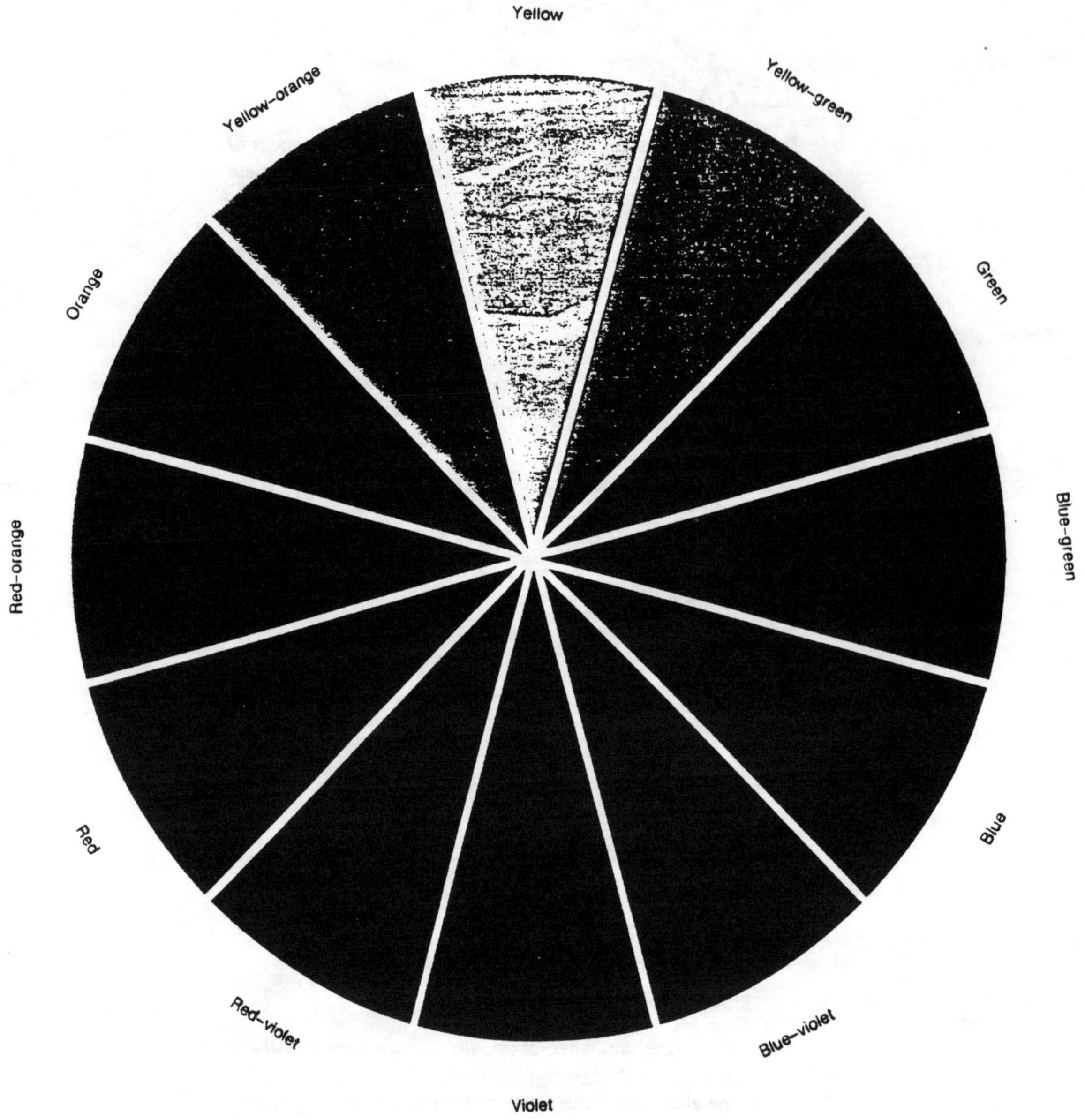

FULL COLOR WHEEL

PRIMARY COLORS

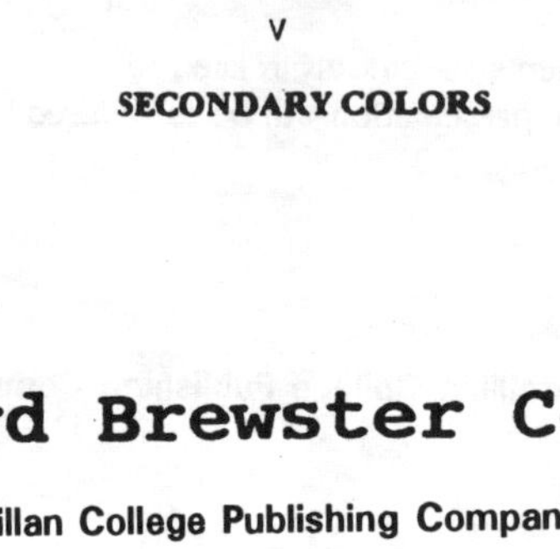

SECONDARY COLORS

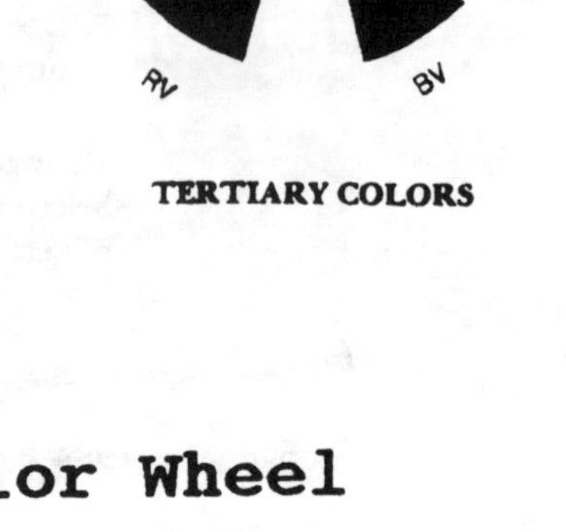

TERTIARY COLORS

The Standard Brewster Color Wheel

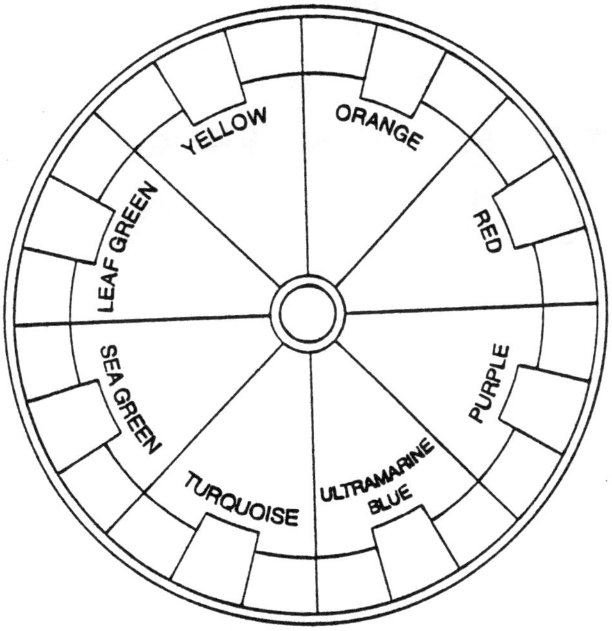

A

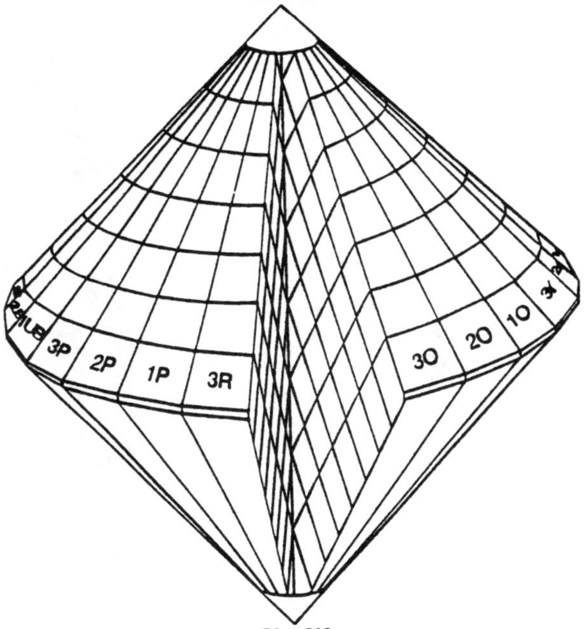

B

The Ostwald Color Wheel and Cone

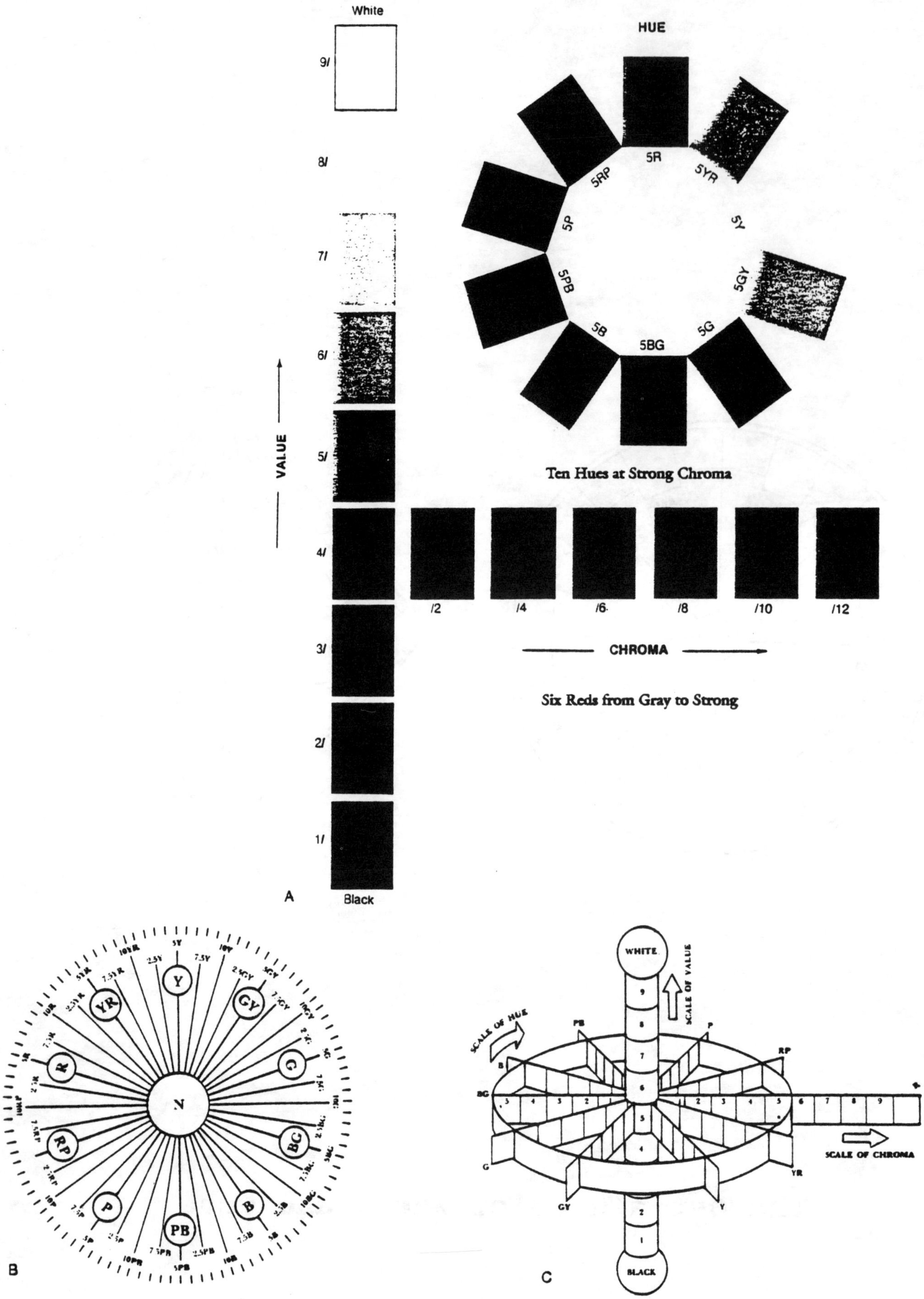

The Munsell Color System

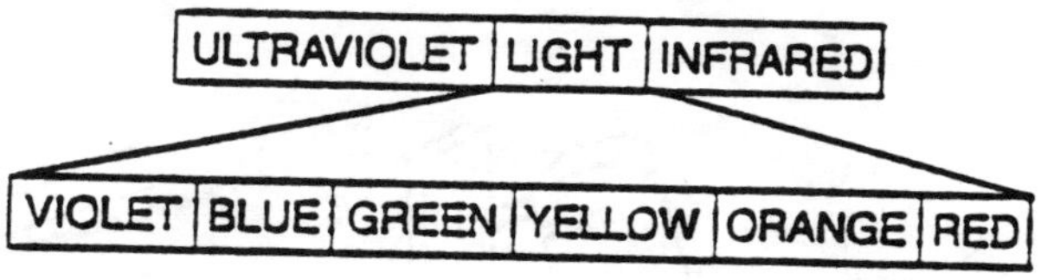

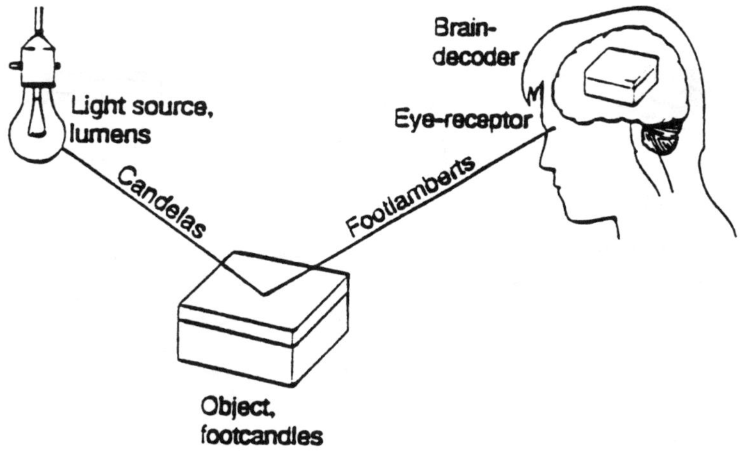

How the Human Eye Sees Color and an Object

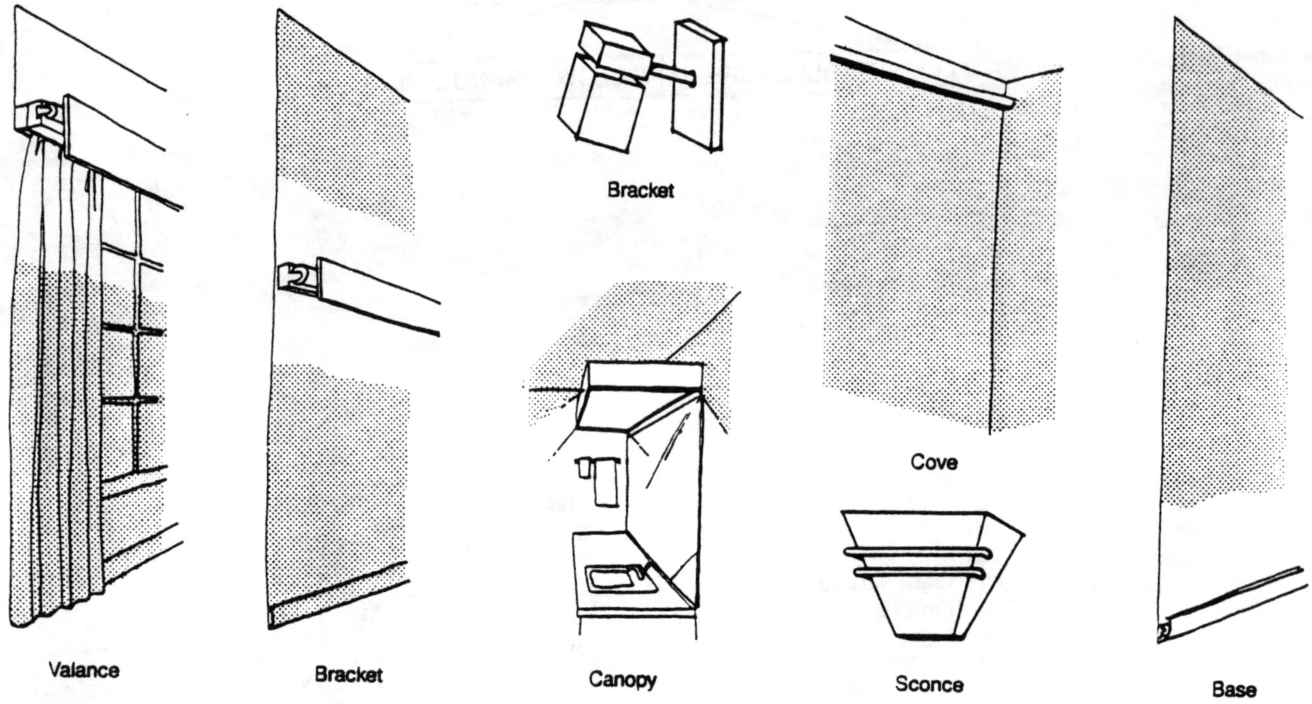

FIGURE 3.19 Common types of wall-mounted fixtures.

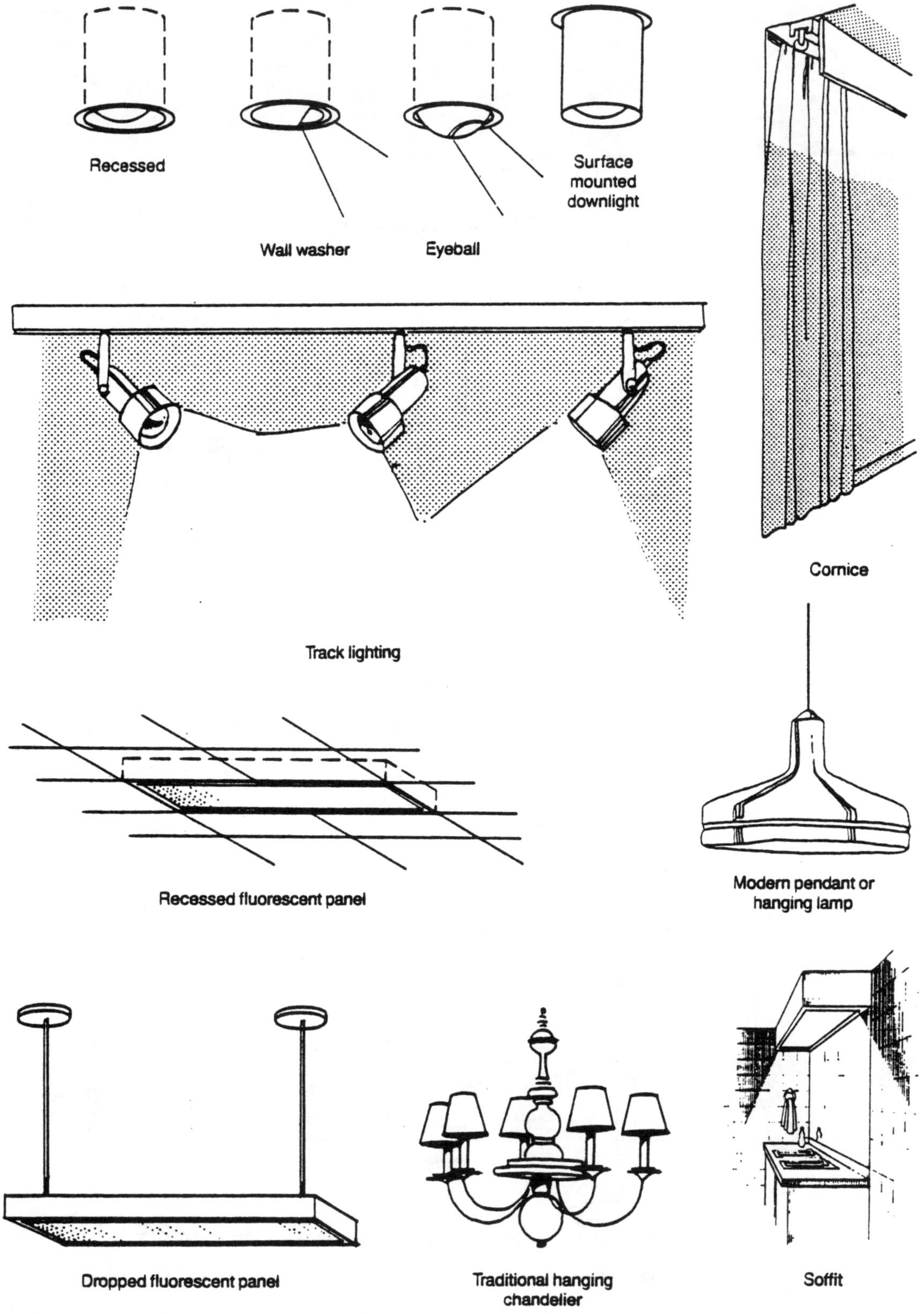

FIGURE 3.20 Common types of ceiling-mounted fixtures.

FIGURE 3.25 Typical portable or standing lamp styles.

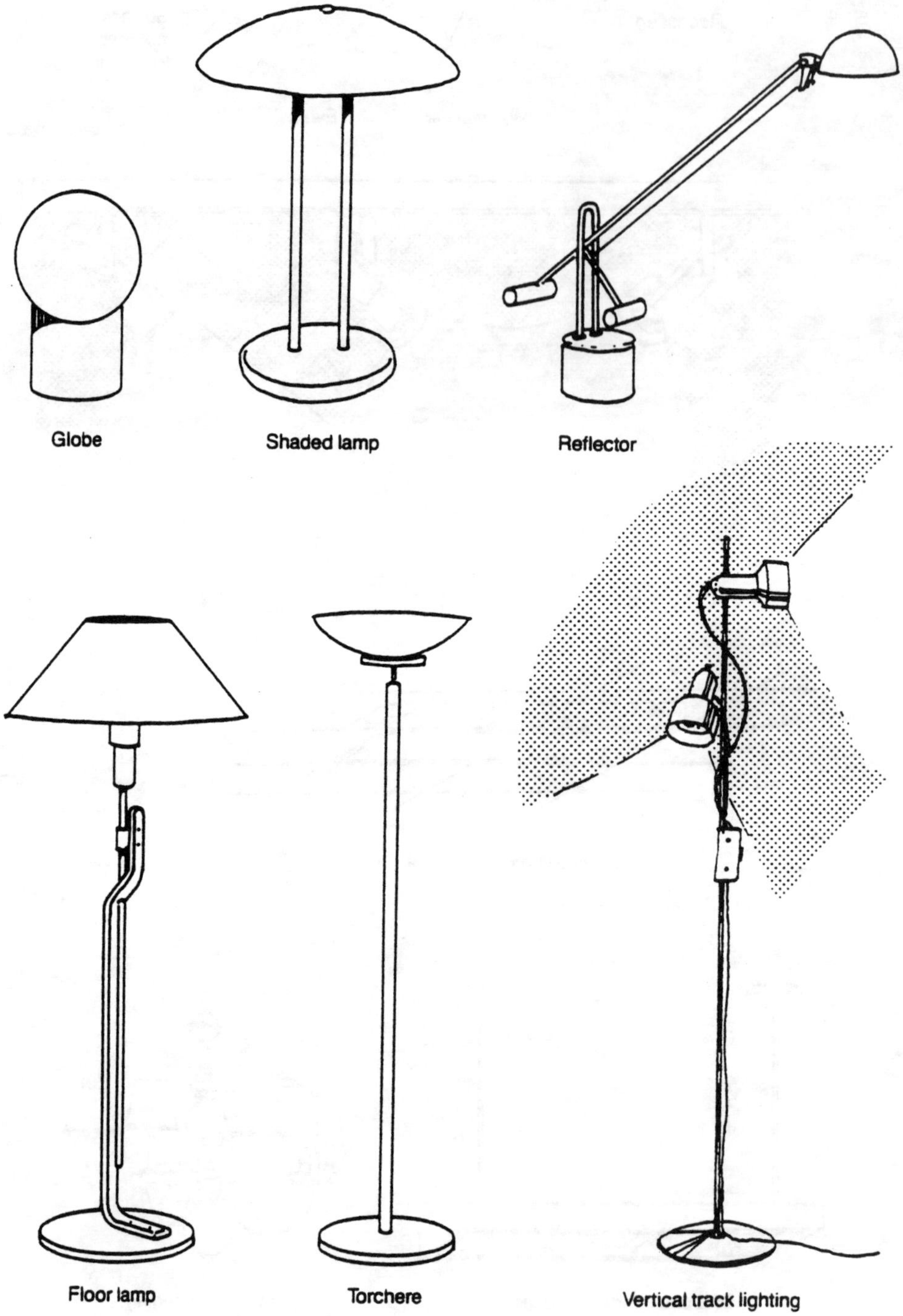

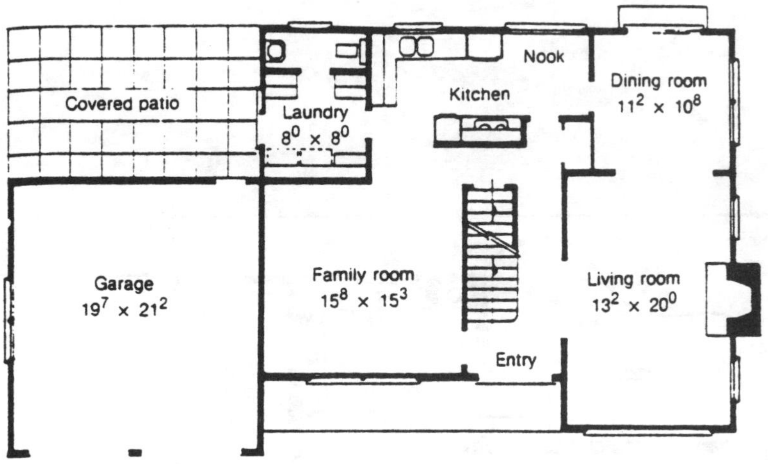

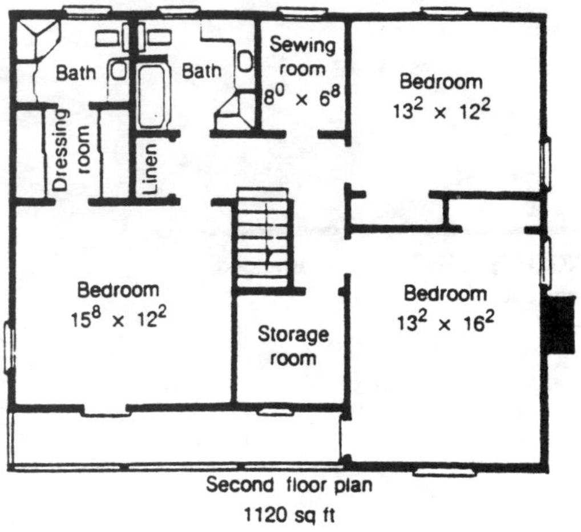

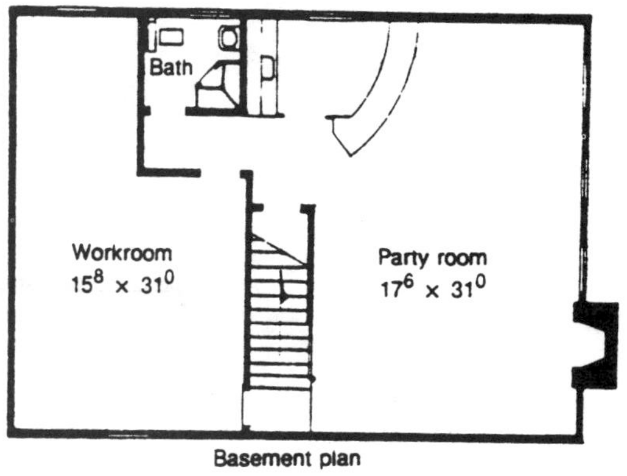

FIGURE 4.32 A well-arranged two-story plan. (Courtesy of Home Building Plan Services.)

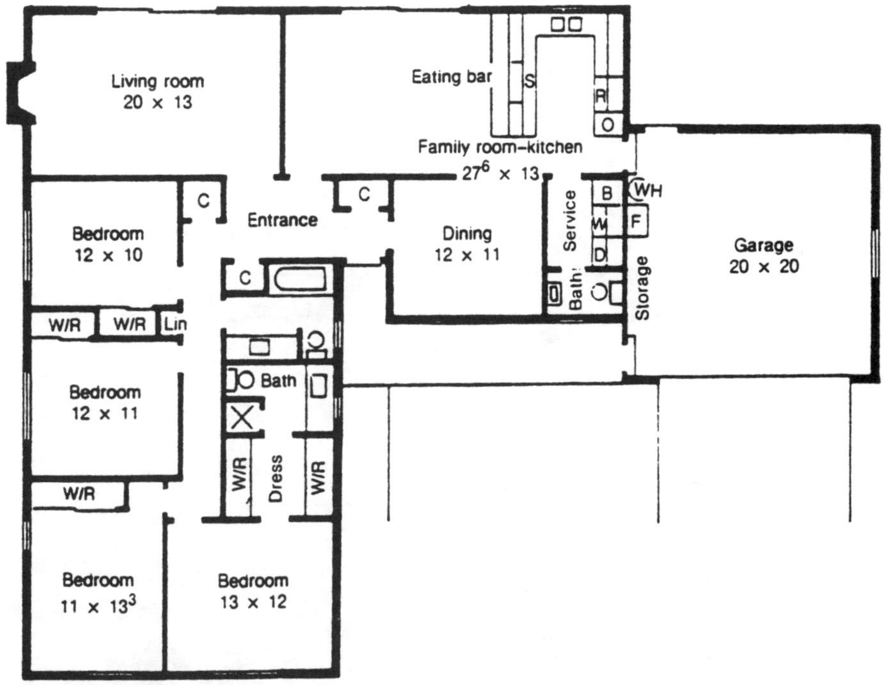

FIGURE 4.33 An economical L-shaped plan.

Floor Plan A

FIGURE 4.36 A poorly arranged floor plan.

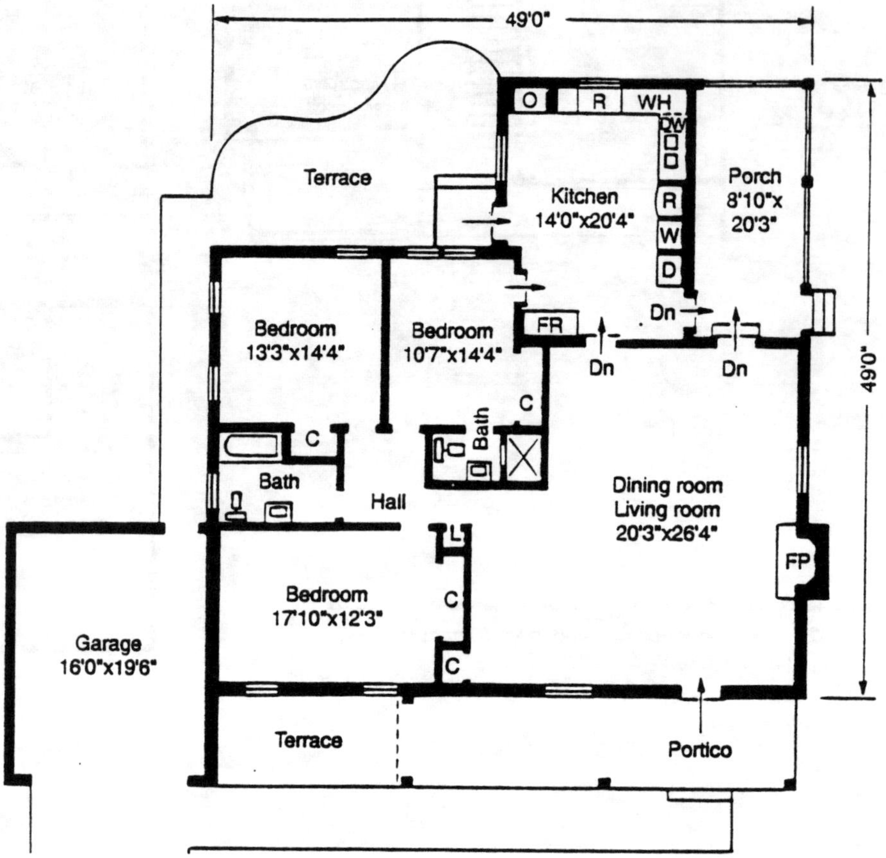

Floor Plan B

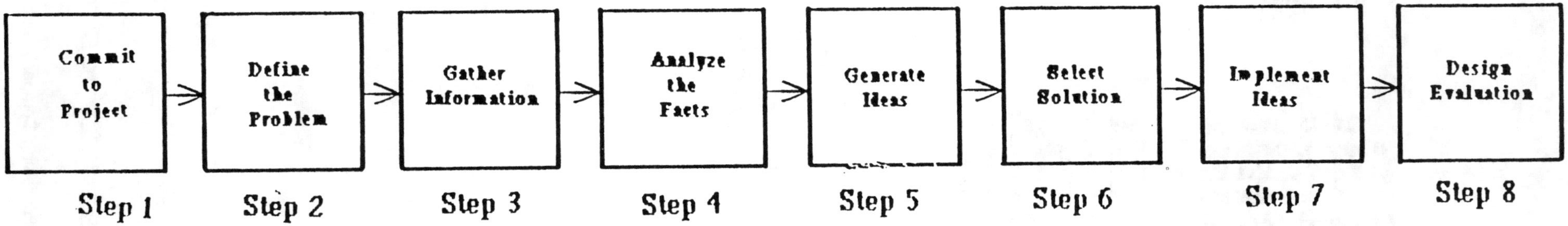

BASIC STEPS INVOLVED IN PROGRAMMING AND THE DESIGN PROCESS

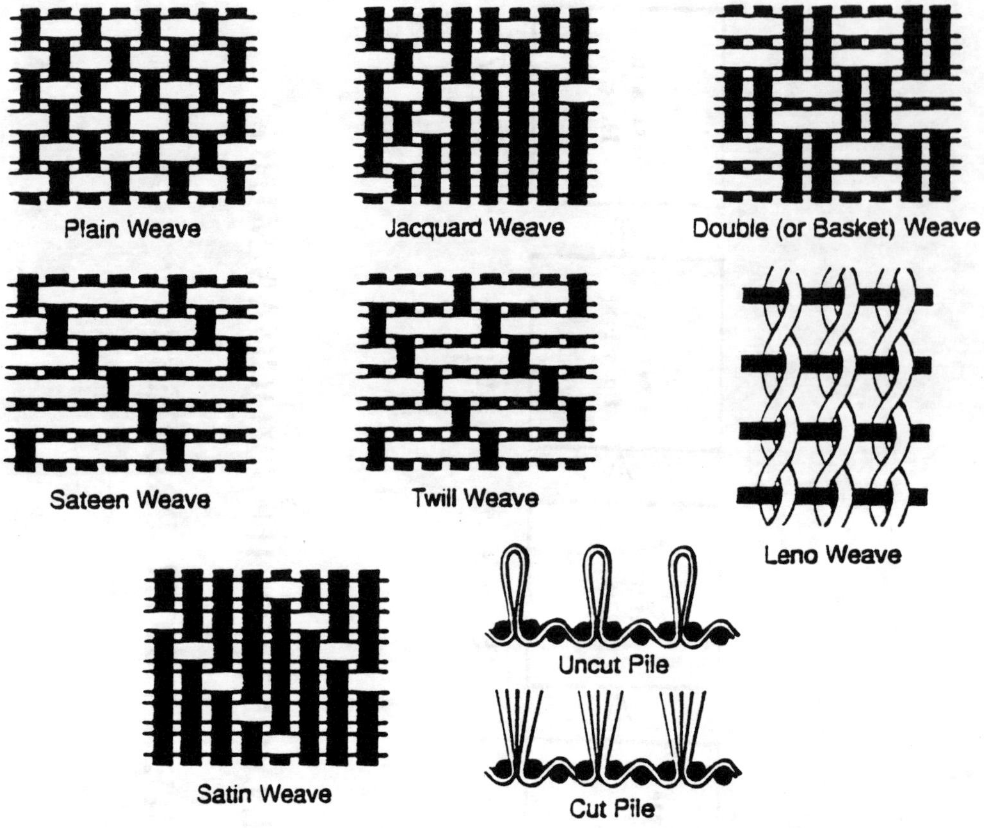

Illustration of Basic Types of Weaves

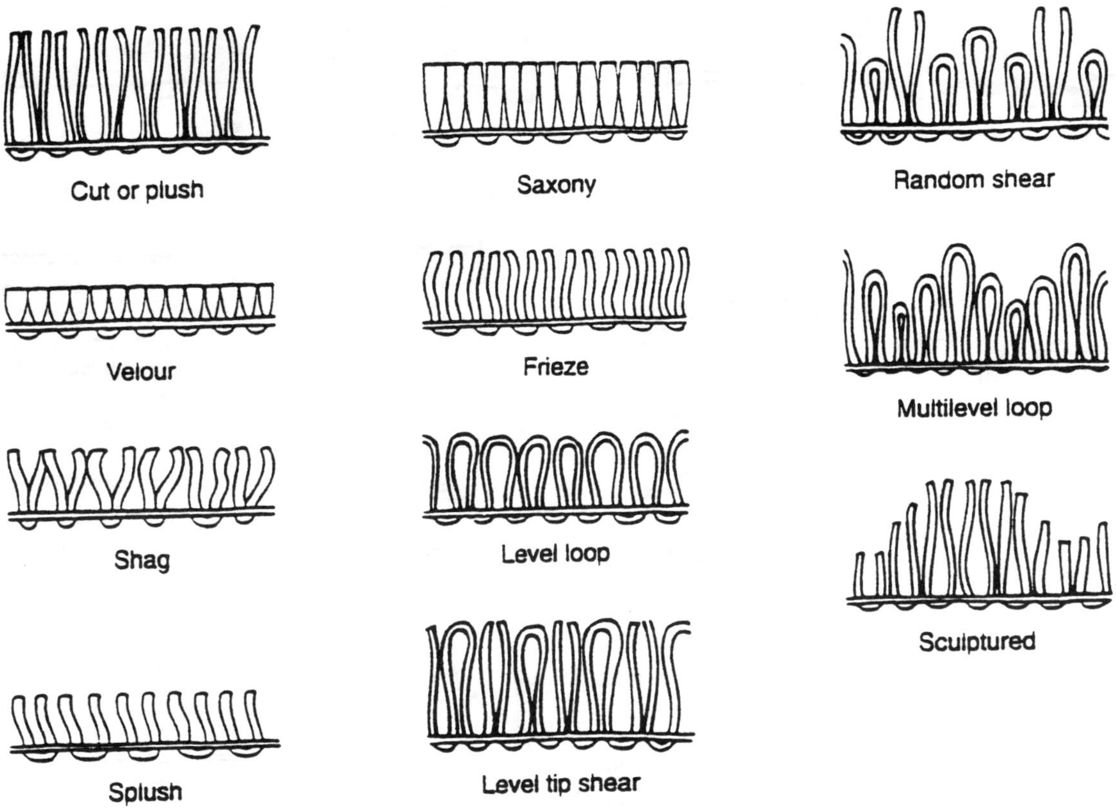

Style Characteristics of Rugs and Carpets

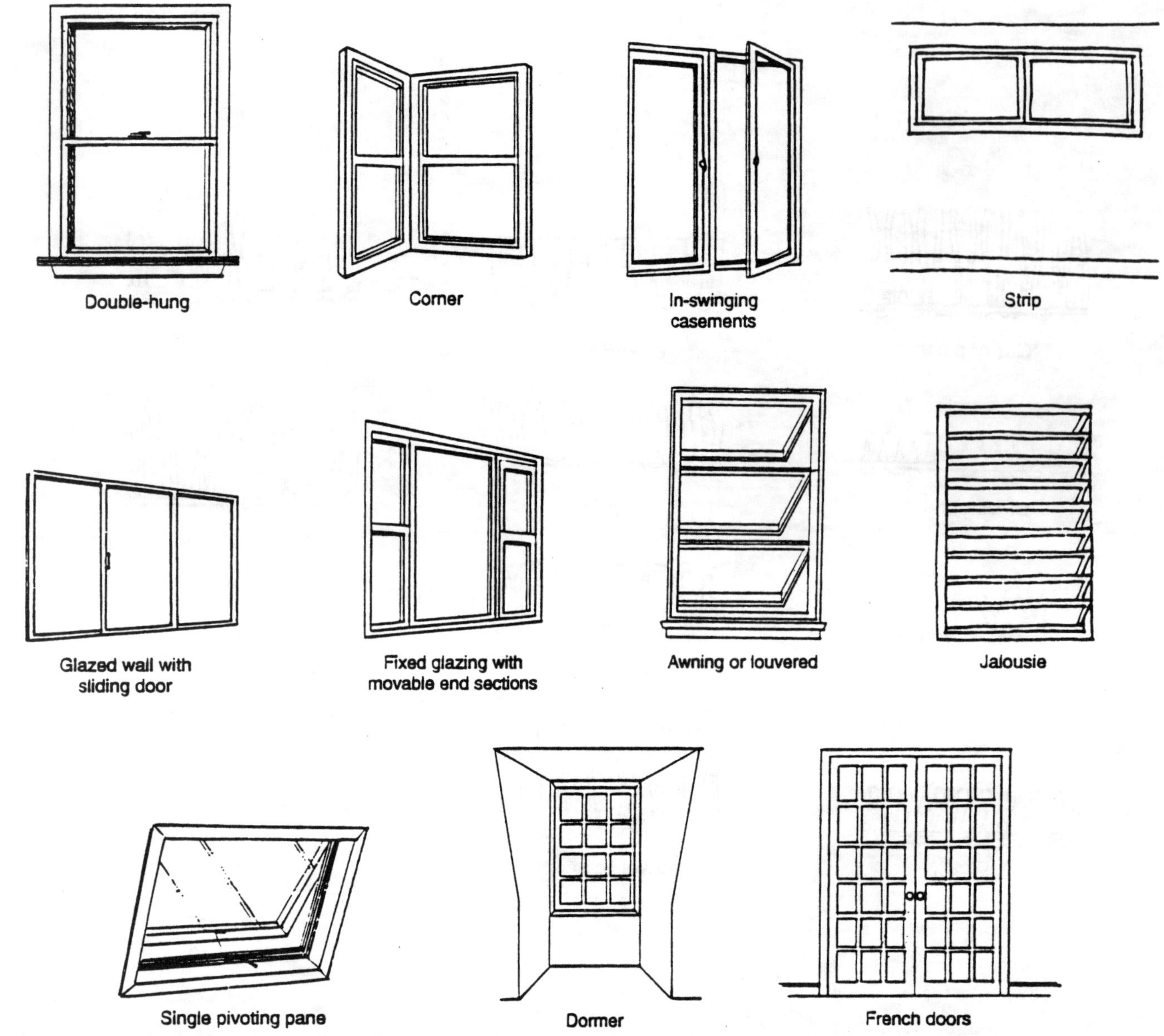

FIGURE 7.2 Types of movable windows.

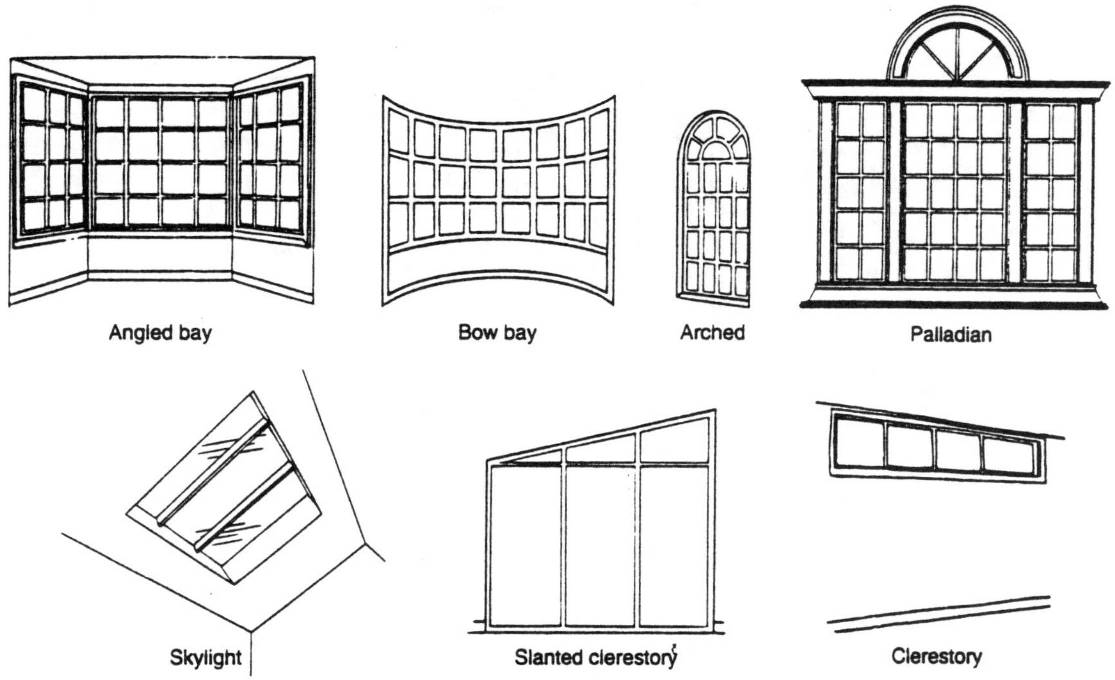

FIGURE 7.3 Types of stationary windows.

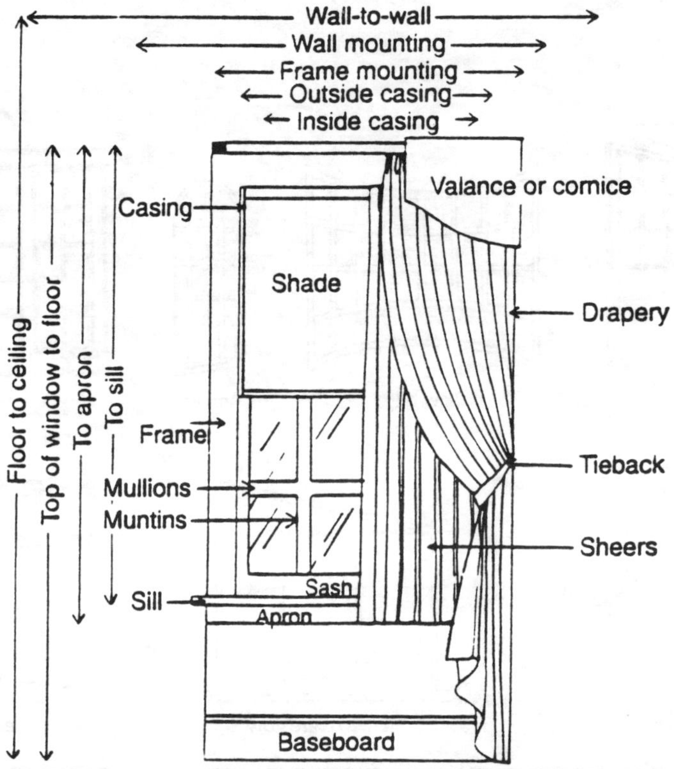

FIGURE 7.5 Window parts and treatment placement.

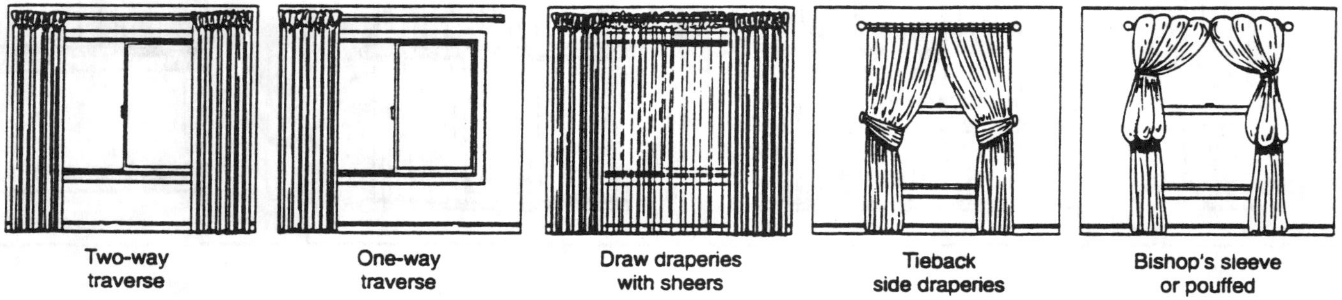

FIGURE 7.6 Types of draperies.

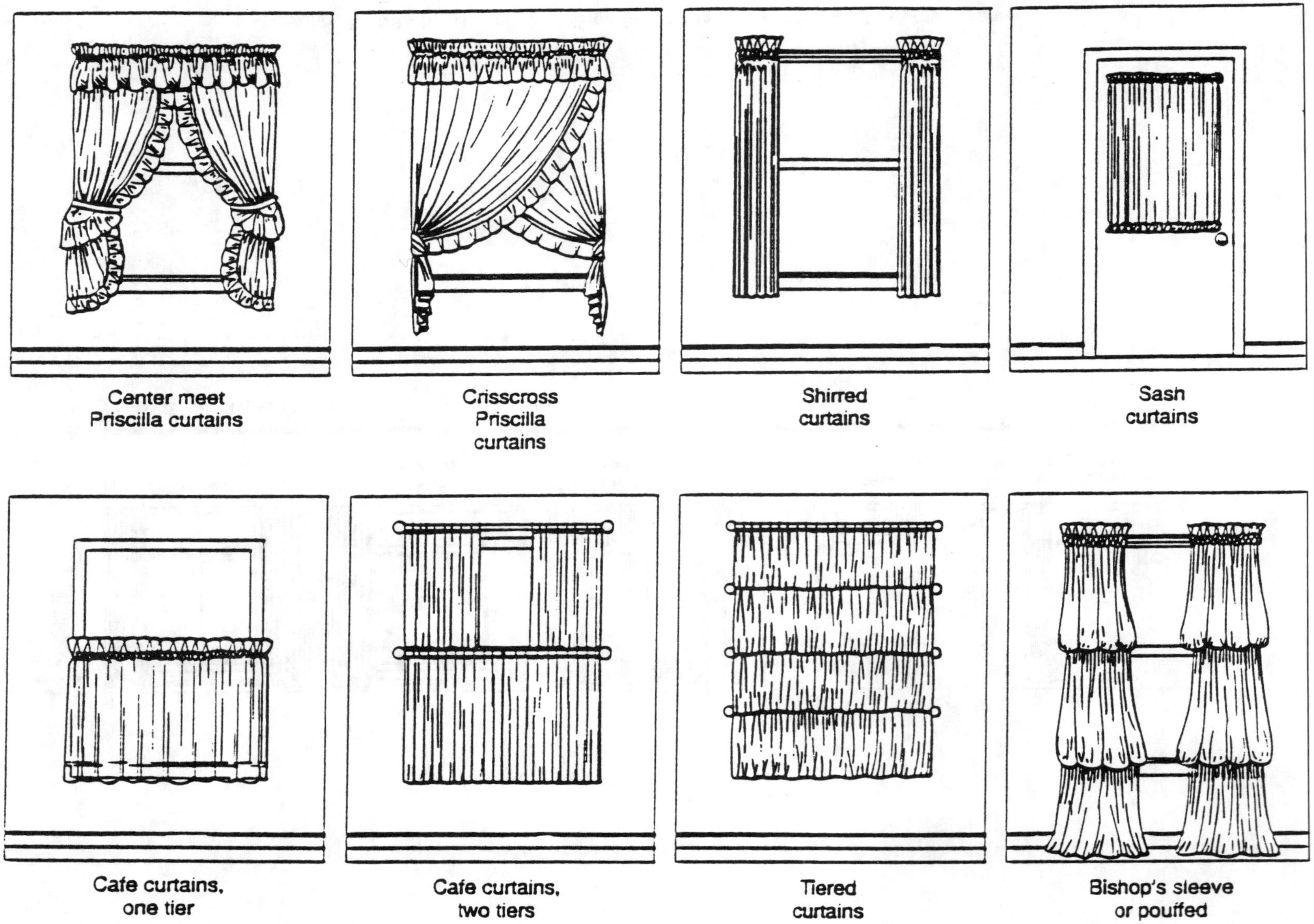

FIGURE 7.9 Types of curtains.

FIGURE 7.11 Types of Roman shades.

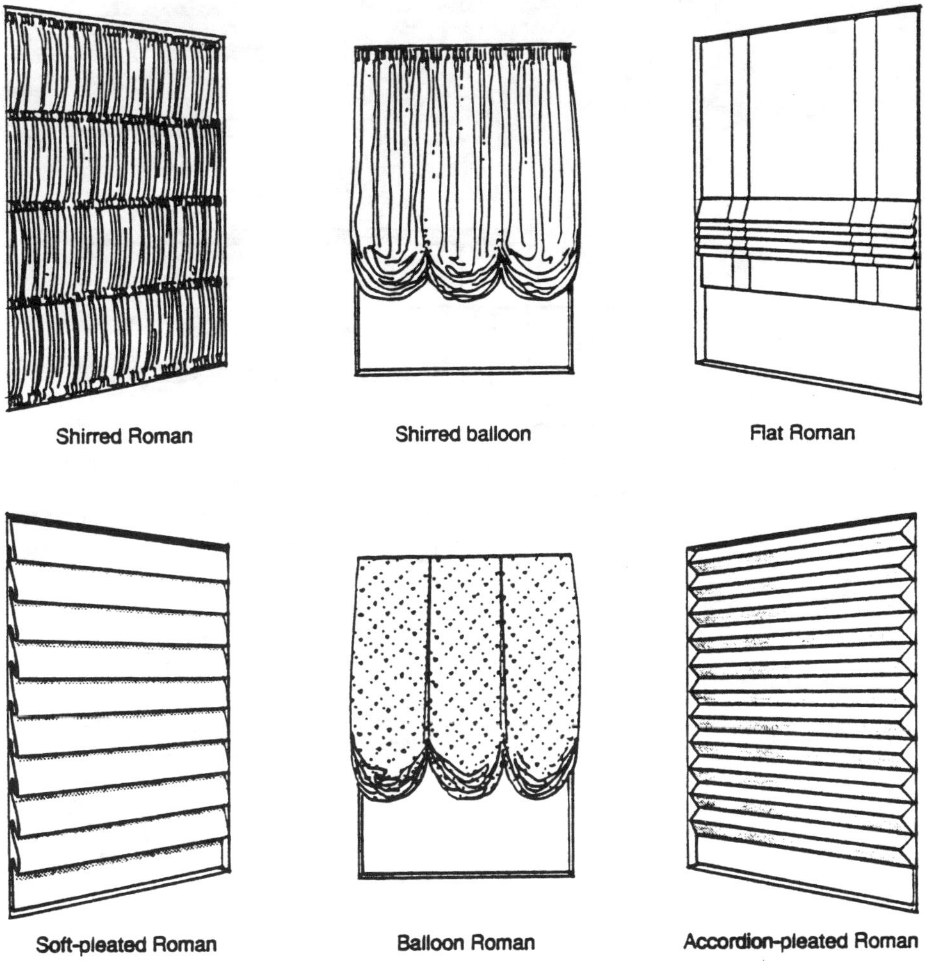

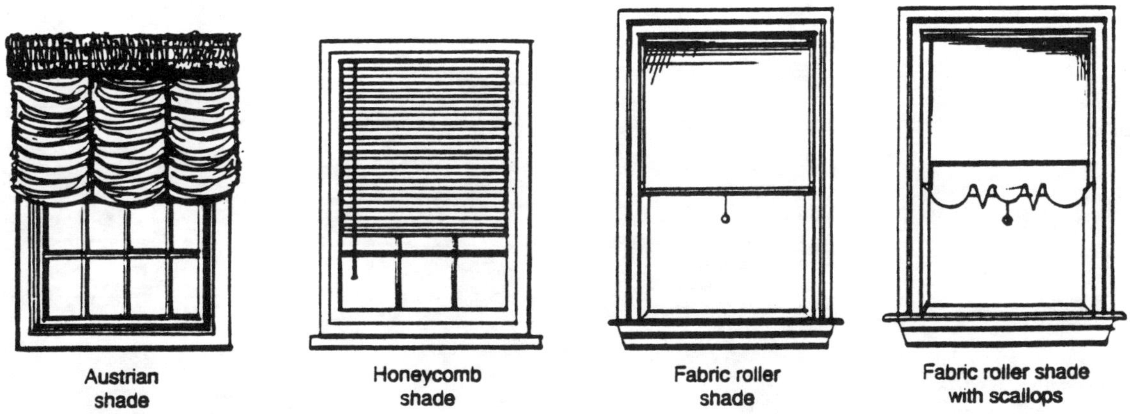

FIGURE 7.12 Other types of shades.

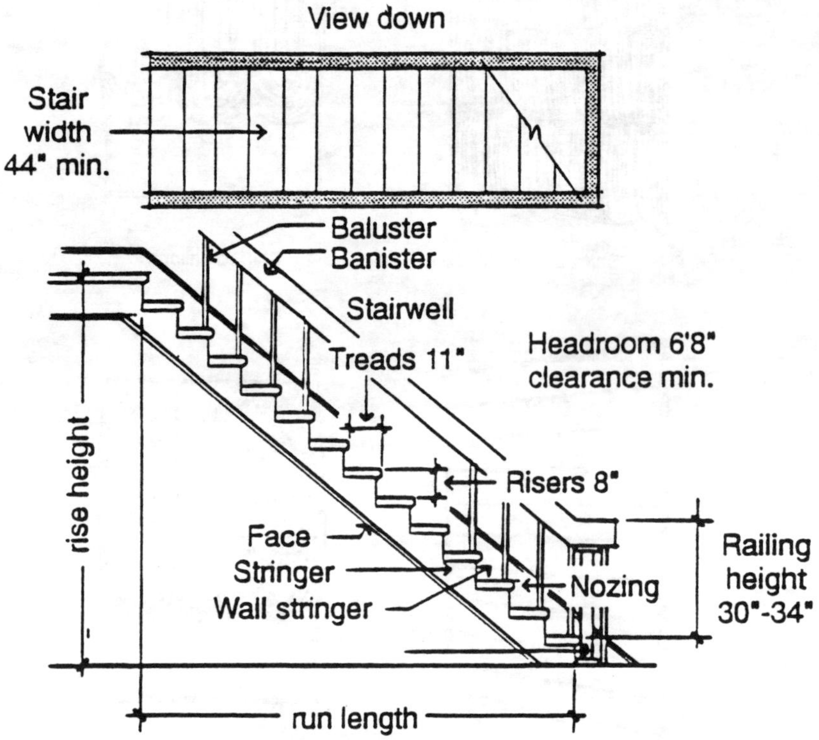

Stairway Terminology

Furniture Types

Furniture Types

Mortise and tenon

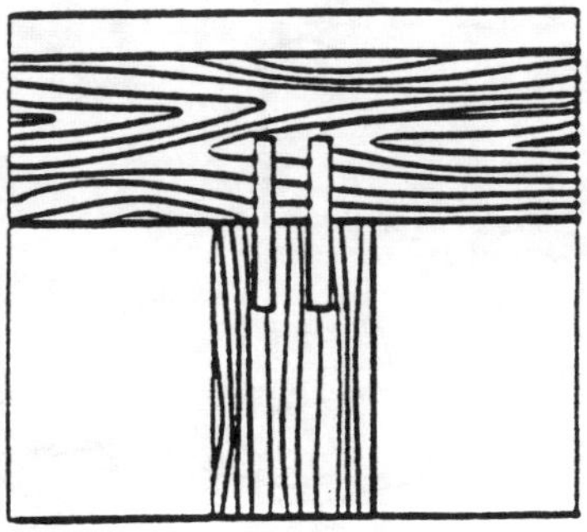

Dowel

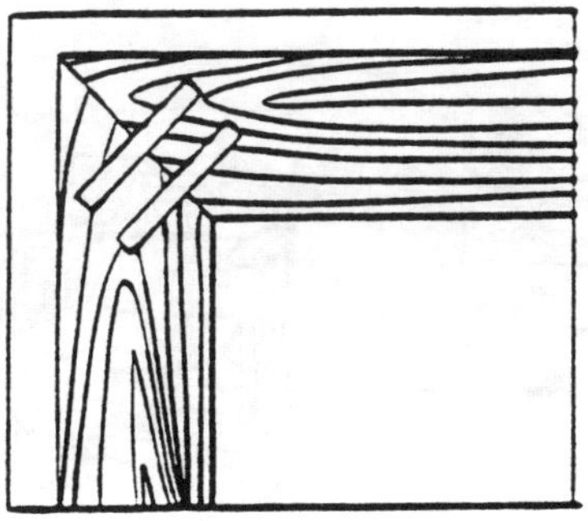

Miter

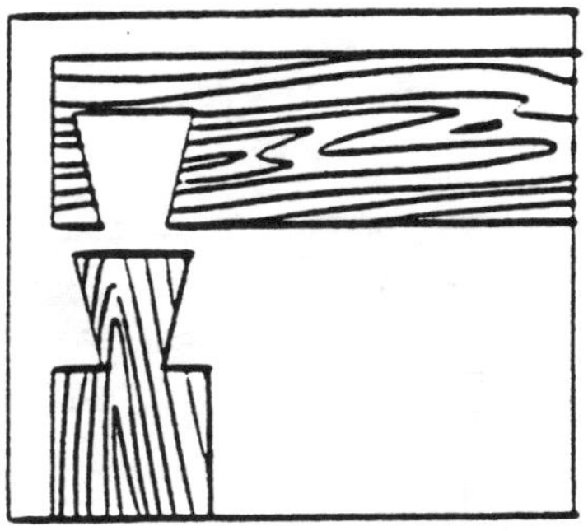

Dovetail

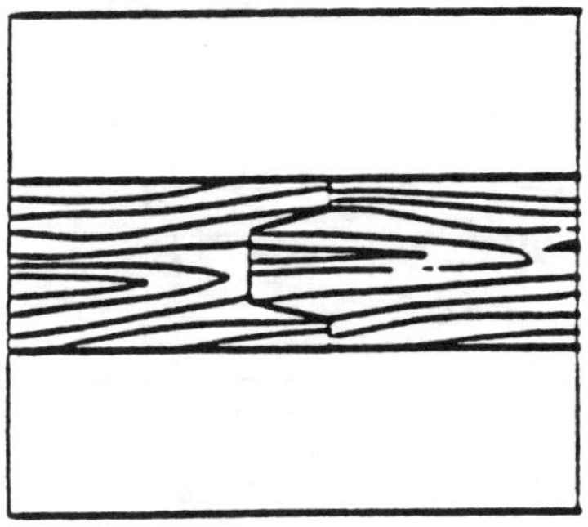

Tongue and groove

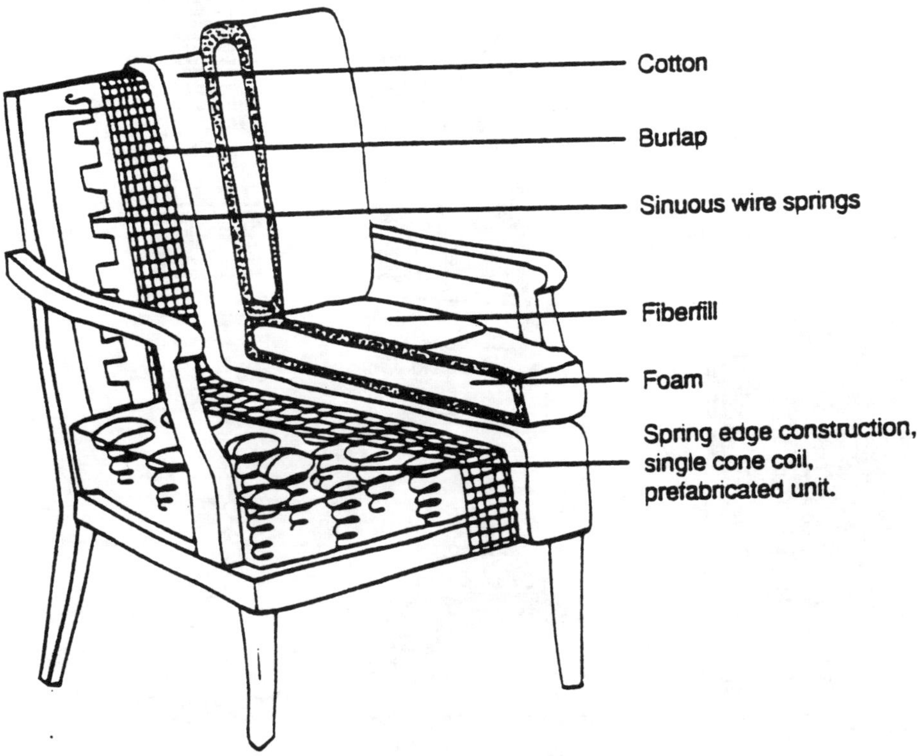

Types of Wood Joining and Upholstery Construction

FIGURE 9.2 Spanish (Colonial/Mission style).

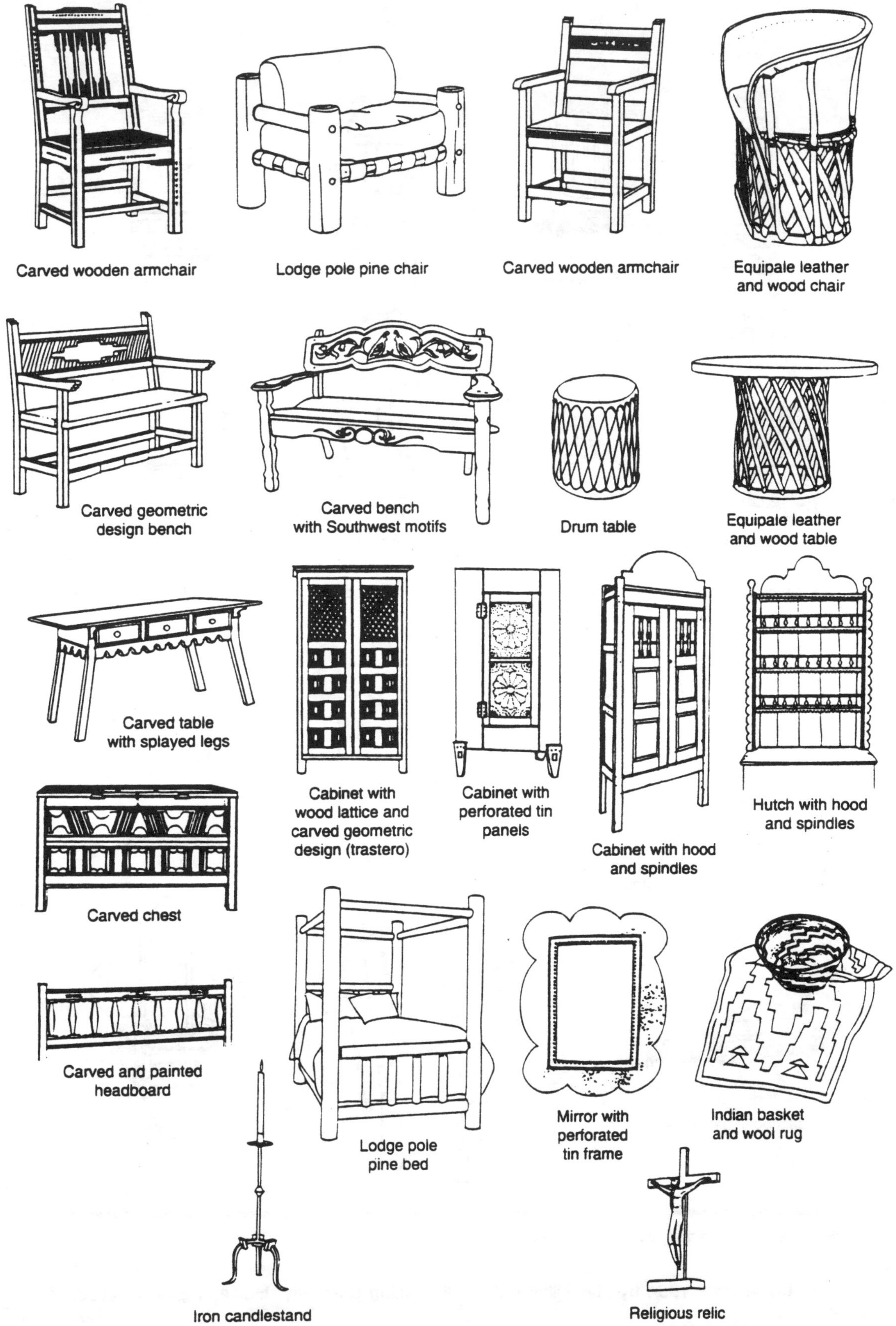

FIGURE 9.3 Spanish (Santa Fe style).

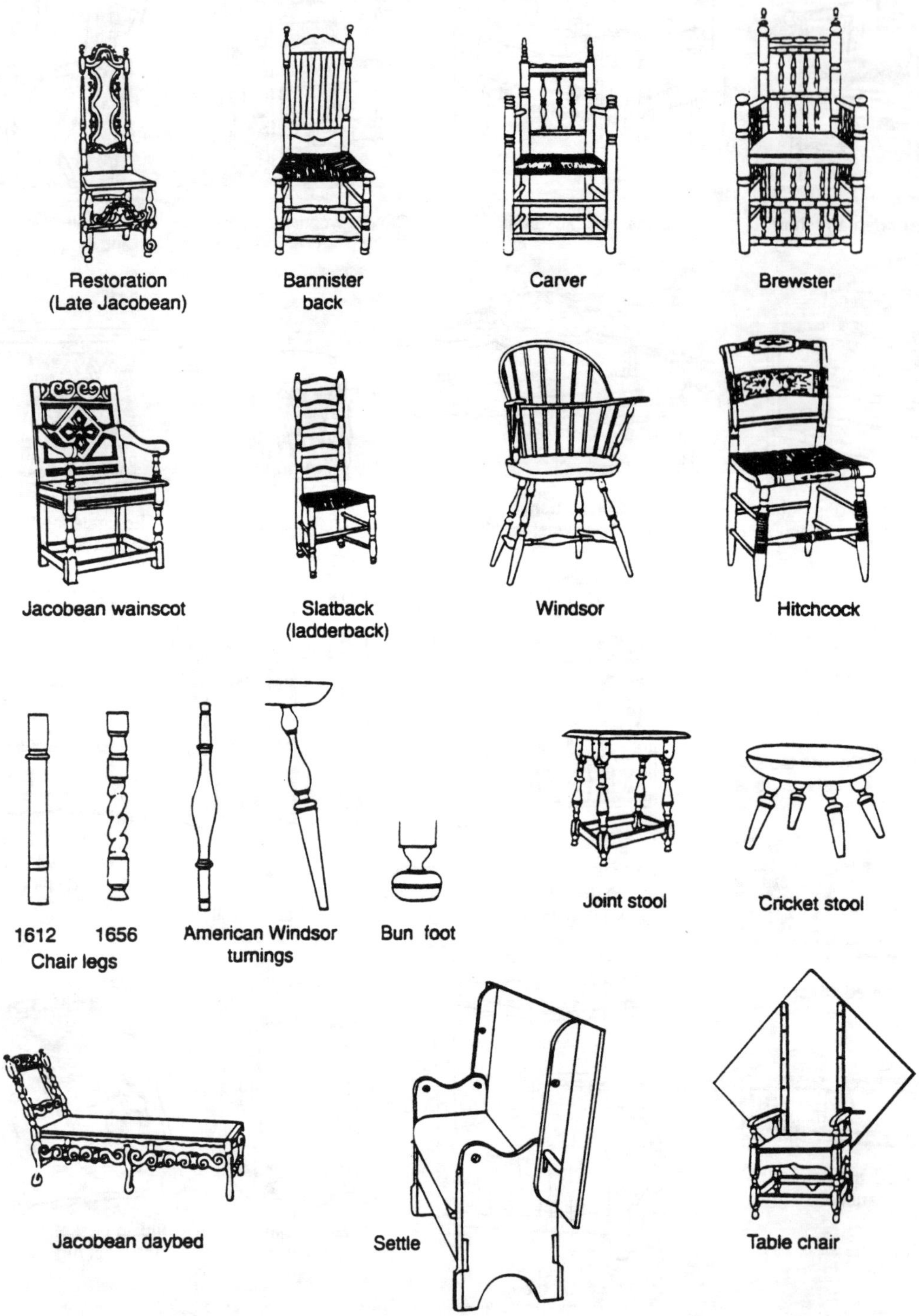

FIGURE 9.4 Early American (17th and 18th century country style).

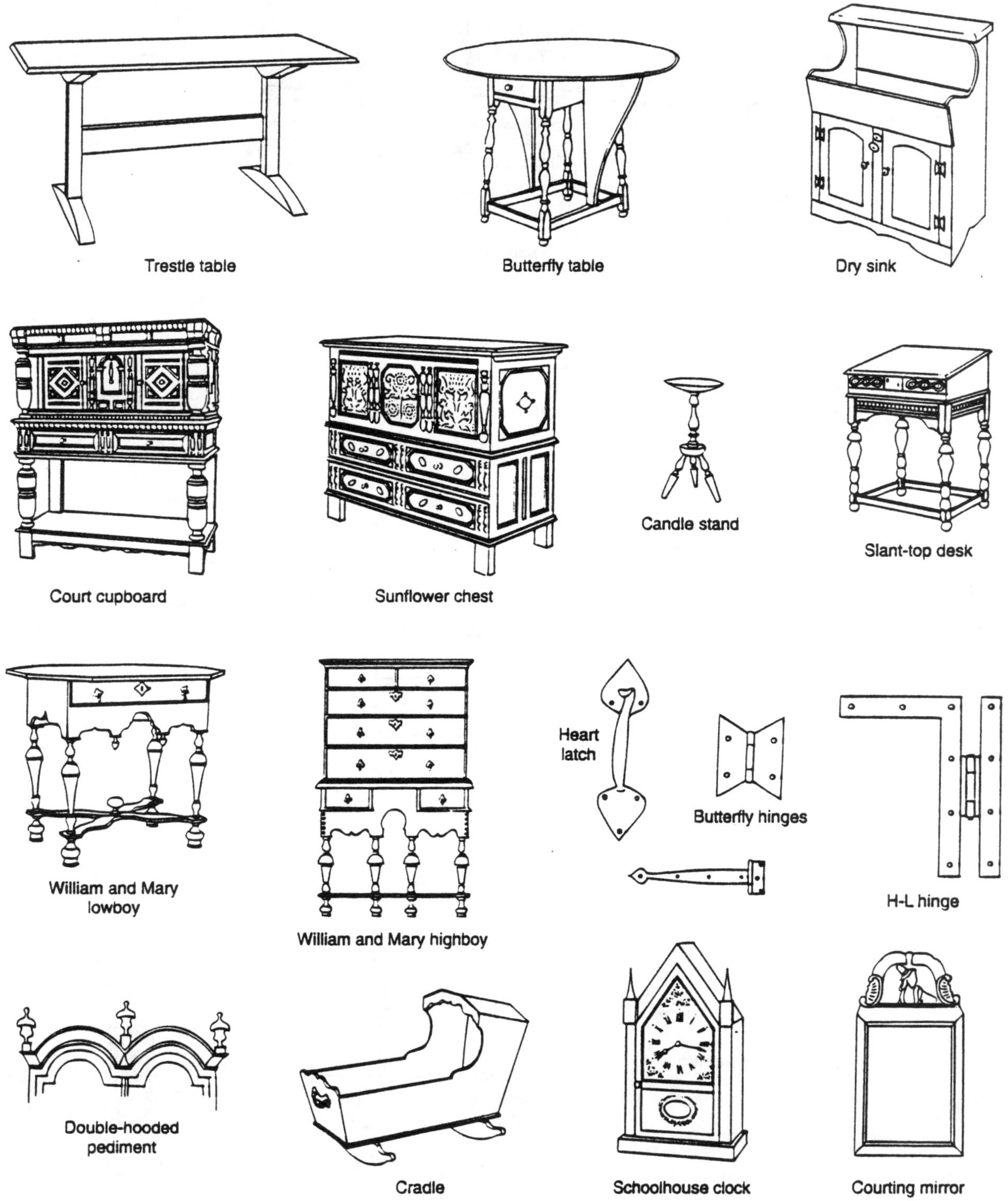

FIGURE 9.5 Early American (17th and 18th century country style).

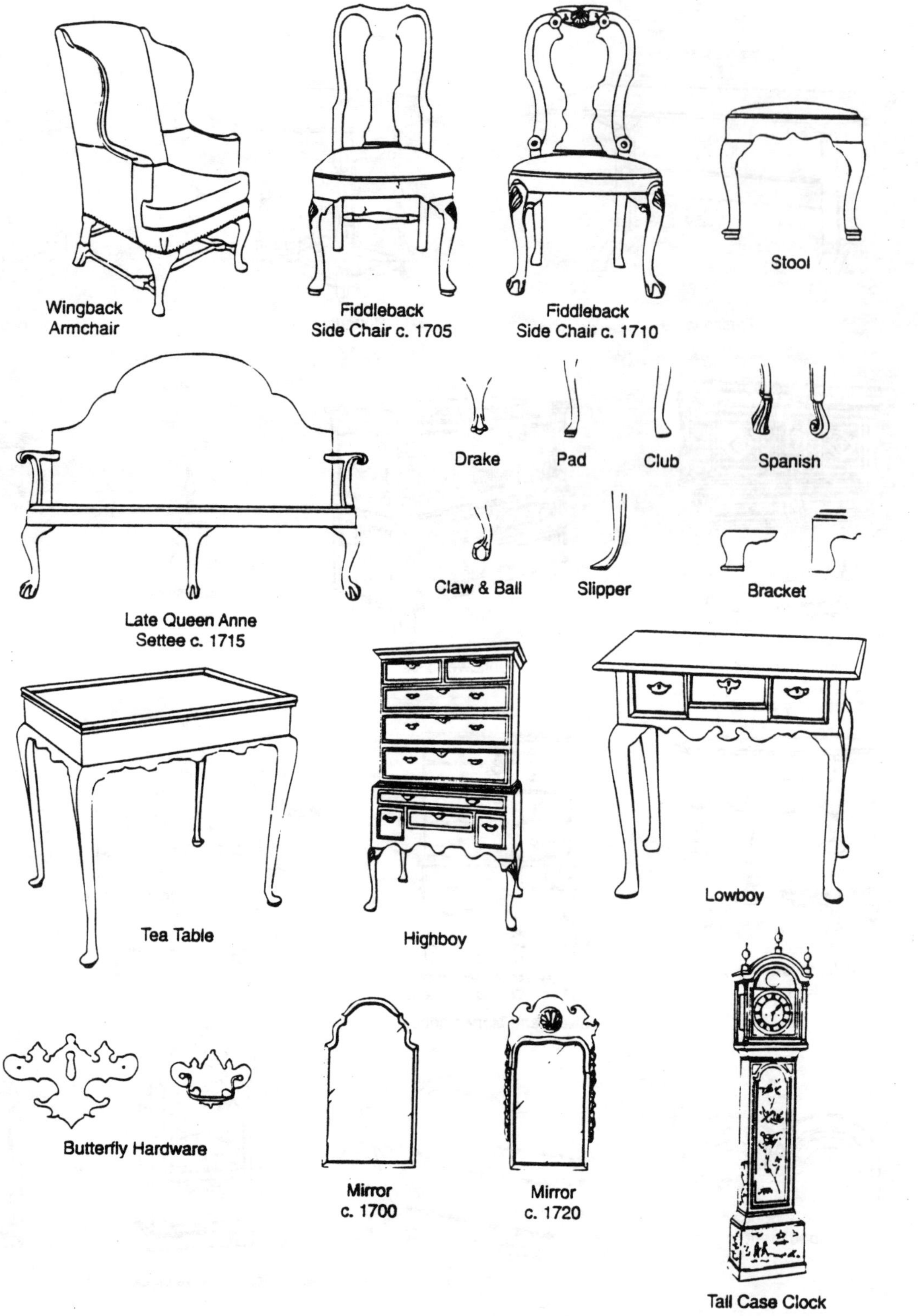

FIGURE 9.6 Queen Anne (Georgian period).

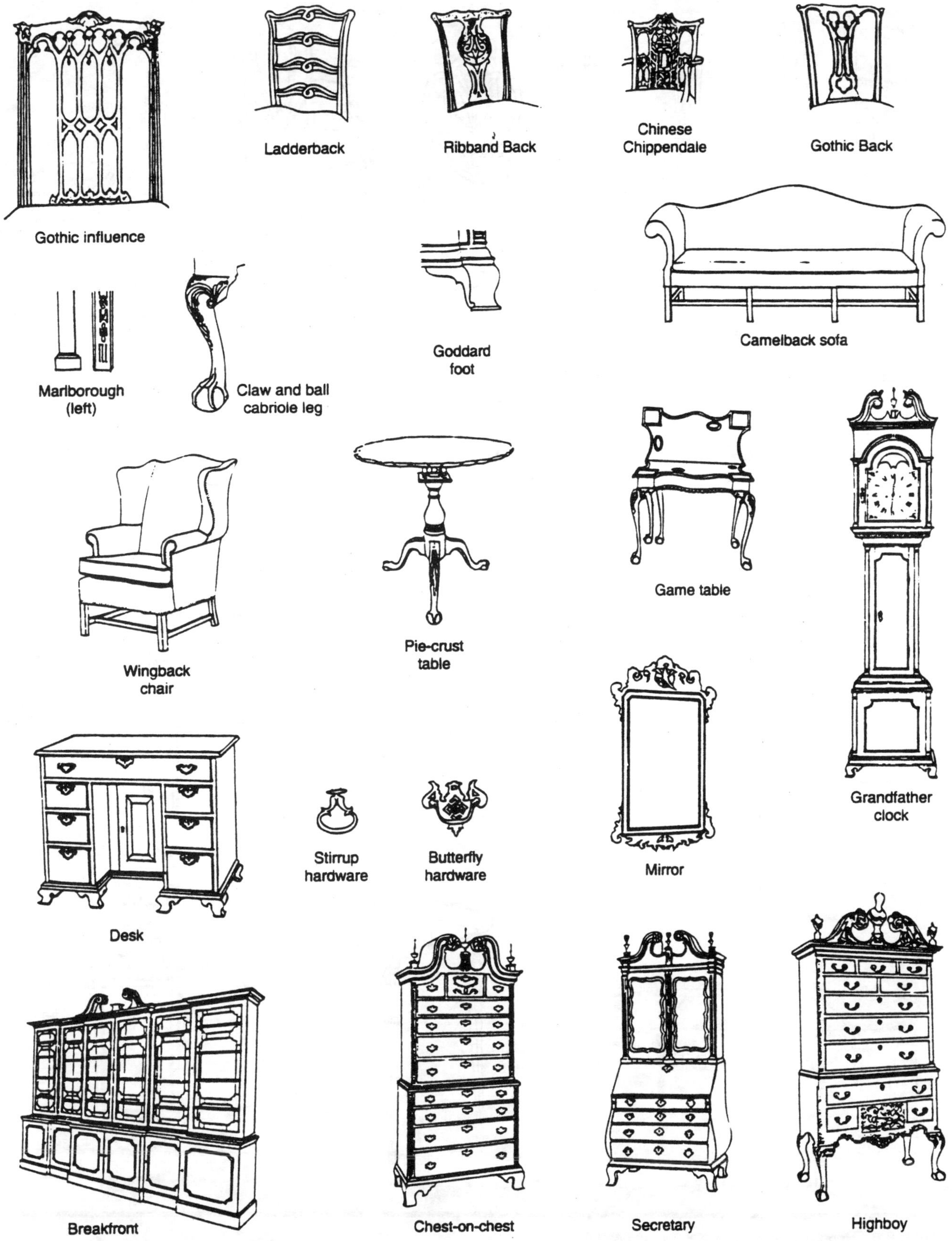

FIGURE 9.7 Chippendale (Georgian period).

FIGURE 9.8 Hepplewhite (Federal/Neoclassic period).

FIGURE 9.9 Sheraton (Federal/Neoclassic period).

FIGURE 9.10 Duncan Phyfe (Federal, American Empire, and Regency period).

FIGURE 9.11 American Empire.

FIGURE 9.13 Louis XV (French style).

FIGURE 9.14 Louis XVI (French style).

FIGURE 9.15 Provincial French.

FIGURE 9.17 Victorian (Belter Rococo).

FIGURE 9.18 Victorian (Eastlake–Renaissance).

FIGURE 9.19 Early modern furniture (Thonet, Arts & Crafts, and Art Nouveau).

FIGURE 9.20 Early modern furniture (Art Nouveau, Secession, and De Stijl).

FIGURE 9.22 Modern furniture (Art Deco and 1930s).

FIGURE 9.23 Classic modern furniture (postwar period–1950s).

FIGURE 9.24 Classic modern furniture (1950s to 1970s).

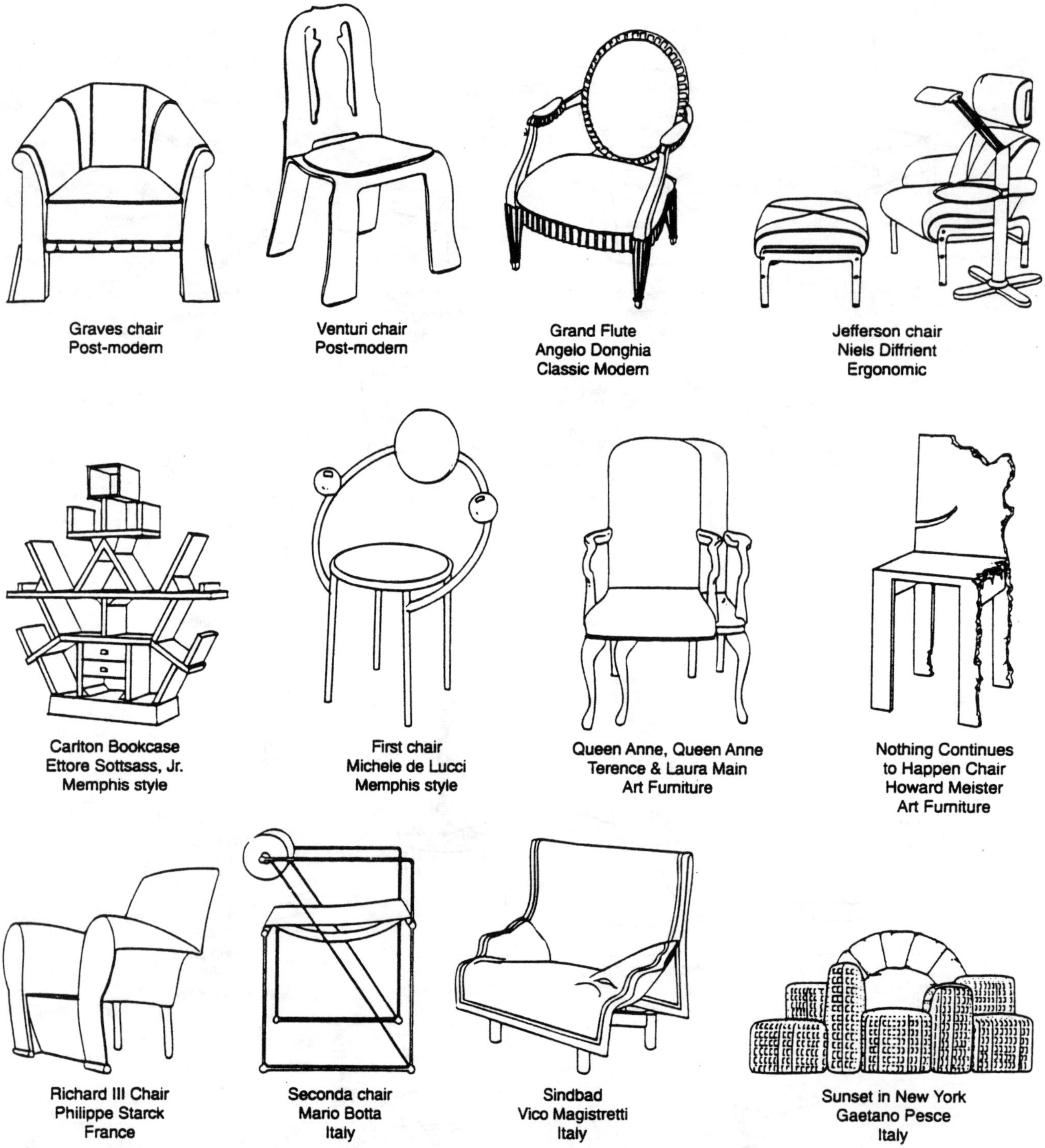

FIGURE 9.25 Classic modern furniture (1980s).

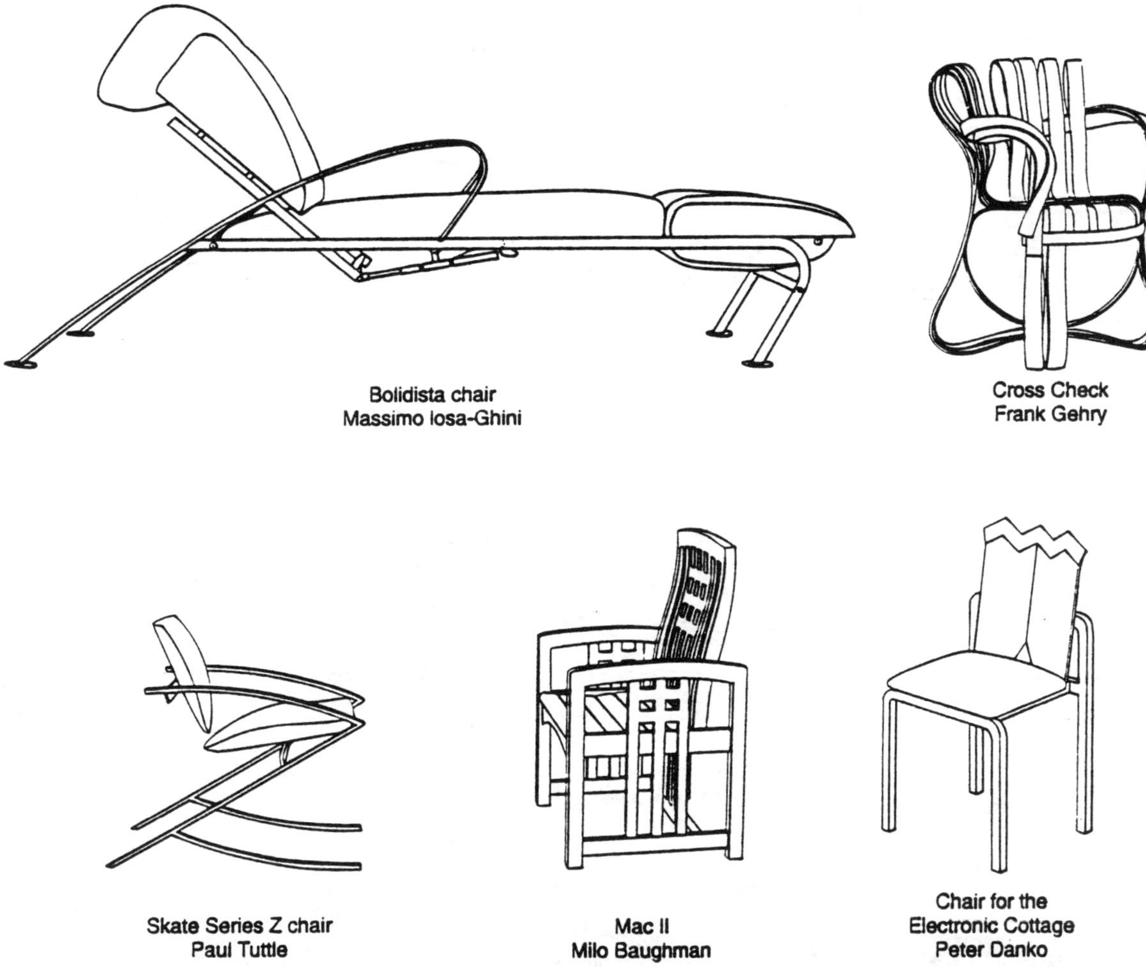

FIGURE 9.26 Classic modern furniture (1990s).

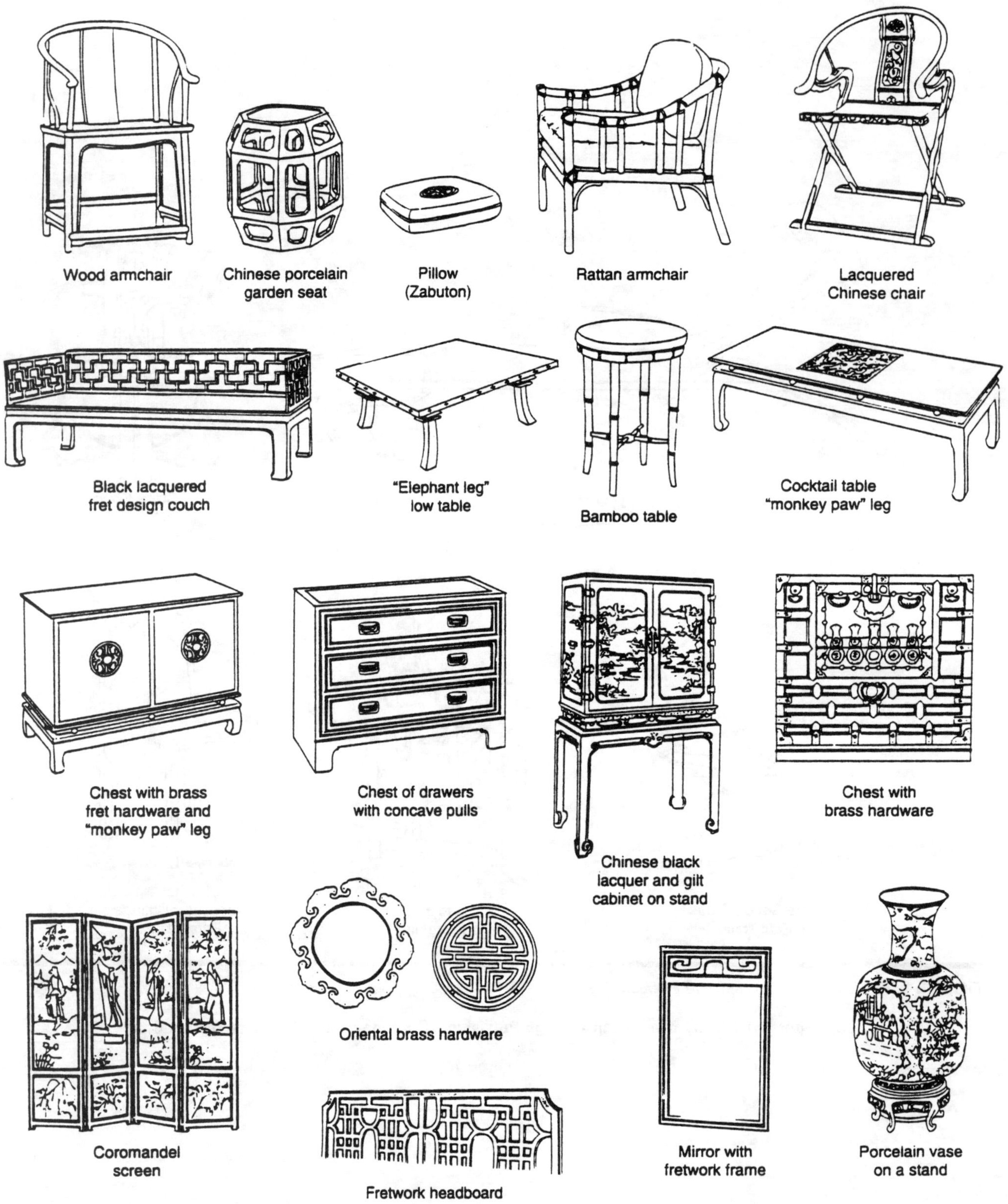

FIGURE 9.27 Far Eastern furniture.

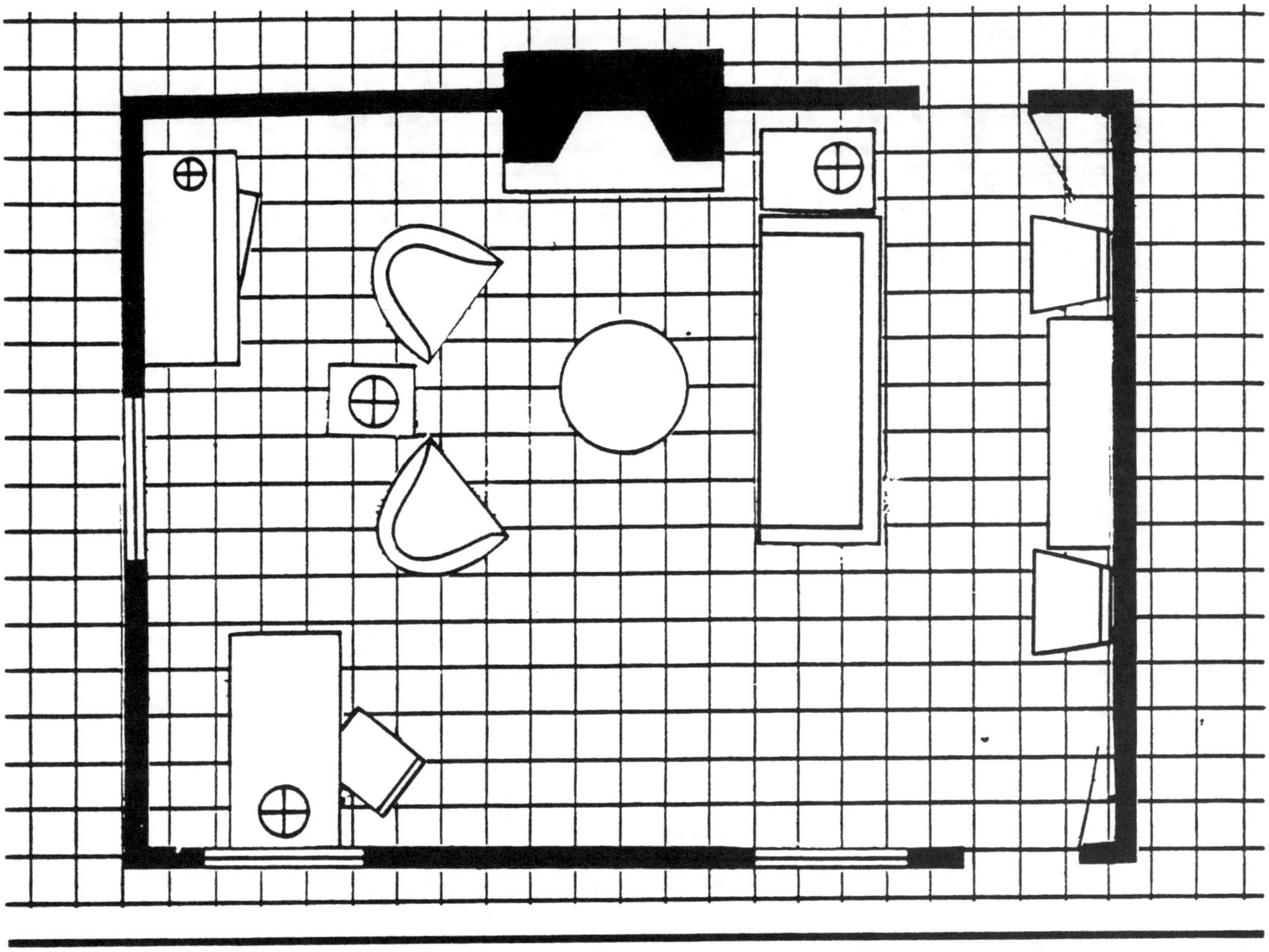

FIGURE 10.5 Furniture drawn to scale is arranged on graph paper using a measurement of $\frac{1}{4}$ in., equaling 1 ft.

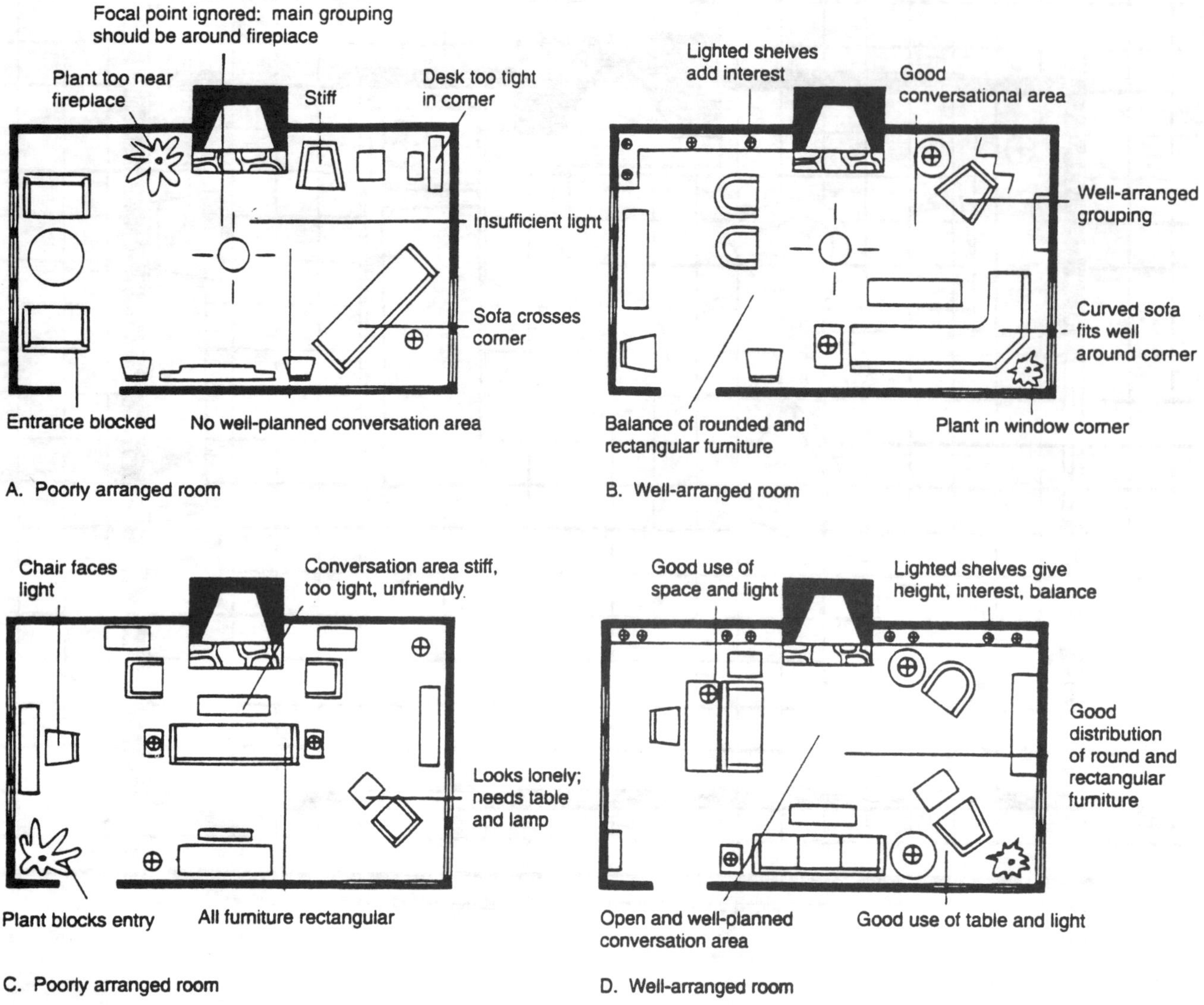

FIGURE 10.16 Four arrangements of a 14 × 24 ft living room.

FIGURE 10.33 Achieving balance in a wall composition.
(A) Bisymmetrical balance may become monotonous.
(B) Asymmetrical balance remains interesting longer.

FIGURE 10.34 Symmetrical and asymmetrical arrangements of art are hung with careful attention to the relationship of positive spaces (the art itself) and negative spaces (spaces between the art pieces).

Animal skins
Aquariums and fish
Arms and armor
Art (two-dimensional)
Ashtrays
Baskets
Bath accessories (soap dish, toothbrush container, towel racks, towels, washcloths, scales, toilet-paper holder)
Birdcages
Books and magazines
Blankets
Bottles
Bowls
Boxes
Brassware
Calendars
Candles
Candlesticks
Canisters
Ceramics
Coat racks
Clocks
Collections (coins, guns, stamps, antique items, etc.)
Cushions
Desk accessories (pen and pencil holders, letter holders, desk pad, address book, small clock, etc.)
Dishes
Dolls
Doll houses
Figurines
Fireplace tools and firescreen
Flowers
Flower and plant containers
Foliage
Frames (for art, photos, etc.)
Games
Glassware
Hardware (door knobs, hinges, racks, pulls, tiebacks, hooks, escutcheons, rods, etc.)
Kitchen and cooking utensils
Kites
Lamps
Maps, charts, and documents
Mirrors
Models (airplanes, ships, etc.)
Mosaics
Musical items (instruments, music stands, sheet music, etc.)
Music boxes
Needlework
Pedestals (for displays)
Pillows
Pitchers
Plants
Plates and platters (decorative)
Photo albums
Pottery
Puzzles
Quilts
Rugs
Screens
Sculpture
Serving carts
Shells and rocks
Shelves (a small, decorative, carved wood shelf, for example)
Silk flower and foliage arrangements
Silverware
Stools
Tablecloths, mats, and napkins
Tapestries
Telephones
Tools (antique rake, for example)
Toys
Toy furniture
Trays
Trophies
Umbrella stands
Vases
Wastebaskets
Weavings
Wreaths

Accessory Checklist

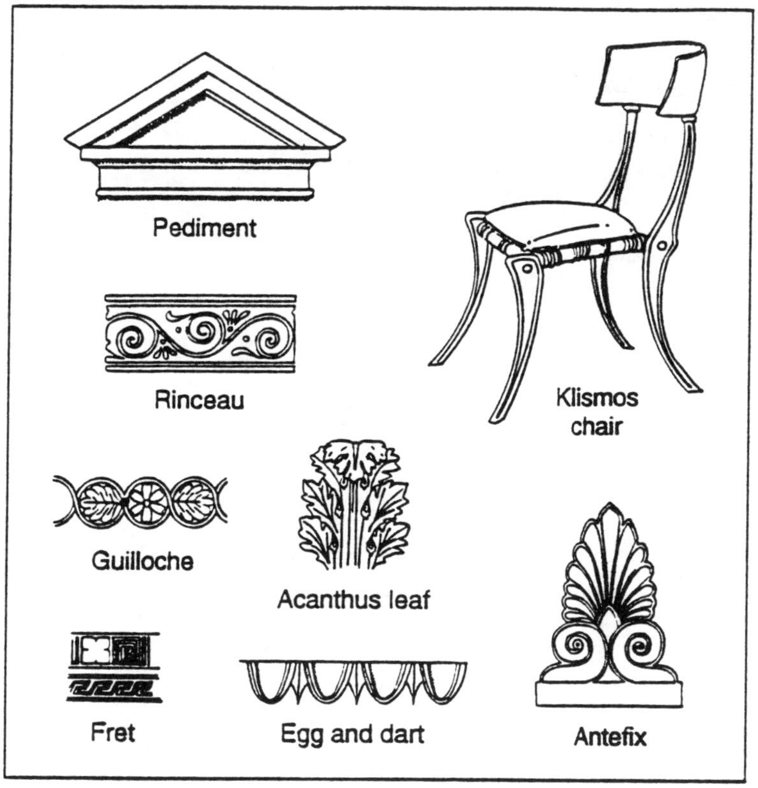

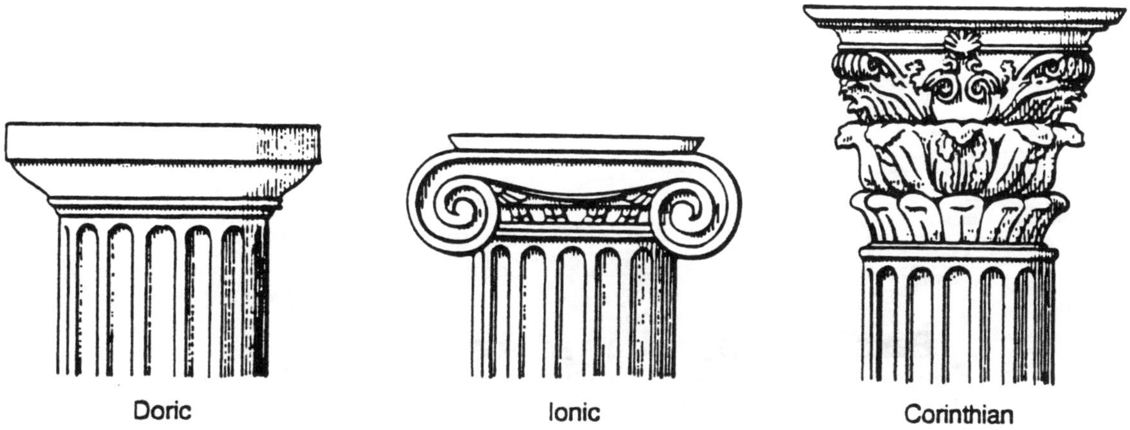

Ancient classical Greece and Classic Greek orders

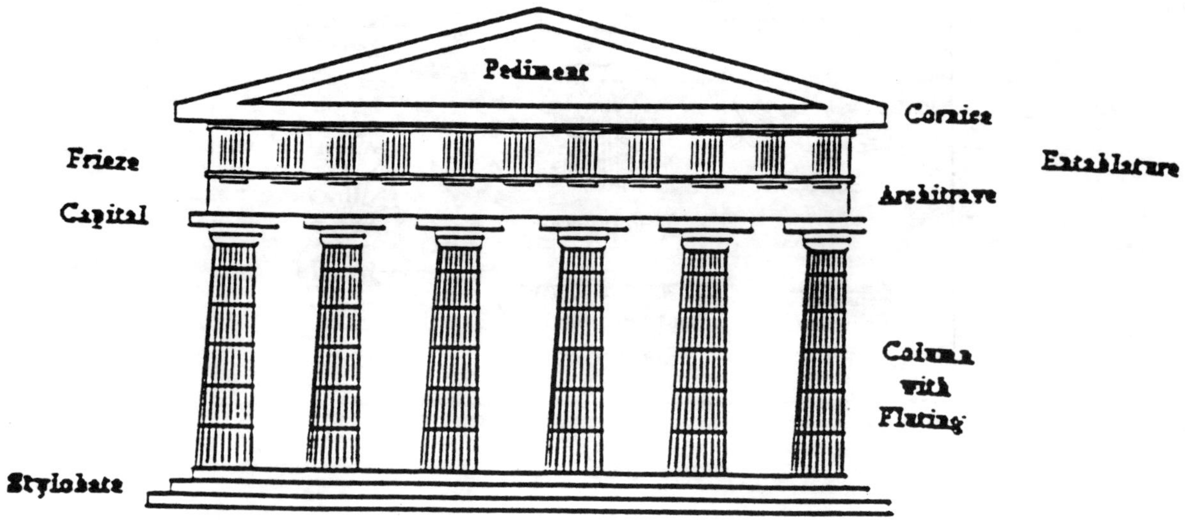

Parthenon in Athens

The Pantheon